POLITICS AND THE ARCHITECTURE OF CHOICE

POLITICS AND THE ARCHITECTURE OF CHOICE

Bounded Rationality and Governance

BRYAN D. JONES

The University of Chicago Press Chicago and London

BRYAN D. JONES is the Donald R. Matthews Professor of American Politics and director of the Center for American Politics and Public Policy at the University of Washington. He is the author of *Reconceiving Decision-Making in Democratic Politics,* and the coauthor, with Frank R. Baumgartner, of *Agendas and Instability in American Politics,* both published by the University of Chicago Press.

The University of Chicago Press, Chicago 60637
The University of Chicago Press, Ltd., London
© 2001 by The University of Chicago
All rights reserved. Published 2001
Printed in the United States of America

10 09 08 07 06 05 04 03 02 01   5 4 3 2 1

ISBN (cloth): 0-226-40637-7
ISBN (paper): 0-226-40638-5

Library of Congress Cataloging-in-Publication Data

Jones, Bryan D.
    Politics and the architecture of choice : bounded rationality and governance / Bryan D. Jones.
        p.   cm.
    Includes bibliographical references and index.
    ISBN 0-226-40637-7 (cloth, alk. paper)—ISBN 0-226-40638-5 (pbk.)
    1. Behaviorism (Political science)   2. Organizational behavior.   3. Rational choice theory.   I. Title.
    JA74.5 .J65   2001
    320'.01'9—dc21

                                                        00-011352

⊗ The paper used in this publication meets the minimum requirements of the American National Standard for Information Sciences—Permanence of Paper for Printed Library Materials, ANSI Z39.48-1992.

CONTENTS

ILLUSTRATIONS

Figures

Tables

Prologue to a Grand Synthesis?

THIS BOOK is about human behavior in formal complex institutions, particularly in political and governmental institutions. Much of the argument hinges on the observation that in politics, as elsewhere in life, people do not process information proportionately. By the phrase "disproportionate information processing," I mean that objective signals from the environment are transformed in the process of thought. Because of this, it is necessary to delve into the human mind and how it processes information. To predict behaviors, it is not enough to know the objective incentives people face in interacting with their environments. We must know also *how* politicians, bureaucrats, and citizens think about politics.

The nature of human thought imparts an essentially episodic and disjointed character to our decision making. We shift our attention from topic to topic in a manner governed by our emotions, which are intimately bound up with setting priorities. Because of attention limits and emotionality, we are poor at making trade-offs. The way we learn and the emotional identification with what we have learned means that we hold too long to outmoded solutions in the face of changing circumstances.

This does not mean that humans are pitiful decision makers, destined to use a cognitive architecture that evolved to solve problems in the Stone Age but is ill-adapted for modern life. This metaphor has become a favorite of evolutionary psychologists, who seem bent on denigrating general problem-solving capacities. No, humans are adaptive creatures, but we adapt in disjointed ways.

This disjointedness has important consequences for modern political and economic life. It is evident in such formal organizations as legislatures, bureaucracies, interest associations, business firms, and labor unions, even taking into account the decision and transaction costs imposed by those institutions. It helps account for bandwagons, fads, grand policy changes after years of quiescence, market booms and crashes, and many other phenomena.

Although I study governments, I hope to speak to a broader critical issue: the failure to link what we know about human behavior from studies in biology, psychology, and parts of political science (public opinion and voting behavior) and experimental economics to the performance of social systems—representative governments, capitalistic economies, and other forms of organized human activity. This failure is a major bar to progress in the social sciences, because as a consequence there is no firm micro- or individual-level foundation for the analysis of social systems.

Is the time ripe for the emergence of a serious synthesis in social science in a manner perhaps comparable to the great synthesis forged in biology in the early years of the twentieth century? That synthesis unified the macro concerns of evolutionary biology with a firm genetic microfoundation. No longer would there be two distinct and irreconcilable languages in biology, one to describe genetic transmission and one to describe the evolution of phenotypes (Mayr 1997).

Rational choice forms the microfoundation of much institutional analysis in social science. It assumes that people have goals and that they act in order to maximize those goals. The rational choice approach is highly problematic, however, because it is clearly an inadequate foundation for the analysis of complex organizations such as democratic legislatures and business corporations. Nevertheless, current critics—indeed, a veritable cottage industry of critical studies has developed—have failed to appreciate the successes of the approach in approximating human adaptive behavior in such complex institutions.

The major problem in forging a critical synthesis is that behavioral and social scientists employ very different perspectives. "Social scientists"—economists, political scientists, and sociologists, along with some anthropologists and a smattering of psychologists—generally focus on the actions of social systems. They want to know why economies perform as they do, how democracies compare with authoritarian systems, and what the role of social status is in organizing human action. "Behavioral scientists"—primarily psychologists and biologists, with some anthropologists, sociologists, and political psychologists—study the behavior of individuals.

Rational choice is demonstratively wrong at the behavioral level. As a direct consequence, it cannot serve as a proper organizing approach for social-level phenomena. Unfortunately, behavioral scientists have not been able to provide a convincing alternative foundation for the study of social systems. We know lots of things about human behavior in the laboratory (less about it in the field). But too often this knowledge falls into the categories of empirical generalization or laboratory effect (or critique of the rational choice-in-practice). Even worse, much of behavioral science today ignores the remarkable adaptive capacity of humans interacting in social systems.

I find the key to synthesis in an old idea: "bounded" or "intended" rationality. Bounded rationality captures the notion that humans are goal driven, or intentional, but not fully adaptable in our current decision-making activities. Most of modern economics and a considerable share of political science are premised on the notion of rational decision making. Rational decision making is fully adaptive decision making. Intended rationality, however, points to those aspects of decision making where rationality (and hence adaptation) fails. This failure is generally due to our biological constitutions. Progress in both rational analysis and in cognitive science and related disciplines offers the opportunity to institute more careful comparisons of adaptive behavior and its failure in particular situations.

I advocate a self-conscious synthesis directed at understanding the deviations from the predictions of rational choice analysis in light of what is understood about human biology and psychology. Let us start, at least when we study behavior in complex formal institutions, with the notion that people are goal oriented and generally adaptive. That said, we must not sweep the failures of adaptability under the rug, but address them forthrightly, using current findings from biology, psychology, political behavior, and experimental economics. What are the "traps" that cause people to fail to adapt in their decision-making strategies? How are they related to our evolved biological inheritance? Is it possible to design institutions that address and even flourish with these psychological and biological limits?

Interestingly, the times are right and the times are wrong for such an undertaking. The times are right because of declining hysteria in social science about biological and evolutionary foundations for contemporary human behavior. The publication of E. O. Wilson's *Sociobiology* in 1975 stimulated a vitriolic reaction from many social scientists claiming that most human behavior could be explained by "culture"—hence learning. That reaction has subsided, replaced by an increasing fascination with the evolutionary roots of human behavior.

The times are wrong because much of the research in evolutionary psychology and human behavioral biology denigrates the general problem-solving mechanism, claiming that domain-specific cognitive adaptations are favored by evolution. Yet that very general problem-solving mechanism must be responsible for the success of humans in the complex and artificial settings of formal organizations. Evidence is all around us every day. As Groucho Marx once commented, "Who are you going to believe? Me or your own eyes?"

Until we understand the tension between our external adaptive capacities and our inherited human natures better, we will not achieve anything close to a synthesis. I suggest an answer in bounded rationality and call for studies explicitly organized around the limits of rational adaptation. Social and behavioral scientists can and should (and in many cases already are, but without much self-understanding of what they are doing) design studies that will distinguish fully adaptive behavior from behavior that is nonoptimal, and link such deviations to facets of human cognitive architecture.

Such a synthesis requires much of social scientists. Psychologists must learn economics and political science; economists must study biology and psychology; political psychology must move beyond voting studies into the realm of the adaptive behaviors of legislators and corporate directors. I find little inclination to make such commitments among social scientists at present, but there are optimistic signs.

The research reported in this book (some of which I conducted with Frank Baumgartner) has been supported in part by the Political Science Division of the National Science Foundation. I appreciate in particular the support of our program officer there, Frank Scioli. I have benefited from comments on this project or from conversations about the nature of social science from Frank Baumgartner, Yorim Barzel, Roy Flemming, Nehemia Geva, Michael Hechter, Mel Hinich, Peter John, Diane C. Jones, Edgar Kiser, Margaret Levi, Xinsing Liu, Jon Mercer, Peter May, Pete Nardulli, Herb Simon, Mark Smith, Fred Thompson, and John Wilkerson. Two of my undergraduate students, Amy Franklin and Casey Dickerson, provided able research assistance. My graduate and undergraduate classes in decision making at the University of Washington wrote extensive reviews of an earlier draft of this work. I learned much humility from these reviews and their comments made this a better book.

PART **I**

MICROFOUNDATIONS

CHAPTER 1

Traces of Eve

IN THE dawning years of the twentieth century, the great Italian sociologist Vilfredo Pareto laid out an ambitious scheme for understanding human behavior in social systems. In his *Trattato di Socilogia generale* he argued that human behavior could be categorized as either logical or nonlogical (he thought that little of human behavior was downright illogical). Logical behavior concerned applying appropriate means in the pursuit of goals; it was the use of the scientific method in problem solving. But much of human conduct, Pareto wrote, was nonlogical, bound up with residues—observable "manifestations of sentiments and instincts" (Pareto 1935, 511). "If non-logical conduct plays such an important role in human life, why has it been so generally neglected?" (499).

It is still neglected. This neglect of nonlogical behavior within the most rational of human inventions—complex formal organizations—has led to an unrealistic understanding of those organizations, and a mischaracterization of behavior within organizations. In particular, the neglect of the cognitive and emotional constitutions of participants in complex organizations has led many social scientists (and, to a considerable extent, citizens in general) to attribute calculating rationality to all sorts of human behaviors that are far more likely to fall into the realm of sentiments and residues. But, interestingly enough, we cannot build an understanding of human behavior in organizations unless we start with the premise that people are goal oriented and adaptive.

In organizations such as government bureaucracies, legislative bodies, and business firms, behavioral patterns have clear structure. A division of labor is imposed, and structures of responsibility established. People know in general what is expected of them. In the terminology of sociologists, they play roles. In a manner analogous to the way in which the behaviors of actors are prespecified by roles in a play, roles in an organization prespecify the behavior of those in positions in the organization. These expectations of behavior are specified by formal rules and informal

3

norms. In all organizations, repetitive, routine, and predictable behavior is a key characteristic—otherwise it wouldn't be an organization.

On the other hand, human organizations represent the high point of adaptation to complex and changing environments. Formal organizations—legislatures, labor unions, business corporations, and charitable foundations—are artificial creations of the human mind. They are deliberately constructed to solve problems. Indeed, the ability to create artificial entities that allow both the coordination of the behaviors of many individuals and the accomplishment of collective goals is a uniquely human trait. To solve problems in changing environments, organizations must be flexible, or adaptive.

The paradox of organizations is that they provide stability, thus allowing people to coordinate their actions to achieve their goals, but they also must be adaptable in the face of changing circumstances, thus disrupting the stability they provide. It turns out, however, that organizations are not smoothly adaptive to changing circumstances. Neither are the people in them. In most situations, human behavior is not consistently maladaptive. But it is often adaptive in an episodic and disjointed manner. Stock markets are subject to bubbles and crashes. Conservatives in politics, having won a close election, proceed to overextend themselves in the legislative process. A once-small business firm becomes a large-scale corporate bully, attracting the attention of government regulators. Again and again we see such excesses brought low by a confrontation with reality. Disjointed adaptations are so characteristic of human action that a single explanation is warranted. That explanation lies in the tension between goal-oriented adaptation and certain biological bounds on human abilities to adapt. This book is about that tension.

Rationalism Ascendant

We live in an era of resurgent rationalism in human affairs. Perhaps at no time since the Enlightenment have we experienced such a faith in the rationalism of science and technology.[1] This does not mean that there are not dissenting voices; far from it. In the humanities, deconstructionism maintains that all systems of human understanding are rooted in power and oppression, and not in rational progress. A vocal resurgence of fundamentalism in religion questions the blind assumption that technology and process are intertwined. But the intellectual zeitgeist of our age is faith in human reason.

Ours is more than just a generalized faith in progress, or the hope that

---

1. Pareto noted the great irony that the worship of logic can be as nonlogical as any other form of unanalyzed worship.

a scientific elite will lead the way to long life and wealth for all. No, we have a renewed faith in the rationalism of the individual. The ascendancy of capitalism and democracy worldwide since the fall of communism represents a victory of Western institutions, based as they are on respect for the choices of individuals, over claims that individual choice is to be subordinated to the "will of the state." A long period of postwar posterity in the Western democracies has faded the memory of the Great Depression, with its political lessons that responsible people can fall into poverty and that government can be a positive force to ameliorate the undesirable social conditions that put good people into bad circumstances. Much public policy in the United States today is directed at restoring individual choice to publicly provided goods and services, under the assumption that enlightened individuals will make rational choices about pensions, about schooling, about health care.

How did we get so smart? The raw material matters: biology and genetics. If there is a genetic basis to being rational, then our rationality is a product of the Stone Age. Our genes have not had sufficient time to evolve in any meaningful way since the dawn of the agricultural era, much less since the development of written communication (and many would say civilization). Cognitive scientist Steven Pinker puts it this way: "Selection operates over thousands of generations. For ninety-nine percent of human existence, people lived as foragers in small nomadic bands. Our brains are adapted to that long-vanished way of life, not to brand-new agricultural and industrial civilizations" (1997, 42).

Traces of our Stone Age past may be found in the operation of our most rationalist institutions: modern liberal democracies and capitalist economies. These systems work because they have evolved to coordinate diverse behaviors and yet still achieve collective goals. They work best when they take into consideration the limits imposed by human nature—requiring neither philosopher-kings in politics nor superhuman planners in economics. Yet they continue to be subject to limitations—they fall prey to vagaries of human foibles. A rational capitalist economy is subject to recessions. A rational democratic polity is subject to misgovernment. Bounds on our rationality show through even in the most cleverly designed institutions.

We must not be misled into thinking that because there is a genetic basis to modern human behavior that there is consequently a direct link between genes and behavior. That is not, and cannot, be the case. First, in the case of complex traits, numerous genes interact to produce the trait. These genes do not act in a simple additive way. Even if a geneticist knew all the genes that produced a trait, he or she generally could not predict the trait, because of the complexity of the genetic interactions.

Second, in the case of almost all the complex behaviors we are interested here, there isn't really a link between behavior and gene at all. As Pinker argues: "Natural selection is not a puppetmaster that pulls the strings of behavior directly. It acts by designing the generator of behavior: the package of information-processing and goal-pursuing mechanisms called the mind. Our minds are designed to generate behavior that would have been adaptive, on average, in our ancestral environment, but any particular deed done today is the effect of dozens of causes" (1997, 42).

Finally, a major part of our human inheritance is the ability to apply means to ends. In this process, it is the tasks we face and the goals we pursue that determine our behavior, not our genetic inheritance. What determines our behavior is the task in front of us, not a gene, a combination of genes, nor any complex interaction among genes. To the extent that behavior is dictated by goals, it will be fruitless to search for a reductionist explanation of behavior. Because behavior is goal oriented but channeled by human biology, we can never reduce behavior to biology (genetics) alone. But neither can we attribute all of our actions to rationality. It is this elusive quality of behavior that makes social science so difficult.

There is no gene or set of genes for voting for the Republicans or for choosing to buy bonds rather than stocks. It is the case, however, that our behavior is canalized by our genetic inheritances (as well as by our social or cultural inheritances). We can get out of the canal, of course, but only with effort (and often education). Because we are subject to canalization of behavior, the manner in which we achieve our goals will be disjointed and episodic. It is not easy to get out of the canal.

Adaptation and Decision Making

It is useful to think of adaptation in general and abstract terms. A system is an entity that may be analytically separated from but still interacts with its environment. Complex adaptive systems consist of a large number of diverse components, or agents, that interact and that produce an aggregate output behavior (Holland and Miller 1991; Holland 1995). Like the earlier general systems approach, the theory of complex adaptive systems seeks to understand general behavior in ecosystems, in the brain, in economies, in polities.[2]

Fundamental to the idea of complex adaptive systems is information processing. Murray Gell-Mann writes that a complex adaptive system (CAS) "gathers information about its surroundings and about itself"

---

2. See also Simon 1995a.

(1995, 120). An adaptive system is purposive, in that it is capable of attaining goals in a range of environmental conditions. It consists of an inner system, an outer environment, and an interface between the inner and outer systems. Information acts as input for adaptive systems, and action in response to this information is output to the environment. "The outer environment determines the conditions for goal attainment . . . the inner system is adapted to the environment, so that its behavior will be determined in large part by the behavior of the latter. . . . The behavior takes the shape of the task environment" (Simon 1996b).

The adaptive system that interests us here is the human decision maker. Humans operate in complex environments in which they have a set of goals and priorities among the goals. Behavioral scientists use the term "task environment" to refer to the opportunities and constraints that affect an individual's efforts toward goal accomplishment. Within the constraints and opportunities in this task environment, people develop strategies for acting on the environment to achieve these goals. If they always choose the best strategy, then our decision makers are rational maximizers. If strategies are unrelated to goals, then the decision maker is illogical. What if, however, there are mismatches between goal and strategy? Over time, will such mismatches be addressed if the gap is severe enough? If so, we speak of adaptive but not fully rational action.

We may distinguish three environments that shape human behavior. The first is the "immediate task environment." A decision maker must match a strategy, either from a repertoire of existing strategies or one developed for the circumstance at hand, to the demands of the task environment. The challenge is to solve a current problem generated by the immediate task environment.

The second and third environments have acted in the past to shape the repertoire of strategies that the individual uses (or may generate) to solve the current problem. The "lifeline environment" provides the opportunities for the individual to learn problem-solving strategies during his or her lifetime. Learning may have been experiential, directly tried in a similar task environment, or social, transmitted via instruction or observation. Finally, the "biological environment" is the sum of evolutionary processes that have generated the human phenotype.

Much of social science is directed at understanding how people adjust to the immediate task environment. If the strategies people use are indeed adapted to the immediate task environment, then understanding the incentives and costs generated by the task environment is enough to understand human behavior. Further, human behavior may be molded by consciously structuring the task environment in order to achieve collective benefits. Social scientific understanding of modern economies and democracies are premised on the idea that the proper structure of incentives will encourage appropriate behavior. James Madison's famous dicta for the separation of powers in political systems—"ambition must be made to counteract ambition"—embodied the notion that governments may be designed to channel the goal-directed self-centered behavior of political leaders in a manner that will achieve collective ends.[3] In the extreme, the American psychologist B. F. Skinner (1962, 1974) argued that incentives can be manipulated in order to construct ideal societies.

But are the incentives of the immediate task environment enough? In *The Sciences of the Artificial,* Herbert Simon makes the following simple yet elegant argument: Most human behavior may be explained by the nature of the task environment. If decision making is complex, it is mostly because the environment is complex. But the inner system is critical to understanding system performance. Only the grossest characteristics of the inner system need to be known to be able to account for behavior, but an account of behavior will be substantially incomplete without an appreciation of the inner system "showing through." The consequence is that it is not normally enough to know the shape of the environment to understand adaptation. Often adaptation is approximate. "Then the properties of the inner system will 'show through.' That is, the behavior of the system will only partly respond to the task environment; partly it will respond to the limiting properties of the inner system" (1996b, 12).[4]

The Paradox of Information Processing

Humans, and the organizations they inhabit, process information from their environments and act on it.[5] But humans do not—cannot—react instantaneously to information and produce a correct response. In the processing of information, people transform it. To react to information, people must attend to it, interpret it, and devise an appropriate strategy to act on it.

As a consequence, humans are "disproportionate information processors," and so are the organizations that they establish to accomplish their

---

3. Madison feared that constitutions embodying paper separations of powers would not be sufficient to contain the drives of ambitious men—that they might conspire to undermine the whole system. While he argued that the system of "checks and balances" could act to stymie a drive toward demagogic power, Madison placed his primary faith in the checks and balances offered by a civil society constituted of numerous diverse interests (Federalist Paper no. 10, reprinted in Fairchild 1966, 16–23).

4. Not only is adaptation imperfect, it takes time. Systems must learn, and learning is never instantaneous.

5. Organizations don't process information of course; networks of people do. But I will use this convenient fiction throughout this book.

goals. "Disproportionate information processing" implies that objective information is transformed in the process of thought. It involves the tendency of people to react differently to identical information depending on the context in which the information is presented. What is essentially identical information provokes different responses in situations that are similar in all major respects except the interpretation that decision makers have placed on the information. In one context, a bit of information is ignored. In another context, it becomes meaningful and stimulates action. A major reason for such discrepancies is the attention people pay to selected parts of the environment, and how that attentiveness may shift, sometimes in response to very subtle changes in the external world.

Disproportionate information processing means that inputs into a decision-making process do not link directly to outputs. As a consequence, there is an imperfect match between the adaptive strategies people devise and the information they receive. This mismatch is the inner cognitive and emotional architecture of the human brain "showing through" in responding to information. *This mismatch may be observed and assessed in certain situations.* The work of observation and assessment has only begun, and remains controversial among social scientists.

Unfortunately, as we shall see, social scientists are not at present able to isolate the factors that distinguish when a particular piece of information will yield a response and when it will be ignored. Sometimes the event cannot be ignored by those making decisions: events can serve as "triggers" for subsequent action. While the nature of the response may be in question, there is little doubt that there must be one. It would be hard to explain a lack of action after the Oklahoma City federal courthouse bombing or the Japanese attack on Pearl Harbor. On the other hand, it is not so easy to explain from objective situations why so many people fear flying but not driving; why Americans seem to have accepted the virulent influenza outbreak of 1918 (500,000 dead Americans) with considerable equanimity but exhibited such panic at the isolated outbreak of Legionnaires' Disease in 1976 (26 dead) (Garrett 1995, chap. 6); or why many European consumers who smoke regularly fear genetically altered grain.

Unifying Social and Behavioral Sciences

Despite a wealth of evidence of disproportionality in decision making, the notion itself is not uniformly accepted. Social scientists are trained to isolate specific causes that lead to specific effects; if different effects stem from what seem to be similar situations, then we assume that the fundamental causal factors are different. People must simply be adapting to different situations. This is the classic logical fallacy of *post hoc ergo proper hoc.*

Logical fallacy or not, the idea that people react disproportionately to information makes many social scientists uncomfortable, and they there-fore argue that the causal factors are somehow to be found in the objective circumstances facing the decision maker.

The tendency of social scientists to search for incentives for human be-havior is a major roadblock to progress in social science. It separates thinking in the social sciences from thinking in the behavioral sciences. Many behavioral scientists adopt the "other side" of this fallacy: that be-havior can be reduced to psychological or biological mechanisms with no apparent need to refer to the immediate task environment. This has led to a problem of parallel languages: discussing the same behavior in two dif-ferent sets of concepts. As a consequence, analysis in the social and behav-ioral sciences has not been sufficiently integrated. Such integration is fun-damental for scientific progress in these fields.

The notion of disproportionality in the processing of information leads us to the dual adaptive process that continually drives human decision making. People must adapt not just to the objective circumstances in which they find themselves, but also to their own inner cognitive and emo-tive constitutions (Simon 1996b). It is this inner environment that is re-sponsible for the disproportionate processing of objective information. How this transformation occurs, and with what effect, is the primary fo-cus of this book.

While more than a few natural scientists have adopted a perspective that in principle reduces most human behavior to genetics, social scientists have erred in an opposite direction. Most have tended to emphasize the malleability of the human spirit in the face of changing cultural and insti-tutional constraints and opportunities. If most sociologists and cultural anthropologists have sided with culture as the determinative force, the more common tendency in political science and economics has been to relegate the debate between nature and nurture to the sidelines. Most social scientists studying advanced forms of human formal institutions simply don't see the issue as relevant. In effect, they have sided with nur-ture, because of the quite proper emphasis on the ability of institutions to shape behavior. In the so-called new institutionalism, an important ap-proach in political science, scholars view institutions as molding behavior primarily though the incentives they create; the older school of the behav-ioral study of organizations emphasizes in addition the role of institutions in providing interpretations and understandings.

There has been a persistent, if mostly ignored, dissenting voice in politi-cal science. A vigorous scholarship on the biological bases of political ac-tion, probably best represented by the research of Roger Masters (1989) has proceeded independently of mainstream political science (Somit and Peterson 1999). Masters is a political theorist, interested in fundamental questions of human nature. Most students of political behavior were much more concerned with opinion data generated by scientific sample surveys. For this or other reasons, the work of those interested in biopolitics has unfortunately had little impact on the empirical study of political behavior and institutions. So the main path is clear: political institutions are studied with only passing reference to the biological nature of the beings that inhabit those institutions.

In many ways, the academic discipline of economics is most interesting in its ambivalence on the nurture-nature issue. On the one hand, the assumption of comprehensive rationality in human behavior is most developed in that discipline. On the other hand, most economists further assume that human selfishness is the primary, if not the sole, motive for behavior, and that institutions and policies failing to recognize this are bound to fail. In this view, humans are supremely rational yet basely selfish, and no institution can modify that fundamental premise of human behavior.

A vigorous movement in experimental economics is challenging the foundations of this approach. And leading economists, including several Nobel laureates, have begun to address the narrow behavioral base of their discipline (Alt, Levi, and Ostrom 1999; Shiller 2000). Economist Viktor VanBerg writes:

> All social sciences share a common subject, human behavior, and they are not at liberty to construe models of man at their own convenience. . . . They can, for instance, not afford to ascribe to humans behavioral traits which according to evolutionary accounts could never have evolved in the selection environment to which the human species was exposed, nor may they suppose capacities of the human mind which, according to the findings of cognitive science, cannot possibly exist. (1999, 3)

Nevertheless, far too many economists seem satisfied with the "supreme rationality" assumption, failing to produce anything approximating a plausible evolutionary story line for the emergence of selfish superman.[6]

The Evolutionary Paradigm in Behavioral Science

At the opposite end of the continuum of approaches to the study of human behavior lie behavioral genetics and evolutionary psychology. Evolutionary psychologists John Tooby and Leda Cosmides lay down a sensible

---

6. Economists justify their approach via a philosophy of science termed "instrumental positivism" (Friedman 1996). The approach argues that microfoundations are irrelevant; the only test of a theory's adequacy is whether its predictions correspond to observation. This approach is highly problematic. It is corrosive of synthesis in the social and behavioral sciences. It denies scientific curiosity about the roots of human behavior. And it does not follow the practices in the more mature sciences, where assumptions are continually probed both theoretically and observationally.

dictum: "Social scientists should be extremely uneasy about postulating an improbably complex structure in the system with the capacity to solve non-biological functional ends, unless that capacity is a by-product of functionality that evolved to serve adaptive ends" (1992, 110). They argue that the conceptual bases of the various social and behavioral sciences should be mutually consistent as well as consistent with what is known in the natural sciences (Cosmides, Tooby, and Barkow 1992, 4).[7]

Current thinking in evolutionary psychology and behavioral genetics emphasizes that human cognitive architecture evolved in a functionally specialized, content-specific way and concomitantly downgrades generalized problem-solving capacities in humans. In particular, the evolutionary psychologists have renewed the attack on equipotential learning: the idea that people can learn most anything via the manipulation of the incentives before them. The notion that anything can be learned through the manipulation of incentives was long a fundamental premise of American behaviorist psychology. Tooby and Cosmides write: "A psychological architecture that consisted of nothing but equipotential, general-purpose content-independent, or content-free mechanisms could not successfully perform the tasks that the human mind is known to perform or solve the adaptive problems humans evolved to solve" (1992, 34).

Underlying all rationality models as employed in economics and political science is a "general problem-solving mechanism" whose basic foundation is equipotential learning. Social scientists are so quick to assume that the incentives available to a decision maker are the cause of his or her action that they often fail to grasp that they have implicitly imposed a process—a point emphasized by Herbert Simon (1997a) in his distinction between substantive and procedural rationality.

The aim of the adaptationist program in behavioral science is sound enough: to debunk the "blank slate" model of human nature that has equipotential learning as its primary foundation. In their zeal to denigrate a general problem-solving mechanism in human cognitive architecture, however, evolutionary psychologists and behavioral geneticists may have overly discounted generalized problem solving in modern social systems.[8] Tooby and Cosmides, for example, are dismissive of laboratory studies of memory, problem solving, and decision making because they assess performance on "artificial, evolutionarily unprecedented tasks such as chess-playing or cryptarithmetic" (1992, 124). A student of complex institutions might ask whether these unprecedented tasks are more or less similar

---

7. This is a weaker criterion than conceptual integration, which may be overly ambitious at the present state of knowledge.

8. Or, more generally, adaptation to universal features of the world. See Shepard 1992.

to crafting a motion to recommit a budget resolution or deciding when to sell a stock option.

Many of the content-specific mechanisms studied by behavioral Darwinists are of little aid in understanding human interactions in modern complex institutions. It is doubtless true that many social scientists fail to realize that "environmental responsiveness requires a complex evolved design" (Tooby and Cosmides 1992, 87). That is, the match between the complexity of the environment and the evolved perceptual mechanisms of humans is both remarkable and clearly a product of evolutionary forces. But students of economic and political institutions need only ensure compatibility of their environmentalist theories with evolutionary theory. It is exactly when the match between the environment and the decisions of humans *fails* that we are most interested in the evolved cognitive architecture of legislators, voters, stockbrokers, and corporate leaders. Otherwise behavior may be most efficiently explained as a consequence of the task environment.

On the other hand, it is critical for social scientists to understand that many of their favorite theories hinge on a discredited notion of learning. No species, including humans, learns solely by the behaviorist notion of response reinforcement (or reward for performance). And the substance of what is learned matters; some behaviors are easier to elicit through response reinforcement than others. We return to the notion of equipotential learning in chapter 2.

None of this obviates the key role of the task environment in human decision making. If the task environment is the most important factor in human behavior, why bother with genetics and psychology? The reason is to understand (1) the causes for mismatches between behavior and goal, and (2) how adaptive behavior emerges in the first place. Here we are primarily interested in mismatches. Mismatches occur because our cognitive architecture did not evolve to solve the problems inherent in modern complex institutions.

There are three evolutionary-based causes of mismatches (or what might be termed "decisional adaptive failures"). First, evolutionary traits are jerry-rigged as a consequence of the evolutionary process itself. Evolution takes as a given the phenotype; it cannot begin anew. So whatever phenotype exists—including human cognitive architecture—is a rigged apparatus from past accretions of random variations winnowed by selective processes. Second, evolution takes time, and a lot of it, to operate. The human cognitive architecture we observe today is a function of the operation of natural selection for tasks performed in a Paleolithic environment. Finally, the cognitive task environment of complex modern institutions is hard. The more difficult the cognitive task, the more the limits of human cognitive architecture will reveal itself through a mismatch between environment and behavior.

Socially Channeled Behavior

There is no doubt that socially constructed ideas and institutions channel human behavior—biology is not destiny in human affairs. Human culture is so powerful in directing human behavior that many evolutionary biologists and anthropologists think that cultural evolution has displaced biological evolution as the major mechanism of human adaptation. Culture, it has been said, allows us to escape our genes.

There is perhaps no more eloquent testimony to this than the declining birthrates worldwide. Italy recently became the first country with more people over the age of sixty than under the age of twenty. If our genes are "selfish," as biologist Richard Dawkins's apt metaphor suggests, striving mightily to maximize their survivability, then how does one account for the declines? At first, many demographers pointed out that the survival of a lower number of offspring could more than offset the decline in the production of the number of offspring. But in northern Italy, women are giving birth to an average of less than one child. The only explanation seems to be that we (or the Italians, at least) have fooled our genes. Nurture wins over nature.[9]

On the other hand, the institutions that exist as a product of human culture seem to work best when the limits and potentialities of human nature are taken into consideration. Human behavior is not infinitely malleable. It is a truism of both common observation and economic theory that market economies work better than planned ones. Planned economies undermine the incentives of individuals to be productive. And the planners, being self-centered themselves, will often use public power for selfish aims. Public policies may be hijacked for private gain, and this possibility is tied fundamentally to human nature. Liberal democracy, with its commitment to open criticism of public officials, reinforced by the constant threat of removal from office through elections, paradoxically requires only sporadic attention from the bulk of citizens while requiring political leaders to justify what they are doing. Public policies are prioritized according to the dynamics of attention, which sets the agenda for public action. No set of governors are procedurally capable of paying attention to all problems simultaneously, even if all are equally deserving of

---

9. There is no great puzzle here. "Human beings, like other organisms, have been designed by selection to strive for *specific* goals, not the *general* goal of reproduction-maximization" (Symons 1992, 139). But it does point to the risks of an undisciplined evolutionary adaptationist program in social science.

action. Emotion and mobilization, as a consequence, are necessary to raise attention to issues and prioritize public action. These examples and many more suggest molding our institutions in light of human nature.

The Biological Heritage of Decision Making

Into every decision we make in life, we take both our biological and our social heritage. Biological heritages are aspects of our biological makeup that affect our current decision making. We may distinguish between two different kinds of biological heritages: procedural and substantive. "Procedural" inheritances are those biological characteristics that affect the processes by which we make decisions, including how we process information about alternatives and make choices among the alternatives. To take one major example: the human brain has almost unlimited long-term memory storage capacity. But it has an exceedingly small short-term (or "working") memory capacity. Psychologist George Miller (1956) wrote a classic article in the late 1950s entitled "The Magic Number Seven, Plus or Minus Two" to emphasize the limited capacity of short-term memory. Even worse, we cannot access our almost infinite long-term memory—at least consciously—except through the bottleneck of short-term memory. We can't think about anything unless we pay attention to it, and that is true whether the relevant stimuli come from the environment or from one's own long-term memory.

There are good evolutionary reasons for the development of attention structures. Any organism unable to "pay inattention" to irrelevant stimuli while focusing on relevant ones is quite clearly doomed. This system works superbly in a world of few relevant stimuli and many irrelevant ones. On the other hand, in an information-rich world with lots of potentially relevant stimuli, attention structures are ill designed to identify and combine the relevant ones and react to them. I refer to this as the "index construction problem" and discuss it further in chapter 7. As long as attention is fundamentally dichotomous (attending/not attending), a decision maker can fall prey to the index construction problem—in particular, how to pick out the currently most salient item in a complex situation and react to it.

Lots of decisional consequences come from the bottleneck of attention, including the difficulty we have in making comparisons in decision-making situations with numerous attributes. We can compensate for the short-term memory problem—we can write down the attributes, like President Nixon did on his ubiquitous yellow pad. We can even combine them via a formula, even if that formula is to some extent arbitrary. But the point here is that our decision-making behavior is canalized by this part of our genetic heritage. It should also be evident that procedural limitations will afflict all goal-directed behavior—that is, behavior will not be affected by the substance of the goals people pursue.

"Substantive" inheritances are those conscious and nonconscious behaviors that affect the content of decisions directly. They affect the goals or preferences people hold. While there are lots of particular goals and preferences that people have, and there are great individual differences among those wishes and desires, we may nevertheless characterize them broadly into two classes: self-centered and other-centered. Self-centered beings will make different decisions than will altruistic ones. On the other hand, much supposed altruism, directed as it is by status rewards, may be explained by rational self-interest. Moreover, other-centered behavior may not be admirable—as may be the case, for example, when soldiers march off to an unjust war because of a sense of duty (rather than a fear of punishment for draft dodging).[10]

It is by no means accepted by many social and biological scientists that truly altruistic individuals exist. Many biologists see altruism as directly related to the propagation of genes. An altruistic act toward one's relatives can be genetically adaptable (Sober and Wilson 1998). Altruism toward kin is consistent with the "selfish gene" argument that postulates that adaptive behavior can be altruistic if it results in an increase in genes passed on. Altruism for your children, or even your nieces and nephews, can be "selfish" in this sense, but altruism toward your post–reproductive age spouse is not explicable in terms of kin selection.[11] It nevertheless seems that humans are capable of considerable altruism toward non-kin. (Sober and Wilson 1998; Simon 1990). Indeed, there is considerable evidence that humans are in general more cooperative than a self-centered rationality can explain, and we discuss this in chapter 5. This "better than rational" cooperative behavior has important implications for human interaction in complex institutions.[12]

The distinction between substantive and procedural inheritances is to some extent arbitrary. Both have a genetic basis, but in each instance we are talking about the transmission of predispositions, not invariable determinants. Both inheritances can be modified through learning. Many of the implications of either can be avoided with conscious effort. Nevertheless,

---

10. Some social scientists distinguish between "thick" and "thin" rationality. Thick rationality refers to self-centered rational decision making; thin rationality to maximization with *any* goal (including altruism). The idea of this approach was to escape the limits imposed by self-centeredness, but the consequence is that no predictions can be made (Simon 1985).

11. See Dugatin 1999 for a discussion of the biological bases for cooperation in animals and humans.

12. The term is Elinor Ostrom's (1998).

it makes much sense to distinguish between those human characteristics that affect the process of decision making and those that affect the ends of decision making. The distinction highlights a major contradiction in the underpinning of economics: substantive inheritances are emphasized (in the motive of self-gratification) but procedural inheritances are ignored (in the assumption of supreme rationality).

Nature, Nurture, or Task Environment?

Many social scientists hold the implicit or explicit premise that humans are very nearly infinitely malleable. As much as social scientists in democratic societies criticized socialism's attempts to create a "New Man," many still harbor a view of human nature that is insufficiently sensitive to its genetic limitations. On the other hand, many psychologists have tended to the opposite extreme: underestimating the adaptability of people to the demands of complex formal institutions.

Discussing genetics inevitably involves discussing evolution. Biologist R. C. Lewontin (1998) has issued a strong warning to those who would speculate (his term) about the evolution of human cognition. Much writing about the evolution of human behavior has involved establishing plausible "story lines" about how cognition and consciousness could have arisen. Stephen Jay Gould (1980) has termed these story lines "just so stories" after the writing of Rudyard Kipling.

While cognitive scientist Steven Pinker (1997) defends these plausible evolutionary stories, Lewontin warns that they do not constitute science. Lewontin notes that traits can't evolve biologically, only organisms can; that traits, once acquired, can affect the organism's further evolution; and that the acquisition of a trait could be an epiphenomenon of a correlated trait that was subject to selection. Add that to the fact that cultural evolution and learning can account for current behavioral patterns and we have a very strong caution against the leap to an explanation of a current behavioral trait in terms of natural selection.

It is a false grail to seek a linkage between the evolution of particular traits and current behavior—simply because people are so adaptive to the current demands they face. That is why there will never be a theory of human behavior that can be reducible to genes or human biology. We must also have theories of the incentives that motivate people and the institutions that provide those incentives.

On the other hand, what I have termed procedural limits on adaptation clearly do influence our current patterns of choice. These limits, as well as the tasks people face, must be known in order to predict human behavior in any given situation. Through observation and controlled laboratory settings, we know that these limitations exist. And these procedural limits are related in a causal fashion to the behaviors of modern complex institutions. The necessity of allocating limited attention and the resulting setting of agendas and prioritizing of problems in liberal democracies are major consequences of the restricted capacity of human short-term memory. So are the resulting inconsistencies in established policies that took shape in different contexts. For many years, for example, the United States discouraged smoking (as a health policy) and encouraged tobacco production (as an agricultural policy). Because policymakers are attentive to different aspects of a situation at different times, inconsistent policies can emerge (and, because attention has never been directed at the inconsistencies, endure).

What I have termed substantive limitations on rational adaptation is a much trickier concept, and more controversial. Used with less than adequate care, the concept could be expanded into all sorts of "just so stories" about the operation of modern institutions. I concentrate primarily on one substantive limitation: people are more cooperative and accept suggestions from others more readily than would be expected based on the formal structures of the institutions they inhabit. There are doubtless other substantive limitations, but cooperativeness beyond what would be expected based on rational self-interest (and much cooperativeness can be explained rationally) is becoming so well established that it cannot be ignored as a key facet of human nature. Several scholars (Wilson 1993; Caporeal 1997) have argued that nonrational cooperation is the basis (but not the determinant) for many aspects of modern-day behavior, including morality.

Analyzing Institutions

Social scientists have often analyzed political and economic systems as if they live an independent existence from the thought processes of human beings. In economics and in public choice approaches in political science, institutions are implicitly viewed in a cognitive, non-emotive vein. In the spare approach of public choice economist Charles Plott, the outcomes from institutions (such as a legislative body) are determined by an interaction between the preferences of participants and the rules that structure the institution. Participants decide what they want, and then use the rules to maximize their utility (what they want). Hence Plott's "fundamental equation" (Plott 1991; see also, Plott 1976):

$$\text{preferences} \times \text{institutions} \rightarrow \text{outcomes}$$

All we need to know to understand the collective outcomes of complex formal institutions is how peoples' preferences interact with the incentives supplied by the institutions within which people interact. There is no room for the cognitive constitutions of decision makers in this approach; only desires and incentives matter. Given a standard set of desires, all actions taken by individuals are determined by the objective incentives before them. The rules that characterize the institution supply the incentives. So in markets, participants maximize wealth; in politics, elected politicians maximize expected votes in the next election.

The approach used by Plott and many other economists and political scientists goes under the label "rational choice." The fundamental idea is that people have fixed preferences, and these preferences are transitive. Transitivity just means that if, for example, in the 1992 U.S. presidential election, a voter preferred Bush to Clinton, and Clinton to Perot, he or she would also prefer Bush to Perot. The only other assumption is that people act according to their preferences—they chose the option that they like best. In the technical language of economics, they "maximize utility."

This seems obvious—so obvious that one may wonder why it is controversial (or maybe why it might be useful). Nevertheless, it has been both useful and controversial. Many empiricists in political science, psychology, and sociology have fumed at the artificiality of the rational choice approach, claiming that human behavior is just not so simple. They have pointed to a variety of observational and laboratory-induced violations of the principles of rational choice (see Slovic 1990 for an excellent discussion). In more complex situations involving uncertainty, people can be induced to make intransitive choices, for example. Many everyday choices involve incommensurate factors that are difficult to compare (see box 1.1). Options are often not clear, searches often incomplete, and when choices are clear but where there is risk or uncertainty, people often violate the axioms of expected utility theory.[13]

But critics of the rational choice approach often miss the point. The rational choice perspective offers a powerful set of tools to analyze economies and polities tied to adaptation to present incentives. People have fixed goals and preferences about what they want. They face choice opportunities, such as voting, or lobbying, or taking a new job. Each alternative offers both benefits and costs. People adapt by choosing the best alternative given the choices they face and the goals they harbor.

The institutions of modern capitalism and democracy structure the

---

13. There has also been a fascination with mathematical manipulations to the exclusion of the empirical tests that are the hallmark of science. Political scientist (and rational choice theorist) Peter Ordeshook takes note of the theoretical breakthroughs accomplished by the rational choice perspective in political science, but warns that "much of this research, like a giant ingrown toenail, is wholly literature-driven and directed in inconsequential matters" characterized by "an intoxication with notation" (1993, 74). A less sympathetic critique has been launched by two Yale political scientists (Green and Shapiro 1994).

Box 1.1: Bush or Clinton? A Multiattribute
Problem

How do voters decide which candidate in an election is a better choice?
Let us take as an example the 1992 U.S. presidential election between
George Bush and Bill Clinton. The choice was not just between two
individual candidates, because each man encompassed many diverse attributes—party affiliation, character, ability in foreign policy, domestic
policy promises, etc. We must make choices by somehow comparing
these diverse attributes. This is easy if Bush is better on all attributes, or
if the attributes are easy to compare. But many times attributes are incommensurate. Choice under these very common circumstances is difficult, because it is difficult for people to rank the choice alternatives.

Some research by William Thompson of Indiana University illustrates the multiattribute problem. Thompson's 1996 study of public
opinion polls shows that Bush was favored on issues of foreign policy
by most voters, and Clinton on domestic policy. Moreover, Bush's ratings on foreign policy exceeded Clinton's by a wider margin than Clinton's advantage on domestic policy.

So why did Clinton win? It turns out that most voters weighted domestic policy higher than foreign policy when they got into the voting
booth. The attentiveness that people give to candidate attributes affects
election outcomes.

decisions we face. In effect, they rule out all sorts of factors that otherwise
would have to be taken into account. For example, in 1503, Luigi Man-
nelli made a speech denouncing the Florentine government. He was tor-
tured and exiled (Masters 1998, 90). Such action tends to limit criticism.
Today, the right of contract means that one can make business deals with
strangers. These and other institutional facets generate different decisions
than would be made in their absence. Lots of behavior can be explained
in terms of such institutional arrangements.

To be useful in understanding modern complex institutions, any nonrational explanation must add explanatory power not just at the individual level, but also at the aggregate, collective level. Rational choice
approaches are powerful tools, setting a standard for human adaptability.
But they do fail, and they fail at important points. Moreover, as I show in
this book, they fail in ways critical to the understanding of complex formal institutions.

Many analysts in the rational choice tradition have tried to find institutional incentives for nonconforming behavior. If behavior exists, they

seem to say, we can find some incentive that must account for it. Sweeping these failures under the rug by claiming "close counts" or by claiming that all sorts of human foibles can still be rational is no longer acceptable given the strong nature of the contrary evidence. Here I pursue a different strategy: using the rational choice approach as a critical standard from which to measure deviations—deviations that must be linked to past patterns of adaptation (genetic or cultural) that interfere with current patterns of adaptation.

In effect, we may classify human behavior—at least human behavior that is goal directed—into two categories. The first is rational, adaptive behavior. This is behavior that may be explained by the task environment—the problem at hand. The second category is behavior that cannot be so explained. This second category of behavior is a set of inherited limits that can be adduced from a comparison of task environments and the procedural and substantive limitations that we inherit. If task environments cannot explain our behavior, then our internal cognitive and emotional architectures must—either alone or in combination with the tasks we face.[14]

Many real-life task environments are essentially ambiguous, so that rational adaptation may not be so easy. And in most cases, adaptation is not simple and instantaneous—people must think and learn. In particular, in environments that are "noisy," confusing, or rapidly changing, adaptation is not smooth, but rather is episodic and disjointed (Lounamaa and March 1985; Jones 1994). Efficiencies in adaptation stem both from internal, inherited bounds on our rationality and on the ambiguity of the world we face.

To the extent that human institutions simplify the task environment, they can minimize the problems of ambiguity. Well-running markets and democracies simplify choices, and thereby reduce the ambiguity of task environments.

The Evolution of Institutions

The problem with the analysis above is that it suggests a static set of rational adaptations and a yardstick for measuring deviations of actual human behavior from the ideal. Indeed, I shall show later in this book how we may begin to develop such a static yardstick (see chapter 7). But human institutions are not fixed; they evolve under pressure from external

---

14. Dividing behavior into that determined by the task environment and that determined by biological inheritances does not address the complexities of how these two facets combine. A linear and additive combination quite clearly is overly simple, but nonlinear interactions get very complex very quickly. In essence, many social scientists simply assume that behavior is determined solely by the task environment. As a consequence, any approach emphasizing a combination will be a substantial improvement.

demands and the activities of participants in them. As they evolve, they evoke different responses from participants.

As a consequence, no study of human behavior can ignore the adaptability of humans to the institutions that they create and modify. What I shall call "laundry list" objections to rational choice seem to miss the point that, by in large, humans are reasonably good decision makers, not benighted ones. On the other hand, adaptability is always a moving target, so that last week's adaptive solution may be today's catastrophe. So any model of rational adaptation must include some understanding of the lags and inefficiencies of adaptation, as well as of the persistent characteristics of individuals that repeatedly interfere with smooth adaptation.

The accomplishments of humankind in the development of institutions, when viewed over the sweep of written history, are indeed remarkable. Modern capitalist economic systems have evolved from systems of barter exchange into highly complex symbolic systems in which money acts as an intermediary for exchange; prices act as signals for complex adjustment behaviors; value can be stored and accumulate symbolically; ownership and control are separate; and prices can be set for things once regarded as sacred or profane: labor, capital, and home. Each of these transactions, and many others, required substantial breakthroughs in conceptualizing how social systems allocate and distribute goods and services.

Similarly, modern liberal democracies have developed processes of thought that are equally symbolic and complex: political leadership is depersonalized; political leadership is transitory; political leadership is accountable, via elections and open discussion; winners and losers are determined through a tabulation of marks on pieces of paper; and the concept of rights for citizens and leaders are defined both substantively and procedurally.

The evolutionary shift from a conception of leadership that is based in charisma or in hereditary rights to a system in which the ability to exercise power is "loaned" for a limited period of time is every bit as revolutionary as the development of the price system in capitalist economies. These remarkable accomplishments cannot be conceived as externally forced changes, driven by "technology." They are conceptual, cognitive "inventions," and are as responsible for human progress as are the technological breakthroughs that are so commonly cited as the causes of progress.

There is no reason to suppose that economies or polities have ceased to evolve; indeed, there is good reason to suppose that evolution in organizational and institutional forms is proceeding at a quicker pace than ever. Let us not suppose that evolution and progress are coincident—the necessity of trial and error and the difficulty of reversing error in human systems is enough to vitiate that notion. The important point here is simply that human institutions are not fixed; that they continue to evolve, and that humans must adapt to that changing institutional environment.

The image this should evoke is a dynamic interchange where people are continually adapting to changing environments that consist mostly of the institutions in which they interact, and where institutions themselves continually adjust (through the intended actions of humans) to changing environments. This means, of course, that there is nothing fixed about the incentives that people adapt to. Stable organizational worlds are continually being undermined by the necessity for the organization to adapt.

The Argument

I make the following argument in this book: (1) Human behavior is mostly adaptive and goal oriented. (2) Because of biological limits on cognitive capacities, however, humans are disproportionate information processors. They tend to react to new information by neglect or overestimation. (3) The formal organizations created by humans aid in adaptation by overcoming inherited limitations in adaptive abilities. (4) Nevertheless, some of our limitations in adaptability will show through in even the most rational of institutions. (5) As a consequence, these institutions will not react proportionately to incoming information, and outputs from the most rational of institutions will be disjointed and episodic.

The development of this argument proceeds as follows. In chapter 2, I detail what we mean by adaptation through the use of rational choice perspectives developed in economics, decision sciences, and political science. I also detail the complaints lodged against the rational choice perspective. In chapter 3, I discuss procedural limits on adaptability, proposing a model of choice that is more consistent with our procedural limitations. I explore the idea of disproportionate information processing in chapter 4. In chapter 5, I examine substantive limitations on comprehensive rationality, particularly the human tendency to "overcooperate" in terms of the dictates of the individually based model of rationality. I turn in chapter 6 to organizational adaptation and its limits, making the case that organizational adaptability and failures of adjustment are causally connected to human adaptability and its failures. I explore how we can assess and measure deviations from comprehensive rationality in economic and political institutions in chapter 7, and in chapter 8, I discuss the evolution of institutions and how they may be designed to evoke more rational behavior from those who participate in them. Finally, in chapter 9, I offer some thoughts for balancing adaptation and human resistance to it.

CHAPTER 2

Adaptation and Its Limits

DECISION MAKING is dynamic. Information comes to people (or they search for it), and they take actions accordingly. How they take action based on this information is key, because the action cannot completely be explained by the information. People do not process information proportionately to the information they receive. Information pushes people to act, but a kind of friction keeps them from acting. That friction can consist of objective costs to action but it can also consist of internal cognitive components. Understanding the dynamics of this information/friction interaction is the subject of the next three chapters.

The mismatch between decision and information can only be understood if we begin with a standard of adaptation—of the "proper" decision. Then we can compare the factors in our cognitive constitutions that influence how we reach a proper decision and how we may deviate from one. Even in the organizations that represent the high point of human rational accomplishment, we are influenced by a genetic past that channels our behaviors, and limits the adaptability of our current choices. How might these traces show through in modern rationalist institutions?

Mental Accounting

An important instance is provided by finance economist Richard Thaler. Thaler thinks that economic decisions are, in his terms, "quasi-rational." There is a strong element of rational adjustment to economic circumstances in individual economic decision making. But people behave as if they have trouble in making choices that will delay gratification and must exercise self-control. Thaler writes that "the very term 'self-control' implies that the trade-offs between immediate gratification and long-run benefits entail a conflict that is not present between a white shirt and a blue one" (1991, 93). The standard theory of economic choice decrees that a choice between present consumption and saving for the future is no different in principle from a choice between a white shirt and a blue one. In either case one compares costs (properly measured) and benefits (properly discounted) and chooses the option that has the highest utility (benefits less costs). For example, Thaler asks, what would you do in the following situations?

1. You receive a $1000 bonus at work.
2. You win $1000 in the office baseball pool.
3. You receive a $1000 raise.
4. You are guaranteed an inheritance in ten years. It has a present value of $1000.

In economic theory, money is money. A household ought to maximize its utility or well-being using all the assets at its command. Traditional economic theory dictates that one should treat the income from each of these events as equivalent. This is the fully rational thing to do; it brings about the greatest total happiness to "number one." But most households don't seem to operate that way. Instead, households "code various components of wealth into different *mental accounts,* some of which are more 'tempting' to invade than others" (Thaler 1991, 97). People employ different propensities to consume in each account, developing rules of thumb to deal with the self-control issues inherent in trading off present consumption against future well-being. So most people would consume a higher proportion of the "windfall" than of the raise.

Other common examples of mental accounting abound. Many of us make sure that our employers withhold more money from our paychecks than is necessary to pay federal income taxes. Many people who work in education are paid for only the academic year—usually nine months. Yet they must budget expenses over the full calendar year. As a consequence, many school districts and colleges offer the option of dividing the annual pay into twelve equal units, keeping employees supplied with a cash flow over the summer. But employees lose the use of the money for this period of time, costing themselves the interest that could have been earned during the academic year.

The mechanism of mental accounting, which has been demonstrated in laboratory experiments as well as in casual observation of household behavior, should not emerge in households employing a completely rational approach to the allocation of its assets. It, as well as other similar mechanisms that people use when they are allocating assets, is at odds with the pure theory of consumer choice. Such observations form the basis of a new field of study in business termed "behavioral finance." [1]

---

1. The field is summarized by Thaler in an fine and accessible book, *The Winner's Curse.* Thaler treats the findings from behavioral finance as "anomalies" given predictions from economic theory. If we think of such decision-making anomalies as stemming from the tension between adaptation to external incentives and adaptation to the internal cognitive

If there is something wrong with the pure theory of consumer choice, then what is the alternative? If we understand that human nature involves a struggle for self-control—what William James termed the "effort of attention" to control an "unwise passion"—then there is nothing at all "irrational" about mental accounting. On the contrary, mental accounting falls into an important class of human behaviors termed "bounded rationality." Since the task is to manage one's finances, one institutes informal "rules" to deal with the temptation of immediate gratification of consumption. Mental accounting is a process that is goal directed and might even be seen as "utility maximization with constraints." But the source of the constraints is human nature itself.

Fully rational decision makers, say many social scientists, maximize utility. Maximizing utility means simply adapting fully to the set of choices one is facing. The decision maker surveys his or her opportunities and costs, and takes the course of action that achieves the greatest gain given the costs of the opportunities.

In theory, achieving such an ideal has to do only with responding to the incentives that are "out there" in the environment. In real life, generating maximum utility is often neither simple nor smooth, and it is affected by the cognitive and emotional constitution of the decision maker. Bounded rationality sees human decision makers as adaptive and goal oriented, but subject to human limitations. It is not just a question of impulse control; it does not just involve "controlling our emotions" in order to maximize utility within the domain of pure, sweet reason. Modern cognitive science has shown definitively that emotions are a necessary component for prioritizing our choices, and hence essential for decision making (Damasio 1994, 1999). Nor is bounded rationality simply a set of "heuristic" devices employed to avoid time-consuming analyses of all alternatives. In many cases, such heuristic decision making is misleading, even if goal directed.

Finally, bounded rationality is not a set of perverse human mistakes in decision making. There has been a tendency for many critics of goal-directed, utility-maximizing human behavior to generate a laundry list of human foibles in decision making. Reading this literature, much of it coming from psychology, one gets the idea that people are really quite flawed at making decisions.[2] My position here is quite the contrary; I think

---

architecture, they become part of a theoretical perspective rather than a set of loosely connected empirical observations that do not comport with rational choice (Shefrin 2000; Shleifer 2000).

2. The pessimism of psychologists on human decision making may come from the "one-shot" nature of the laboratory experiments they generally use. It is not that such settings are

people are mostly pretty good at it. Humans are goal directed, understand their environment in realistic terms, and adjust to changing circumstances facing them. But they are not completely successful in doing so—because of their inner limitations. Moreover, these cognitive limitations make a big difference in human affairs—in the affairs of individuals and in the affairs of state and nation.

General or Specific Problem Solving?

Consumer choice theory, as well as most theories current in economics, sociology, and political science, implicitly or explicitly postulate general problem-solving mechanisms. Social scientists generally assume that decision makers adapt to a situation in light of goals and constraints—whether they are "utility maximizers" or "bounded rationalists," they adapt to the environment by processing information and solving problems.

There is another side to this coin. A vigorous debate in evolutionary biology and psychology concerns the extent to which mechanisms in the mind are directed at domain-specific rather general-purpose problem-solving mechanisms. Evolutionary psychologists Tooby and Cosmides write: "General mechanisms turn out to be very weak and cannot un-assisted perform at least most and perhaps all of the tasks humans routinely perform and need to perform" (1992, 39). David Buss continues the argument: "There can in principle, therefore, be no fully domain-general solution mechanism—one that can be used across all adaptive domains, by all ages, by all sexes, and under all individual circumstances" (1995, 7). He reasons that "adaptive problems that humans had to solve in their environment of evolutionary adaptedness were many, complex, and different from one another"—hence the solutions that evolved are "many, complex, and different." Buss lists such specific mechanisms as fear of snakes, spiders, and strangers; benefits of color vision, particular sensitivity to perceiving animal motion, and ability to predict the intentions of others; reasons for child abuse by stepparents and the causes of marital dissolution, mate preference, male and female differences in risk behavior, and morning sickness (8–9).

These domain-specific postulates have replaced an emphasis on cognitive plasticity as the primary adaptive path for *Homo sapiens*. Our adaptive path was previously seen as intelligent problem solving—processing information from the environment and acting on the environment in

---

artificial. It is that experiments generally do not last long enough to allow the feedback and adjustment processes that keep people from falling into the traps into which their cognitive limits would otherwise lead them. For a defense of field research in assessing these correctives in the real world, see Laitin 1999.

response to that information. Because of consciousness, humans were supposed to be better information processors than other species.

While the evolutionary psychology emphasis on relating evolved traits to current behavior is laudatory, the approach has some problematic aspects. First, many of the alleged mechanisms listed by Buss and others are but tenuously demonstrated. Second, many of these tenuously demonstrated effects may or may not be products of evolution (rather than cultural, learned artifacts). Most important, the approach is fundamentally static; it cannot explain dynamics in human behavior. Women of high reproductive value are supposed to be more intensely monitored than those of low reproductive value (Buss 1995, 9). That sort of monitoring behavior is on the radical decline all over the world. What explains these changes (and many, many more) other than adaptability and general problem solving? We are better served by starting with the assumption of a general information-processing and problem-solving capacity, and then tracing just where the evolved domain-specific cognitive systems affect current decision making.

Prepared Learning

It is unlikely that we will get very far in understanding human behavior in complex institutional settings through the lenses of evolutionary psychology, at least as currently constituted. That's because so much human behavior is goal directed and governed by current incentives.

On the other hand, there are enough examples of failure at seamless adaptation that social scientists would be foolish not to examine the behavioral underpinnings of modern complex institutions. Indeed, the behavioral approach to organizations, developed at Carnegie-Mellon University in the 1950s, is directed at just that process of examination. Unfortunately, the influence of this approach has become muted in the social sciences under the contradictory influences of rational choice theory, which denies human limits, and evolutionary psychology and behavioral genetics, which ignores human adaptability.

In particular, the explosion of findings in cognitive science has not been integrated into a new understanding of human behavior in organizations. To achieve this integration, we need to ask to what extent limitations in our human nature interfere with our adaptive ability. Or, stated slightly differently, how are the demands to adapt canalized by our biological makeups? This implies beginning with the premise of general-purpose adaptation and problem solving rather than the domain-specific approach advocated by the evolutionary psychologists.

Even given the remarkable flexibility inherent in general problem solving, humans possess certain predispositions to behave in certain ways—

a bias in behavior that psychologists call "prepared learning." During the mid-twentieth-century heyday of behaviorism, psychologists posited two kinds of learning: classical conditioning and instrumental learning. Both are characterized by an association between stimulus and response (hence the term "associative learning"). In instrumental learning, experimenters controlled the reward structure, and conditioned a response to the desired stimulus by reinforcing it. Laboratory observations suggested that instrumental learning was characterized by "trial and error" by the animal.

Underlying this approach was the "equipotentiality" premise, the notion that "all responses and reinforcers can be associated about equally well" (Seligman and Hager 1972, 3). "Give me control over a reward, and I can condition any stimulus to it" was the rallying cry of the Skinnerian behaviorist.

There was a major problem with this approach, however. Laboratory animals learned some associations much quicker than they did others. Seligman and Hager, in their introduction to a volume entitled *Biological Boundaries of Learning,* write: "In addition to sensory-motor apparatus [the inherited biological phenotype], the organism brings associative apparatus which also has a long and specialized evolutionary history. This specialization may make certain contingencies easier to learn about than others, more difficult to forget, more readily generalizable, and so on" (1972, 3).

Learning psychologists were unprepared to accept the implied attack on the equipotentiality premise. The first studies of prepared learning in rats, by John Garcia and his colleagues, met with outright hostility from the psychological learning theory establishment. All the major journals rejected the papers, and they were finally published in "out of the way journals" (Seligman and Hagar 1972, 8).

It is important to understand what prepared learning is and is not. Prepared learning is not hardwired instinct. Rather, it involves an ease of learning some stimulus-response associations, and a resistance to learning others. As a consequence, the same set of rewards will be more efficient in eliciting a response where the organism is prepared to learn it than where it is not.

There is a critically important lesson for the development of bounded rationality and behavioral organization theory (if one is willing to apply at least some general principles across species). It is this: the nature of external stimuli is not enough to predict the behavior of an animal. Something of the animal's biological makeup must be known in addition. Moreover, there is a developmental aspect to prepared learning; there are critical periods for learning particular behaviors during the life of an organism. These associations can become virtually hardwired causes of behavior, a process called "experiential canalization." For example, the attractiveness of a duck's maternal call is not innate; only if the animal experiences the sound at the right developmental moment will the association work (Gottlieb 1996).

Garcia and his colleagues, however, never thought to replace prepared learning with a domain-specific evolutionary psychology. In 1972 they wrote: "We were not concerned with upsetting learning theory. . . . The behavioral techniques served us well. . . . Only the 'empty organism' theories proved to be totally inadequate" (Garcia, McGowan, and Green 1972, 23). Even in the study of rats in the laboratory, the assumption of a general learning mechanism was supported, at least when supplemented with some appreciation of the idea that animals came to the laboratory setting better prepared to learn some associations than others.

Conscious thought gives humans the option of overriding such canalized, habitual behavior. Human habitual behavior, like the apparently innate fear of snakes, can be overcome—self-consciously and with effort (Wilson 1998, 79). Thaler's mental accounting can be seen as a set of self-conscious devices employed to overcome learning biases—in this case, the bias toward immediate gratification of basic wants. Gratifying essential and immediate wants is adaptive, in the Darwinian sense of conferring survival value. But such gratification can interfere in the long run with the economic well-being of a modern household. Mental accounting offers a set of heuristic decision rules that work to balance current desires with long-term utility.

Garcia and his colleagues captured the problematic nature of discerning the limits of a general learning mechanism when they wrote that "[o]perant techniques employing immediate reinforcements have been used to manufacture wondrously complex habits . . . but the associations which cannot be formed, given perceptible signals and effective reinforcers, may be more informative since they reveal the biased differentiated structure of the organism" (Garcia, McGowan, and Green 1972, 40). In the laboratory, given strong and clear signals from the environment and effective incentives for responding to those signals, subjects nevertheless find some associations impossible (or very difficult) to establish or maintain. Some behaviors in some situations cannot be conditioned. For many species, escaping canalized behavioral responses, whether established genetically or by experience, can be a nearly insurmountable task.

Response to environmental rewards and punishments is unlikely to be effortless and smooth, because of habituated behaviors. In the case of canalized behaviors, a proper response to the environment may not be forthcoming at all.

Box 2.1:   The Language Organ

Is language learned via a process of trial and error, reward and punishment? Quite certainly not—at least when it comes to grammatical structure. Since the work of Noam Chomsky in the 1950s, linguists have recognized that the learning of language by children cannot be explained by environmental factors alone. Mechanisms of trial-and-error and reward could not account for the rapidity of language acquisition nor for universalities in the structure of grammar across languages and cultures. On the other hand, language does not come to us the way that right-handedness or eye color does. It has an important acquired element to it. Developmental psychologists speak of a "readiness to learn" language and other skills, a notion that ties prepared learning to developmental sequences.

There continues to be considerable controversy over the inheritance of language. There seems to be general agreement that simple mechanisms of operant conditioning cannot account for many facets of learning a language and probably other developmental skills.

Implicit Learning Theories in Social Science

Though long abandoned by psychologists and biologists, many social scientists have adopted, perhaps implicitly, the equipotentiality premise in studying human behavior in complex institutions. Clearly institutions provide incentives for people to act in certain ways. The equipotentiality premise as employed by many economists and political scientists implies that people can be conditioned to any arbitrary incentive generated by an institution. Here is the way political scientists Arthur Lupia and Matthew McCubbins put it: "*People choose* what and when to learn. . . . We define rationality to mean all human behavior that is directed toward the pursuit of pleasure and the avoidance of pain. . . . If pain and pleasure correlate with environmental factors, and if people desire to avoid pain and experience pleasure, then they have an incentive to learn about their environment and base their choices on what they learn" (1998, 22–23).

This definition of the causes of human behavior harks back to Jeremy Bentham and the British Utilitarian school of thought, ascendant in the early nineteenth century. So there is nothing new about it. Humans, in this view, are connected to their environment by pleasure and pain. All an analyst need do is to figure out what in the environment causes pleasure and pain, and the behavior of the individual is determined. Quite clearly the approach accounts for a great deal of human behavior. Unfortunately, it fails at important places, because it has no role for prepared learning and other biologically influenced factors that are critical to understanding human behavior.

E. O. Wilson sees prepared learning as the essential building block for what he calls "epigenetic rules": "As employed in biology, epigenetic rules comprise the full range of inherited regularities of development in anatomy, physiology, cognition, and behavior" (1998, 150). Epigenetic rules are usually adaptive, in the sense of conferring advantage to the organism in survival and reproduction. But in the case of humans, the adaptive advantage was conferred on a Stone Age brain, and may not be adaptive in postindustrial society. Moreover, where the problems of survival are complex, epigenetic rules may conflict, with one rule being adaptive for one set of problems, but maladaptive for a second. So the application of the rules in current situations is a critical component of decision making.

Preparation versus Deliberation

Prepared learning may be a very general phenomenon, fundamental to intelligent systems, human or artificial. Computer scientist Allen Newell writes of a "preparation vs. deliberation trade-off":

> At some point a response is required. Then two types of processing enter into determining that response. The system can *deliberate*—engage in activities to analyze the situation, the possible responses, their consequences, and so on. . . . The system can also have various responses already *prepared*. To use such preparations, the system must access the memory, retrieve the prepared material, and then adapt it as appropriate to the case at hand. (1990, 102)

Many of these preparations are creations of learning and culture, but many are consequences of our evolutionary past. Prepared learning can be seen as evolutionary and adaptive. It facilitates the learning of a standard response in a rapid and efficient way, but it allows the ability to override that response in the face of demands from the task at hand. Moreover, prepared learning addresses certain cognitive processing limits that stem from the "quick read, slow write" facet of human memory. In general, it is difficult to learn a new strategy (that is, it is not easy for a person to learn and store into long-term memory a new approach (the "slow write" component). Once stored, however, it is relatively easy to retrieve the strategy. The more the preparation, the more quickly the system can respond to a current problem. Unfortunately, the more prepared the organism, the more likely it is to fail to respond correctly to a novel situation.

It is, of course, possible to prepare lots of different strategies. However, this can also complicate retrieval, because of our tendency to draw on the most vivid strategies for retrieval. Of course, the more one thinks about the proper strategy, the less one is likely to fall prey to such complications, but then we are back to deliberation.

Many of our responses to stimuli may be "hardwired," and numerous domain-specific psychological and physiological mechanisms may influence our daily existences. On the other hand, such mechanisms cannot explain most of human political and economic behavior, governed as they are by complex institutional arrangements and informal understandings. These institutional arrangements provide the current incentives and deterrents—positive and negative consequences—that are the most immediate causes of behavior. Democracies encourage politicians to seek votes, to be responsive to the electorate. Markets encourage people to exchange goods and services.

The most reasonable approach, given the existing literature in biology and developmental psychology, is that the rules of behavior act as canals, essentially constraining behavior. If, however, the canal can be escaped, albeit with effort, then we come closer to a model appropriate for the study of behavior in complex institutions. When will people not behave according to clear signals from the environment indicating rewards or punishments? Can we account for such exceptions using the canals imposed by our cognitive architecture?

Simon's Basic Principle of Adaptation

A major issue in the study of human institutions concerns the limits on adaptability of humans to the rapidly changing demands of modern society. There are, of course, individual differences, but we focus here on general propensities. While there currently is no general answer to the issue, there is nevertheless substantial evidence to support a guiding principle, articulated by Herbert Simon: "There are only a few 'intrinsic' characteristics of the inner environment of thinking beings that limit the adaptation of thought to the shape of the problem environment. All else in thinking and problem-solving behavior . . . is learned and is subject to improvement through the invention of improved designs and their storage in memory" (1996, 54).

When humans face a problem, we tend to solve it adaptively. We may do so directly, through a process of reasoning based on past experience or learning, or we may do so through the development of better and better designs over time, designs that are stored in memory for future use. Only a few human characteristics will limit our ability to adapt to the problem-solving environment, but these characteristics are critical.

These limiting characteristics correspond to E. O. Wilson's epigenetic rules—or, rather, they are those epigenetic rules that may have been adaptive at one time or may still be adaptive in a different place, but are not relevant to the current problem-solving task. They not only limit instantaneous adaptation (the immediate solving of the problem), but they also may interfere with the acquiring and storing of strategies that can be used in the future.

Thinking systems organize their responses to the environment according to the preparation-deliberation trade-off. But the approach is not fully efficient. The preparation-deliberation trade-off affects current adaptation by ensuring that the preprogrammed solution (preparation) is not quite right for the current problem. The old aphorism "the generals are always prepared for fighting the last war" defines this issue.

Preparedness can come via genetic inheritance (a genetic tendency for an organism to respond to a particular stimulus in a predetermined way) or via individual learning (storing the strategy in memory for future use). The consequences for current decision making are not particularly different. In either case, if the current demands from the environment are severe, then the preprogrammed strategy is likely to be reexamined and replaced (in effect, the decision maker will shift to the deliberation aspect of cognitive processing).

What is true of humans is also true of organizations. Formal organizations, established as they are to address human problems and opportunities, are as a consequence generally adaptive. But organizational adaptation is often limited by characteristics of the internal environment, just as humans are. We return to organizational adaptation in chapter 6.

Rational Choice and Adaptation

If we are to be able to discuss the limits on adaptation imposed by genetically based epigenetic rules, then we must have some standard of comparison by which to judge adaptation. Fortunately one exists: the models of decision making developed in economics, political science, and the decision sciences.[3]

Human choices are adaptive to the extent that they confer benefits on

---

3. The extent to which rational choice in political science is simply a matter of "economic imperialism" is an interesting issue. The analytical tradition in economics was established at the end of the nineteenth century—much earlier than the political or decision sciences—with the "marginalists" interested in using calculus and tailoring economics to the standard of physics. Early work using rationality assumptions in political science, from the late 1950s, was clearly influenced by economics. But political science more rapidly incorporated game theory and offered a unique perspective on spatial choice. In particular, political scientists saw the potential for agenda manipulation by strategically placed actors; hence the rational choice work in political science incorporated notions of multiple equilibria or even nonequilibria that were capable of being manipulated. See Amade and Bueno de Mesquita 1999.

the decision maker. This description doesn't go far enough, however, because lots of different choices may confer benefits on a decision maker, yet not be very good choices. We may enjoy the new car we decided to purchase, but come to regret the decision (and others like it) when, a few years later, we are forced to continue working when we would like to retire. As a consequence, in discussing good decision making, we must include the concept of "opportunity costs." Opportunity costs are benefits forgone: that is, they are benefits that we do not enjoy because of a choice that we have made. By choosing to enjoy the car now, we have not been able to set aside money for a comfortable retirement. So the best decision is the decision that confers the greatest benefits when we take into account opportunity costs.

Good decisions are adaptive decisions. The best decisions are maximally adaptive: they confer the greatest net benefits on the decision maker. As a consequence, in the words of experimental economists John Kagel, Ray Battalio, and Leonard Green, "adaptive behavior commonly coincides with the 'rationality' requirements of consumer-demand theory" (1995, 18).

Fully rational decision makers are characterized by the following qualities:

- Fixed, transitive preferences for alternatives. Social scientists say that the decision maker has a "utility function" that relates the alternatives he or she faces to the benefits that accrue from each alternative. Utility functions not only specify the benefits of each alternative, they also specify the trade-offs between choosing one alternative over another.
- An ability to calculate costs in terms of forgone opportunities.
- An ability to compare future and present benefits, a process termed "discounting." In real markets, interest rates reflect this trade-off.
- A comprehensive utility function that integrates all aspects of the decision maker's life. (Weaker forms of the assumption of rationality drop this requirement.)

What we will refer to as "comprehensive rationality" assumes that people at all places and all times have transitive preferences and respond to incentives by maximizing. In this view, each human possesses a universal utility function that encompasses all of life's domains.

A vigorous proponent of the comprehensive rationality approach is University of Chicago economist Gary Becker (1976). Becker insists that markets simply involve exchange and occur whenever scarcity exists. Economists see scarcity as occurring everywhere, because of unlimited human wants and limited supply of valuable things. Becker sees underlying markets in marriage choice, status seeking, and a variety of other "commodities" that may be characterized by "shadow prices." Shadow prices are implicit indicators of how much one is willing to sacrifice for a commodity—including time, effort, and opportunities forgone. Because people employ shadow (or monetized) prices for all aspects of life, they are able to make trade-offs between all sorts of things that might be viewed as incommensurate.

Comprehensive rationality is the extreme form of a general problem-solving mechanism. It highlights adaptability and ignores the "traps" of prepared learning and other barriers to adaptability. Domain-specific psychological mechanisms are (implicitly) relegated to preference structures, and are treated as givens for the purposes of analysis. Becker's approach has the real value of pointing to the ubiquity of exchange mechanisms in social life, and the concept of shadow price allows the careful study of exchange behavior where it was previously ruled out. On the other hand, the postulate of an unrealistic set of behavioral assumptions makes more difficult a unified social and behavioral science.

Below I discuss the use of rationality assumptions in economics and political science. The treatment is a summary, as it must be: rationality forms the core assumptions in economics, and forms the basis for a very large body of work in political science. I concentrate on models of individual decision making, ignoring for the present models of interactive choice captured by game theory. Game theory models how two (or more) make decisions in response to each other. In the sections that follow, I want only to offer a flavor of the analytical approaches currently in use.

Consumer Choice Theory

To analyze choices made by economic actors, economists use an approach known as "consumer choice" (or "consumer demand") theory. In its simplest form, a consumer is presented with two goods: good 1 and good 2. These can cover any choice faced by a consumer: two automobiles, two different vegetables at the grocery store, two HMOs. Or they could represent a choice between life insurance and a new car. Moreover, while it is easier to visualize a choice between two goods, consumer choice theory applies as readily to the choice among many goods and services.

Economists assume that wants are unlimited—the more one has of a good or service, the better off one is. The choices made by consumers are limited only by their budget constraints—how much money is available to spend at the time of the choice. Becker's shadow price approach allows economists to generalize the consumer choice model to the more general "choice under constraints" model. The budget line simply indicates how much time, energy, and money one is able to allocate to the choice.

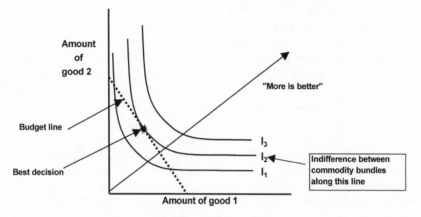

Figure 2.1   Consumer Choice Theory

Figure 2.1 depicts this system of economic choice. Here we have a consumer choosing between two goods. The consumer can chose any of a number of "commodity bundles," or combinations of the two goods.

The consumer's preferences are depicted through a series of "indifference curves." Each indifference curve indicates how he or she will substitute one good for another. The trade-off rate at any one point along an indifference curve (say I_2) is known as the "marginal rate of substitution"—marginal, because the trade-off occurs "at the margins." By "at the margins," economists mean how the would-be consumer trades off one *more* apple against one *more* orange (to use the classic Economics 101 example). Good decision making means taking into consideration how many oranges and apples you already have before buying yet one more. Indifference curves are concave (in relationship to the origin, which represents none of good 1 and none of good 2) to define the tendency for many goods to be subject to diminishing utility as one acquires them. It takes more and more apples to compensate for getting one more orange when one has lots of apples.

Figure 2.1 depicts three indifference curves, not just one. In reality, an infinite number of such curves can be imagined. A consumer would rather be on a higher indifference curve than a lower (because he or she could then have more of both goods at once). But this is not possible, because of budget constraints (as shown by the budget line in fig. 2.1). The budget line shows what particular commodity bundles the consumer can afford.

Now it is easy to define the optimal decision. The consumer should choose the combination of goods that is on the highest indifference curve that still falls under the budget line. This is the point where the budget line is tangent to (just touches) an indifference curve. Given the choice system, this is one and only one point; as a consequence, this point maximizes utility. It generates the highest level of benefits, given the consumer's preference. It is the most adaptive decision possible under the circumstances.

The rationality of the consumer is matched in economic theory by the rationality of the entrepreneur, the supplier of goods and services that the consumer chooses, who maximizes his or her profit.

Political Choice

Politics in some ways looks like economics: it is about allocation of scarce things. But in two ways it is very different. Markets, in theory, involve exchanges between two or more willing participants. But government involves some element of coercion—how many people are "willing" taxpayers? Second, politics is about reconciling diverse preferences. People have different ideas about what government should do, and politics is about managing those differences.

There is a lot of silly writing by conservative economists about the "inefficiencies" of politics and "democratic failure." They tend to be cynical about democracy while lauding capitalism. They worry about misinformed voters, manipulative politicians, and selfish bureaucrats. One economist, Donald Whitman of the University of California at Santa Cruz, has provided a systematic antidote to this cynicism. Whitman (1995) argues that, given what democratic governments are supposed to do, they do it efficiently—indeed, as efficiently as markets.

Because institutions evolve, and because intendedly rational people don't always succeed, in the real world neither markets nor democratic politics are fully efficient. But each institution evokes reasonable behavior from participants. And judging reasonable behavior can hinge on models of comprehensive rationality in economics and politics as standards of comparison.

Voting Choice

Political scientists use a variant of consumer choice theory in the study of voting choice. In politics, it is assumed that the rational voter wants a particular bundle of issues (similar to the commodity bundle of consumer choice theory). Unlike consumer choice, however, it is typically assumed that on any issue a voter can become "saturated"—they can get too much of the issue. As a consequence of political saturation, political scientists depict indifference curves as closed circles or ovals.

A second complication is that, unlike consumers, democratic politics does not offer direct access to issues. Rather, in an election, candidates offer differing levels of the issues. One candidate may offer radical welfare

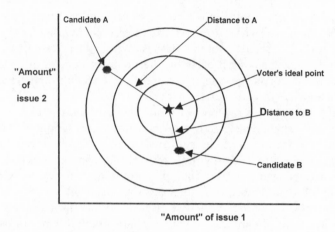

Figure 2.2   Rational Voting Choice

reform, the other only modest reform. This occurs across the whole panoply of political issues. The voter can choose only among candidates. This choice is depicted in figure 2.2, which represents the contest of two candidates vying for the vote of a citizen by offering two different combinations of two issues. The voter's ideal point is the combination of issue 1 and issue 2 that he or she would choose if that bundle were available. But the ideal point is not possible, because the candidates are not offering that choice. From the voter's point of view, candidate A offers too little of issue 1, but too much of issue 2. On the other hand, candidate B offers about the right amount of issue 1, but too little of issue 2.

Political scientists assume that the rational voter will choose the candidate that minimizes the distance between the voter's ideal point and the candidate's position. That is, the voter will choose the candidate who is closest in "issue space." As can be seen in figure 2.2, voting for the candidate closest in issue space is the same as picking the candidate on the highest indifference curve.

In both variants of choice theory, the shape of the indifference curve indicates the marginal preference for a good or issue. The steeper the indifference curve as one moves away from the origin (in consumer theory) or away from the ideal point (in voter theory), the relatively more desirable the commodity. In the example of political choice depicted in figure 2.2, the circles representing the voter's indifference curves indicate that the issues are equally important in the voter's eyes. If one issue were more important, then the indifference curves would be depicted as ellipses.

There is a second set of actors in democracy: politicians. In the rational

model of democracy, politicians serve the role of entrepreneurs in economies. The politician wishes to maximize the probability that he or she is
elected. A side consequence of that wish is to bring the preferences of voters into the policymaking process by offering them bundles of issues for
consideration. Voters respond by accepting or rejecting the package of
issues offered by entrepreneurial politicians.

Finally, models of democracy also include bureaucrats, but it has not
been so easy to pin down exactly what bureaucrats are supposed to maximize. Early work in public choice, which involves the use of the formal
tools of economics to study politics, saw the heads of bureaus as maximizing the sizes of their budgets. That assumption has been strongly questioned in subsequent research. More recently, research has focused on the
issue of control of bureaucracies by elected officials through the use of
explicit incentives. In any case, the issue is not simple; we return to it in
chapter 6.

Objections to Choice Theory I

How well does actual human choice stack up to the demands of rational
choice theory? A number of objections have been lodged. They fall into
two categories: analytical and empirical. Analytical objections are those
that suggest that choice theory fails to incorporate certain elements that
adaptive, rational decision makers face. Empirical objections claim that
people can't (or don't) make decisions according to the specifications of
the rationality requirements of choice theory. We tackle the analytical issues first.

Risk and Uncertainty

Critics have pointed out that very rarely do individuals know with certainty exactly what benefits they are getting. There is a strong element of
risk and uncertainty in any decision we make, economic or otherwise.
Economists point out that expected utility theory, in which decision makers maximize *expected* utility rather than certain utility, addresses this
objection.

In expected utility theory, the goods of consumer choice theory (now
termed "decision outcomes") are weighted by the probability of their occurrence. Suppose you are trying to decide whether to buy a state lottery
ticket with a prize of $1 million for $5. It is easy to calculate the approximate expected utility in such a situation: all you have to know is
the approximate number of tickets that will be sold. Let us say that, for
this lottery, eight million tickets have been sold. The probability that
your ticket wins the lottery is one out of eight million: $1/8,000,000 =
0.000000125$. To get the expected benefits of this choice, we multiply the

probability of occurrence by the benefit (0.000000125 × $1,000,000 = $0.125, or 12.5 cents. Now subtract the cost of the ticket, $5, and we get −$4.875. That is, one can expect to lose, on average, $4.87.

Exactly what does this number mean? Either we win a million or we lose five bucks. "On average" means that, if one were to play the lottery repeatedly many, many times over, added up gains and losses, and divided by the number of plays, one would get −$4.875. So the answer is, don't play. You not only fail to maximize utility by choosing the best outcome among many possible outcomes, you actually suffer a decline in utility.

In most decision-making situations, probabilities are not as easily defined as in the lottery example. The expected utility framework applied to less objective probability estimates is known as "subjective expected utility." The extension of choice theory from the concept of maximizing utility to the concept of maximizing expected subjective utility addresses the analytical issues of risk and uncertainty. Unfortunately, it opens up empirical problems, because it turns out that people are not very good decision makers under risk and uncertainty, as we shall see shortly.

The "Gestalt" of Goods

Consumer choice theory treats goods as holistic. People compare the overall worth of good 1 versus good 2. But any good has numerous attributes that must be combined somehow before the good is compared with other goods. Utility, or the benefit derived from the good, is some combination of these various attributes. Two houses differ by quality of construction, by commuting distance to work, by neighborhood prestige, and by any number of other potentially relevant attributes. As any decision maker knows, oftentimes the difficult part of choice is deciding the relative importance of these attributes. Economist Kelvin Lancaster has incorporated multiple attributes into a more general theory of consumer choice, and Gary Becker has extended Lancaster's notion to choice situations in which normal markets do not exist. As Lancaster puts it, "Individuals are interested in goods not for their own sake but because of the characteristics they possess, so that the demand for goods is derived and indirect and depends on preferences with respect to characteristics and on the technical properties that determine how characteristics are embodied in different goods" (1979, 17).

Whatever the relative merits of the various attributes, the typical market for housing will ensure that the consumer will have to make difficult trade-offs. If one house is better on all attributes, you can rest assured that it will cost more. As a consequence, the nature of the trade-offs between attributes is fundamental, because consumers are always having to decide what attributes are most relevant to the decision.

The Rationality of Not Voting

Special problems come up in voting rationally, because voting really involves two steps: deciding *whether* to vote and deciding *how* to vote. In any election with an electorate of more than a few dozen, the probability of affecting the outcome is extremely low. Recall that an expected utility approach to choice factors in the probability that a desired outcome actually will occur. In deciding whether to vote, a rational decision maker would estimate the benefits expected if his or her preferred candidate wins, and multiply that by the probability that one's vote will influence the outcome. Then the prospective voter would compare that result to the costs of voting (learning about the candidates and issues, getting registered to vote, and going to the polls).

Since an election of any size means that the probability of any one voter making a difference in the election is vanishingly small, it would seem that the rational decision is to abstain from voting. The so-called paradox of voting implies either that there is lots of irrationality in democracies or that something is missing from the analysis. Usually political scientists have postulated that utility can come directly from the act of voting itself rather than just through the election of one's candidate. These benefits can be expressive (one gets enjoyment from cheering one's team on to victory) or civic duty–based (one gets utility from performing one's duty as a citizen). The postulation of such direct utility opens up interesting issues, to which we return in chapter 4.

Multidimensionality in Politics

If voting occurs in a single dimension, say, from the most liberal to the most conservative alternative, then the outcome can be predicted with certainty, at least in theory.[4] One-dimensional voting systems mean that voters can be ordered from the most conservative to the most liberal voter. The alternative (which could be a candidate in an election or a bill in a legislature) that will invariably win is the one closest to the median voter. Voting systems that incorporate but one dimension are in equilibrium.

If more than one dimension is involved, as in the case represented by figure 2.2, then the analysis breaks down, in the sense that no prediction can be made. The outcome, it turns out, is dependent on the order of presentation of the alternatives. This means that no equilibrium prediction can be made in multidimensional voting systems. (Riker 1982 summarizes the evidence.)

---

4. Given the reasonable assumption of "single-peaked" preferences among the voters: that a voter does not prefer an alternative further from his ideal point than one closer to it.

How can a voting space be multidimensional? Actually, there are two distinct ways. First, agenda setters (such as legislative leaders in Congress) can assemble a series of more or less unrelated items that will be put to a vote in the chamber. This can make a previously one-dimensional bill (say, a bill to increase farm subsidies) into a multidimensional one (by adding environmental or health protections to the bill). This might be termed "artificial multidimensionality." In theory, this multidimensionality allows leaders great flexibility in determining the outcome. In practice, most omnibus bills are constructed to attract support across coalitions of potential supporters because each dimension is valued differently by the different groups. Representatives from agricultural constituencies may not prefer the environmental provisions, but will vote for them to obtain the farm subsidies.[5]

A second way a voting space can be multidimensional is fundamental. Some issues involve multiple consequences. A bill to reduce taxes can involve both macroeconomic effects (it would be stimulative) and programmatic effects (it would reduce the revenue available to fund programs). Conservatives might want to reduce government programs but not to stimulate the economy in boom times. In theory, this trade-off should be easy to make—the indifference curves of consumer choice theory could be applied here. In practice, however, it is not.

Attributes and Alternatives in Decision Making

Lancaster's approach to preferences, which incorporates the characteristics of goods into the consumer's preferences, is similar to psychological theories of decision making that are based on a distinction between alternatives and attributes. "Alternatives" are the objects of choice: the candidates in an election, for example. "Attributes" characterize the alternatives: the issues that the candidates promote, for example. This leads to the decision matrix depicted in table 2.1.

In the matrix, the b's stand for benefits that stem from an alternative's contribution to an attribute. One might, for example, be evaluating candidates in a multicandidate race. In that case, the candidates would be the alternatives—the objects of choice. The attributes could be the issues advocated by the candidates, or other candidate qualities, such as party affiliation, personal competence, or moral rectitude. In that case, b_{32} would stand for the "score" of candidate 3 (alternative 3) on attribute 2. The task for the decision maker is to score each candidate on each attri-

---

5. The problem of "issue cycling"—the inability of any coalition of legislators to secure an equilibrium victory in a multidimensional issue space—disappears or is severely attenuated when the dimensions have different saliences to participants.

Table 2.1. The Decision Matrix

	Attribute 1	Attribute 2	...	Attribute M	Benefits from Each Alternative*
Alternative 1	b_{11}	b_{12}	...	b_{1m}	[Sum of row 1]
Alternative 2	b_{21}	b_{22}	...	b_{21}	[Sum of row 2]
Alternative 3	b_{31}	b_{32}	...	b_{31}	[Sum of row 3]
	...	...	...	...	...
Alternative i	b_{i1}	b_{i2}	...	b_{im}	[Sum of row i]

*The best alternative is the one with the largest "score" in this column.

bute, combine the scores for each candidate, and then choose the candidate who receives the highest score. Of course, if some attributes are more important than others, then the voter will also have to weight the attributes appropriately before combining the scores.

Decision making thus conceived involves two tasks that people tend to find very difficult. The first is isolating the relevant attributes in trying to understand a problem. One may omit critical components in a decision-making situation and thus misunderstand the nature of the problem one is facing. Specifying the relevant attributes in a problem-solving situation is termed the "design problem" (Simon 1977). Getting the attributes right means making the correct abstraction from a complex reality. To the extent that the situation one faces is ill structured, specifying the relevant attributes is difficult.

Second, once the problem design is specified, one must compare the alternative solutions to the problem on all attributes. Comparisons across attributes are complicated by limitations in short-term memory. Moreover, some attributes are inherently difficult to compare, especially when they involve core values (Alvarez and Brehm, in press).

Objections to Choice Theory II

With the decision matrix in hand, we can turn to the second set of objections to choice theory, which concern the difficulties humans have in conforming to it. Numerous empirical studies of human decision making, from experiments in the laboratory, to large-scale social surveys, to observational studies in the field, have demonstrated that humans often don't conform to the strictures of choice theory. Even defenders of choice theory have retreated. According to Peter Fishburn, expected utility theory "is no longer regarded as an accurate descriptive theory" (1988, 25). R. Duncan Luce comments that "although a fair consensus exists that SEU [subjective utility theory] is normatively adequate in certain highly static situations, an at least comparable consensus holds that it fails to be descriptively adequate, even in those static situations" (1995, 6; see also Luce 1992).

Some of these objections are quite fundamental—so much so that it seems impossible to develop a serious empirical theory of choice without taking them into consideration. They address both the limitations of humans to comprehend and act on inputs from the environment, and the fundamental complexity of the environment, which is vastly underestimated in standard rational choice theories.

The Nature of the Decision Maker

Empirical objections to rational choice are so voluminous that they are, in effect, a laundry list of problems. The first set has to do with the nature of the decision maker.

Search behavior. In general, people don't consider all aspects of a decision facing them. They must factor the decision to make it manageable, examining only relevant aspects. They don't do complete searches for information, and they ignore available information—especially if it is not relevant to the factors they have determined to characterize the structure of the problem. A great deal of research demonstrates that selective search is related to value premises and hence is not determined only by the objective problem at hand (Gerber and Green 1999). That is, people allow biases associated with their value premises to influence their search behavior.

The decision matrix discussed above sensitizes us to the fact that any decision search must include both alternatives and attributes. Different physiological and psychological mechanisms probably underlie the search for attributes (which is equated in ordinary language with understanding a problem) and the search for alternatives (which involves a choice given a particular decisional structure, design, or understanding).

Calculations. People generally cannot perform the calculations necessary even for a reduced set of options in a decision-making situation. Although much emphasized in discussions of our cognitive limits, this is actually the least problematic limitation in decision making—given our ability to write down and manipulate the numbers.

Cognitive illusions and framing. When identical options are described in different terms, people often shift their choices (for example, if a choice is described in terms of gains, it is often treated differently than if it is described in terms of losses). The concept of "framing," developed by psychologists Daniel Kahneman and Amos Tversky, refers to situations in which decision makers allow descriptions of a choice in different terms to affect their choices. Kahneman and Tversky claim that this tendency violates a major, if often unstated, assumption of rational choice: the axiom of invariance, which states that the "preference order between prospects should not depend on the manner in which they are described" (1983, 343). They bolster their claim with numerous convincing experiments indicating that decision makers tend to choose different alternatives when they are described in positive terms (for example, in terms of the number of lives saved with a vaccine) than in negative terms (the number of people who will die). Kahneman and Tversky state that "[i]n their stubborn appeal, framing effects resemble perceptual illusions more than computational errors" (343).

Self-control. People often seem to need to bind themselves in some way to establish self-control over their behavior in the future. A major mechanism for dealing with likely future lapses in self-control is to establish binding rules that prohibit the unwanted behavior—such as in Thaler's description of mental accounting. Such rules may or may not work; the point is that the widespread existence of such behavior indicates difficulties in the full-blown maximization model (Lowenstein and Elster 1992).

Design. People have trouble figuring what factors are relevant to a given decision-making situation. To respond in a proper fashion, people must construct a roughly appropriate mental model of the circumstances facing them. Some facets are relevant, and others are not. This determination is not straightforward where the decision-making environment is at all complex.

Incommensurate attributes. In multiattribute situations, people often have severe difficulties in making the trade-offs that look simple in consumer choice theories. They tend to use a variety of shortcuts that avoid making the direct trade-off (See box 2.2). Evidence from psychological perception studies shows that people have great difficulty attending to two or more attributes simultaneously in a situation (Shepard 1964). The bottleneck of short-term memory, which allows active conscious manipulation of only limited information, further constrains comparisons.

Updating. People are "incomplete Bayesians." In uncertain situations, they do not update their choices in light of incoming information about the probability of outcomes in the manner that calculations from probability theory indicate that they should (Bayes's rule is the relevant yardstick) (Piattelli-Palmarini 1994).

Identification with means. In situations of repeated decision making, often people come to identify both cognitively and emotionally with the means, or subgoals, of a decision-making process (Simon 1947). In effect, process becomes more important than product—following the rules becomes more important than solving the problem. This leads one to become too conservative in shifting to a more effective means for solving a problem.

Box 2.2: Dealing with Incommensurate Attributes

Of all the limitations cited in people's ability to put rational choice theory into practice, the most important is probably the difficulties people have in handling incommensurate attributes. Somehow the "scores" of each alternative on each attribute must be combined (the hard part) and then compared (the easier part).

The rational choice ideal is the "net benefits equation." Decision making according to the net benefits equation has been termed "compensatory decision making" or sometimes "linear modeling" because a low score for an alternative on one aspect or dimension may be offset by a positive score on a second.

In the net benefits model, the decision maker would assign weights to attributes relative to their importance. Then he or she would take an alternative's score on each attribute, and multiply it by the weight. The next step is to add the score of the alternative on each attribute together. This obtains a final score for each alternative on all the attributes. The easy part is then to compare the total scores of the alternatives, simply picking the one with the highest score.

An example of the net benefits approach is college admissions policies. Here students are the alternatives, because they are the subjects of choice; the choice is whom to admit. Sometimes schools will use a formula that takes twice the grade point average and adds it to the standardized test score (ACT, SAT, GRE, LSAT, etc.). The grade points and the standardized test scores are standardized so they will be measured in the same units:

Student's admissions score = 2*(grade point) + 1*(test score).

One may ask where in the world this weighting scheme came from. And where are the other factors that might relate to success in college? This is the key problem of the incommensurate attribute problem, and it's why people have so much trouble with the idealizations of choice theory.

But consider this. Decision theorist Robyn Dawes (1988) thinks that people's decision-making biases are so pronounced that even a flawed linear model like the example above is better than relying on one's informed judgment in combining the attributes! Dawes's delightful book, *Rational Choice in an Uncertain World,* is an introduction to the "traps" one needs to avoid in order to make better decisions. His general suggestion is that our biases are so severe that a system that binds one to an arbitrary but reasonable course of action is better than relying on one's intuition or even on expert judgment. Note how this argument comports with Thaler's mental accounting, as well as with such financial advice as "buy and hold."

The Nature of the Environment

Other objections to rational choice theory involve the nature of the environment.

Ambiguity and uncertainty. Proponents of limited rationality suggest that the environment is fundamentally more uncertain than is understood in prevailing choice models. Uncertainty, in rational choice models, is not knowing the probability of decisional consequences. In limited rationality models, uncertainty also involves lack of knowledge of the attributes that characterize the problem (such problems are described as "ill structured"). Furthermore, uncertainty can involve ambiguity, which itself has two connotations. The first involves situations in which the attributes are clear, but we are unclear about the weights that we should attach to them (Chong 1993). The second is more fundamental and occurs when "alternative states are hazily defined or in which they have multiple meanings, simultaneously opposing interpretations" (March 1994, 178).

Ambiguity and uncertainty in the environment feed back into the preferences of the decision maker. Preferences are desires about end states. In the rational choice model, people maximize the probabilities of achieving a desired state. But if end states are ambiguous, then our preferences must be ambiguous! If our preferences are ambiguous, then that mainstay of rational choice, fixed, transitive preferences, cannot hold. (See March 1994, chapter 5, for an extended discussion.)

A great number of what were previously thought to be limitations in voters' abilities to conceptualize complex political reality turn out on further investigation to be associated with ambiguity. Where difficult value trade-offs are involved, considerable response volatility to public opinion questions may result—even for well-educated citizens (Alvarez and Brehm, in press). Cognitive limits can be overemphasized; some problems are just essentially hard. This is to be expected when goals are in conflict, and a decision requires a trade-off.

Repeated decisions and ends-means causal chains. People never make decisions in isolation. They interact with others, who themselves have decision strategies. They must modify their goals in light of the social milieu that they find themselves in. Indeed, some analysts have argued that preferences should be viewed as fluid, not fixed, because of the necessity to be flexible in the face of changing circumstances (Wilson 1980; Stone 1993). It is common for decisions to exist in complex ends-means causal chains (Simon 1983). In many problems, as we take one step down the path toward solution, we preclude other options, and we open new opportunities. That is, problem solving is an ongoing process involving interacting with the environment, which changes the set of constraints and opportunities we face.

Box 2.3:   The One-Dimensional Legislator

A prime example of an ends-means hierarchy is the classic reelection-driven legislator. This legislator has one goal: to get reelected (or move to higher office). The legislator simply maximizes the probability of his reelection.

Political scientists have traditionally assumed that legislators were motivated by elections, but the notion that it is their sole goal may be traced to an essay by David Mayhew of Yale University in the mid-1970s (Mayhew 1974).

At first glance, it would seem that this assertion tells us very little. How might a reelection-driven legislator go about achieving his goal? Any act the legislator may take is characterized by multiple attributes. Each attribute may have varying impacts on his reelection chances. Each choice made tends to preclude others. Any vote may please some constituents, alienate others, and not reach the consciousness of most. And any vote that benefits, say, the elderly may or may not motivate them to vote for the legislator's reelection. Raising lots of money from interest groups may subject the legislator to criticism of cronyism. Being too flexible in supporting benefits to constituents may leave the legislator liable to charges of inconsistency.

Even when a goal is clear, the network of means that connect actions to goals may be quite unclear. Because of the existence of complex ends-means causal chains and the emergence of constraints and opportunities in an ongoing decision-making process, simply postulating a reelection incentive tells us little about behaviors in specific choice situations.

Nevertheless, the assumption has proved very useful. In particular, it has led to an understanding of democratic politicians as "opponent anticipators"—fallible decision makers relying on diverse sources of information to anticipate the likely consequences of their actions on the probability that the action will be exploited by an opponent in the next election (Arnold 1990).

Sometimes these ends-means chains are intertwined, adding complexities to the design problem. Sometimes, however, they are hierarchical. That is, an overarching goal structures an actor's choices (box 2.3).

Heuristics and Decision Making

In assessing the empirical objections to choice theory, we need to distinguish between (a) "can't," (b) "won't," and (c) "has trouble doing so." If humans "can't," then they must be genetically or biologically limited in some fashion that precludes fully adaptive decision making. If they "won't," then they must be pathological. If they "have trouble doing so," they may be subject to limitations that either have a biological or social base and that they can only overcome with effort.

Most of the objections fall into class (c): "have trouble doing so." Humans have designed (or have inherited) all sorts of strategies for dealing with the cognitive and emotional limits that interfere with adaptive behavior. Mental accounting is but one of many that might be cited. This kind of strategy is known as a "heuristic": "a simple and approximate rule— whether explicit or implicit, conscious or unconscious—that serves to solve a certain class of problems" (Piattelli-Palmarini 1994, 19).

Heuristics function to simplify decision making by limiting either the construction of the problem space or the search for solutions. Laboratory studies in problem solving and decision making suggest that these heuristics don't always simplify in a manner that leads to more efficient decision making; indeed, often they mislead. Moreover, in laboratory problem-solving experiments, people tend to employ the same heuristic search procedures even when they are clearly problematic (Newell and Simon 1972).

One important decision-making heuristic leads people to evaluate gains and losses differently (Kahneman and Tversky 1983). This leads to decision-making that conflicts with the dictates of expected utility theory, the standard for rational decision making. One can, with effort, overcome this tendency, hence making better decisions. Differential evaluation of gains and losses seems a fine example of prepared learning.[6]

What can account for the use of heuristics in decision making that are not helpful in addressing the immediate problem? The answer lies in the cognitive constitution of the decision maker and its probable evolutionary path. In dynamic environments, even heuristics that once led to efficient decision making can become maladaptive. It may take time to eliminate malfunctioning rules, for both individuals and organizations, especially if selection pressures are weak. Change is also often frustrated by the tendency of people to identify both cognitively and emotionally with the rules they employ.

Mice Do It, Birds Do It...

The standard models of consumer and voter choice make demanding requirements of the individual decision maker's cognitive abilities. A considerable amount of research has shown that these requirements are not met

---

6. Differential evaluation of gains and losses may well have an evolutionary basis. In the Paleolithic era, threats were often immediately life threatening. Indeed, in the Paleolithic period, losses were *not* equivalent to gains.

in either laboratory or field observations. But there is another side to the coin: oftentimes, adaptive decision making need not be fully and comprehensively rational.

One example of this aspect of decision making comes from experimental economics. Whatever the objections to consumer choice theory, experimental economists have shown that mice, pigeons, and college undergraduates can perform quite respectably in laboratory economies. Kagel, Battalio, and Green have studied extensively the choices made by laboratory animals between two goods (food and water). In the experiments using rats, lever presses represented the "price" of a good. Income was allocated to the rats by experimenters and signaled to the rats by white lights over the levers. Subjects quickly learned that the levers would not deliver the "good" (food) when the lights were on. The authors summarize: "[O]ur subjects responded quite rapidly to changes in price and income parameters. Usually within three observation periods (days), the data revealed major adjustments in their response behavior" (1995, 19). (The experimenters have also conducted studies of simulated markets using undergraduate students, prompting Ray Battalio to comment that his undergraduates performed every bit as well as his pigeons!)

Given an appropriate market structure, one that is either set by omniscient experimenters or that evolves in real time, adaptive consumer behavior is reasonably easy to elicit. It can be elicited from animals as well as humans. Computer simulations suggest that decisions based on very rudimentary "dumb" programs can lead to market equilibrium (Gode and Sunder 1993). In short, comprehensive, global rationality on the part of economic actors is not required; some basic preferences and some simple learned associations will do the trick.

Even Humans Do It

On the other hand, the markets established by experimenters, at least, will deliver only predetermined goods. If the experimenters do not intervene, they cannot satisfy preferences not explicitly included in the model economy that even rats apparently enjoy—sex, companionship, and curiosity. Real markets operate to satisfy a diversity of human preferences, preferences that are not dictated by an omniscient being but are nevertheless satisfied by "an invisible hand." Well-performing economic markets can "bring it about that the producing, consuming, buying, and selling behaviors of enormous numbers of people, each responding to personal selfish interests, allocate resources so as to clear markets (Simon 1996b, 32). That is, markets have evolved to canalize our selfish motives in a productive fashion, both coordinating the behaviors of many actors without explicit formal control and adding to the collective well-being of society.

Systems of Multiple Decision Makers

Thus far we have proceeded as if there exist but two entities: a decision maker and the environment. The decision maker adjusts to his or her environment by being intendedly rational, but at some times and some places, bounds on rational adaptation show through to the current decision-making situation.

On the other hand, the decision maker/environment dichotomy can lead us astray at important points. In particular, we must consider the following qualifying factors:

• Much of the environment of modern decision-makers consists of other decision makers.
• These decision makers may or may not share similar preferences. In economic trades, all participants are willing: each is doing what he or she thinks adds to utility. Because no transactions are coerced, we may generally assume that such trades are imagined to be mutually beneficial by all parties at the time of the transaction. Politics, however, is fundamentally about reconciling diverse preferences, and may involve the use of coercion.
• Decision makers are not independent and free floating. They are grouped in formal organizations. Transactions occur within organizations and across organizational boundaries, and these transactions fundamentally differ.

The introduction of multiple decision makers having contradictory preferences placed within social organizations complicates the picture enormously. With complex environments, it can be very difficult to decide where people are responding to environmental decisions and where they are responding to internal states that can interfere with rational adaptation. We are not at the point of fully understanding the impact of such complex environments on human behavior. We concentrate in chapters 5 through 7 on the organizational components of adaptation, and how organizations paradoxically increase human capacity and fall prey on a larger level to human foibles.

Adaptive Inefficiencies

Adaptation in decision making means responding optimally to the incentives present in the environment. The result would be a direct connection between the environment and the decision—and we would need no theory of decision making, only a theory of the environment. Even if rational adaptation determined decisional choices, however, adaptive inefficiencies would exist. This is especially true in systems of interacting decision makers. James March (1994, 235–36) details several such adaptive inefficiencies.

Lags in matching. Adaptation cannot be instantaneous, and it is difficult to know whether an observed environment-decision match is "between equilibria" or whether the match has reached equilibrium and hence is optimal.

Multiple equilibria. There may be a number of local equilibria—choices that are not perfect, but are better than any other "nearby" choice—and hence the decision-making process may not reach global adaptation.

Path dependency. Adaptation may have occurred relative to past environments, which preclude certain present choices.

Networks of diffusion. Information is contingent on "who talks to whom." This means that certain decisions within a network may be suboptimal at the same time that others are optimal.

Mutual adaptation and coevolution. In their actions, decision makers—particularly political decision makers—change the environment that they are adapting to. So there is not just a feedback between the environment and the decision maker, with the environment sending "cues" via incentives and costs. Decision makers mold their environments, and hence affect the cues that they receive.

Decision Making and the Structure of the Environment

This chapter has examined adaptation, showing how models of rational decision making are designed to explore maximum adaptability by a decision maker to the environment. The problem is that people are limited in their abilities to adapt completely. Many, many studies in psychology, sociology, business management, political science, and economics have demonstrated the failure of people to follow procedures that would result in maximization of utility or expected utility.

To some extent, the critics of rational choice have engaged in a game of "gottcha!" By using the rational choice approach as a target of criticism (albeit an easy one), critics have failed both to acknowledge adaptability in human choice and to produce a convincing alternative model. Real and experimental markets seem to elicit reasonable behavior on the part of participants. Similarly, for all the literature in political science on "rational abstention" and agenda manipulation, legislatures, committees, and other institutions of collective choice seem to work reasonably well. The nature of the environment must matter in the conduct of decision making.

To explore the (mis)match between actual behavior and ideal adaptation, we need to explore the sources of deviations from adaptive behavior. We do this in the next two chapters.

CHAPTER 3

Procedural Limits on
Adaptive Choice

FULLY ADAPTABLE decision making in economics and politics corresponds to models of rational decision making under constraints, such as consumer and voter choice models. Human nature and the fundamental complexity of the environment in which we make choices, however, limit our ability to pursue fully rational decision making. Two kinds of fundamental limitations exist: genetically hardwired limitations and prepared learning. Because the evolutionary pathway of humans has emphasized plasticity and consciousness in problem-solving skills, it is likely that most of our cognitive limits are of the latter variety. That is, we can overcome our limitations but only with effort.

The inheritances we carry into our decision making may be procedural, affecting the processes by which we make decisions, or substantive, affecting our choices directly. In this chapter, we will concentrate on procedural limits on adaptive decision making. The aim is to connect the limitations set out in chapter 2 to biological characteristics of our species in a way that will move us from a laundry list of objections to rational choice toward a positive model of human decision making.

Intended Rationality

Stressing the many failures of humans to achieve the cannons of strict rationality has had the unfortunate consequence of downplaying perhaps the key principle of decision-making: intended rationality. Decision theorist James March writes: "Although decision-makers try to be rational, they are constrained by limited cognitive capacities and incomplete information, and thus their actions may be less than completely rational in spite of their best intentions and efforts" (1994, 9). Rationality does not come free; oftentimes it takes a while to get there. In his discussion of intendedly rational behavior, Allen Newell argues that "given sufficient time, an intelligent system moves toward the knowledge level, where the signs of the struggle to think fade away and only the adaptive response to the task environment remains. At this point the system may be said to have gained the peaks of rationality. But getting there takes some doing" (1990, 363).

Newell and other students of computer modeling of intelligent behavior have been mostly concerned with the process by which intelligent systems adapt to a task environment. Some task environments are easier to master than others. It follows that the "peaks of rationality" evoked in human behavior are in part a function of how human cognitive limits interact with the task environment. We are more rational in some environments than in others, even if we intend to be rational in all environments. This implies that we can design institutions that evoke more rational responses.

Intendedly rational behavior implies the occurrence of systematic mistakes. In a particular task environment, people tend to make the same mistakes repetitively, and different people make similar mistakes. When people are instructed about their mistakes, they can correct their actions, but they tend to fall back into the same traps if they do not monitor their behaviors continually. These are the kinds of situations in which our intuitive understandings of what is rational go awry.

Psychologists have uncovered all sorts of biased information processing and cognitive illusions (Piattelli-Palmarini 1994). Let us take an important example of this phenomenon. "Biased assimilation" is the process by which one's current acceptance of evidence is affected by one's prior beliefs. Prior beliefs are themselves colored by one's social status, race, and reference groups. As a consequence, the same objective information will be received differently by different people. This looks far from rational. On the other hand, as political scientists Alan Gerber and Donald Green (1999) emphasize, generally people do update their beliefs in response to information—that is, they adapt to the changing circumstances they find themselves in—regardless of their starting positions or prior beliefs.

The study of the role of these biases on adaptive decision making is in its infancy. We know these biases occur with great regularity, but we have not detected the extent to which they interfere with adaptation. Indeed, the issue has too often been misstated: either the decision maker is fully rational or is a failed decision maker. The proper conception of decision-making behavior is to conceive of mistakes as relative deviations from the fully rational expectation, and to view the correction of mistakes (and the generation of new ones) in a dynamic perspective. This is in effect what Gerber and Green ask us to do when they compare, not the static biases of voters, but changes in their choices when confronted with new information.

It is possible that one need not have superhuman powers of rationality and computation in order to make decisions that, if not perfectly adaptable, at least approximate adaptability. It is likely that deviations from rationality are serious and systematic, but that they can be corrected. Human institutions either are explicitly designed to or evolve in order to compensate for the shortcomings of individuals in comparison to the requirements of rational choice.

Reductionism

Some may ask why social scientists need to delve into the realm of cognitive science. Isn't this a reductionism that will ultimately lead us into the world of brain scans and neuronal synapses? The answer is, not at all. The late cognitive scientist Allen Newell developed a framework that solves the reductionism issue. Newell noted that the cognitive architecture of humans is most visible at the lowest level of temporal action. That is, cognitive architecture is most obvious where action occurs at short time scales. As one moves toward actions that take longer times, cognitive architecture is less and less in evidence, and the nature of the task takes on more and more importance in explaining actions. "The fading occurs because of adaptive behavior, which to the extent it is successful operates to obscure the internal mechanisms by making behavior exclusively a function of what the system's goals depend upon, namely, the external environment" (Newell 1990, 237).

Intentionality solves the reductionism problem. If we move toward the level of conscious decision making, we find that less and less of human action is influenced by cognitive architecture, and more and more by the incentives and deterrents generated by the external environment. Goal direction shifts the locus of causation in human behavior from the internal system, human cognitive architecture, to the external environment.

Because of the principle of intended behavior, we need not examine every aspect of human cognitive architecture. Most will not be important, fading from relevance because of the role of intended rationality. However, two facets ensure that human cognitive architecture will "show through" in goal-directed behavior. The first is the limited amount of time available to devote to thinking—analyzing the task environment, constructing an appropriate problem space, and searching for solutions. To the extent that task environments are incompletely analyzed, human cognitive architecture will show through. Second, some task environments are more difficult to comprehend—to construct a problem space for—than others. The challenge may simply be that the task is difficult. Very few cognitive limits show through in playing a game of tic-tac-toe, but playing chess is a different matter. Cognitive architecture may also show through in complex environments where the task faced is essentially ambiguous.

Table 3.1. A Time Scale of Human Action

Scale (sec.)	Time Units	System	World
10^7	Months		Social band
10^6	Weeks		"
10^5	Days		"
10^4	Hours	Task	Rational band
10^3	10 minutes	Task	"
10^2	Minutes	Task	"
10^1	10 seconds	Unit task	Cognitive band
10^0	1 second	Operations	"
10^{-1}	100 milliseconds	Deliberate act	"
10^{-2}	10 milliseconds	Neural circuit	Biological band
10^{-3}	1 millisecond	Neuron	"
10^{-4}	100 μsec	Organelle	"

Source: Newell 1990, 122.

Table 3.1 reproduces Newell's time scale. The shorter the time available, the more severely the limits imposed by human cognitive architecture influence action. The longer the time span, the more the nature of the task environment influences behavior.

At times of less than one hundred milliseconds, only biology is operative. This Newell termed the "biological band" of human action. The neuronal level is the stopping point. There is no gain to be had in understanding immediate human action pushing below this level, because the neuron is the critical building block for human action. Moreover, very few attributes of the interaction of neurons are important for higher-level cognition. Newell sees only the characteristic operating time and speed of transmission as important (124–25). The next level in the biological band is the neural circuit level, involving interactions between neurons. Because of the time constraints imposed by the biological band, no cognitive behavior can occur at time scales of less than one second.

Above a hundred milliseconds, deliberation—"to bring available knowledge to bear to choose one operation rather than others" (123)—can be performed. In the "cognitive band," knowledge can be brought to bear on a problem, but problem search is constrained—the response is preprogrammed at the level of the deliberate act or involves rapid pattern recognition at the level of operations and unit tasks. "It is fast, there is no control, it is exhaustive, and there is no detailed awareness" (138). In the higher levels of the cognitive band, simple operations are strung together in more complex operations, but the essential character of no problem search remains.

In the (intendedly) "rational band," the task becomes the critical element—human action is designed according to the task that the person faces. The task becomes increasingly determinative of the action. Problem solving is the modus operandi. People construct models of the problems facing them, perform heuristic searches, and draw on existing knowledge.

Finally, in the "social band," people interact in complex formal organizations. They must communicate, understand the intentions and problems faced by others, and cooperate to achieve aims.

The distinction between the cognitive and rational bands corresponds to the automatic/controlled distinction (Shiffren and Schneider 1977). "An automatic process can't be inhibited from being initiated. It is relatively fast. It takes the same time (or almost so) independent of the stimulus load. It cannot be terminated as a function of internal decisions. No detailed awareness exists of what processes are being carried out" (Newell 1990, 136). Nothing in the cognitive band can be rational because the individual is not thinking about his or her response and cannot control it (although a response can be interrupted). We may judge a response's *appropriateness,* in the sense of its match to the environment, but we cannot adjudge its *rationality.*

The Preparation-Deliberation Trade-Off

The armadillo has a startle response that causes the animal to jump straight up to a height surprising for such a small and slow-moving creature. This strategy clearly had evolutionary value in a threatening world, but is quite maladaptive on the highways of Texas. Jumping straight up into the path of an oncoming automobile is not the best way to ensure the survival of the family genotype.

Any intelligent system—human or artificial—is subject to a participation-deliberation trade-off. It can search and deliberate, or it can select from a repertoire of prepared strategies. The prepared strategies may have been learned or inherited (in the case of organisms) or preprogrammed (in the case of computers). These strategies are adaptive, at least in the environment in which they evolved (for hardwired strategies) or were learned (VanBerg 1993, 1999).

The more the system deliberates, the more time that it must consume to construct a problem space and search for solutions. The more it prepackages, the less time is consumed, but the more likely the solution that emerges will be inappropriate. The more simple and stable the task environment, the more prepared strategies can be used. The more complex and dynamic the task environment, the more likely there is to be a mismatch between the task environment and the solution that is applied.

Figure 3.1 displays this trade-off as a set of isobars similar to the indif-

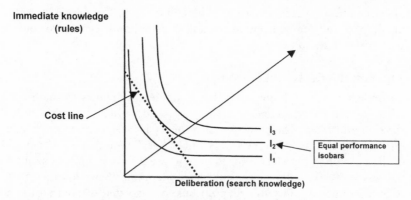

Figure 3.1   The Preparation-Deliberation Trade-off
Source: Modified from Newell 1990, 103

ference curves described in chapter 2. If the time for search is limited, then an organism can improve performance only by acquiring knowledge, learning more prepackaged strategies. This has the effect of moving performance out to a new isobar.

Prepackaged strategies to fit frequently encountered stimuli may have a physiological locus—the cerebellum. The cerebellum, at the head of the brain stem and one of the first parts of the brain to have evolved, was once thought to have been involved only in motor control. Some recent research suggests that the automatic responses to patterned stimuli, learned or not, may be packaged in this region of the brain (Thatch, Goodkin, and Keating 1992). The advantage to the organism is quicker response— higher brain functions (conscious thought) need not be involved. This prepackaging can be highly sensitive to local variation in the organism's environment, thereby allowing considerable flexibility in its behavioral repertoire. The preparation-deliberation trade-off is so pervasive that it affects not just organisms and artificial systems, but human formal organizations as well. We return to this point in chapter 6.

There are sound evolutionary reasons for reducing search behavior in order to allow an organism to react quickly to a threatening situation. On the other hand, having only a limited number of prepackaged strategies curtails current adaptability—as the case of the startled armadillo shows. An efficient evolutionary solution could involve prepared learning: an organism is prepared to learn certain associations, but will not be burdened with prewired and irreversible strategies such as that leading to the demise of many armadillos on the highways of Texas. To the extent that prepackaged solutions are learned behavioral responses to stimuli, they can be unlearned. But unlearning can be a difficult process. Flexible adaptability in complex and changing environments at some point comes into conflict with speed of response.

The Behavioral Model of Choice

To understand how human cognitive architecture shows through even when people are intendedly rational, we need a theory of what shows through and when. The basis of such a theory is Herbert Simon's "behavioral model of choice." In the 1940s and 1950s, Simon developed a model of choice intended as a challenge to the comprehensive rationality assumptions used in economics. Simon continually reminded behavioral scientists of human intentionality in organizations, but isolated where that intentionality failed.

Unlike perhaps any other social scientist in the modern age, Simon is a synthetic thinker. He has made major contributions not only to his initial field of academic study, political science (as the founder of the behavioral study of organizations), but also to economics (as a Nobelist), psychology (as a founding father of cognitive psychology), and computer science (as an initiator of the field of artificial intelligence). Indeed, as we will see, Simon sees bounded rationality as the foundation for his contributions in organization theory, economics, computer science, and psychology.

Bounded rationality and the associated behavioral theory of choice were born from a comparison between academic theories of decision making and observations of real people in real policymaking roles. As an undergraduate at the University of Chicago, Simon returned to his native Milwaukee in 1935 to observe budgeting in the city's Recreation Department:

> I came as a gift-bearing Greek, fresh from an intermediate price theory course taught by the grandfather of Chicago-School neoclassical laissez-faire economics, Henry Simons. . . . My economics training showed me how to budget rationally. Simply compare the marginal utility of a proposed expenditure with its marginal cost, and approve it only if the utility exceeds the cost. However, what I saw in Milwaukee didn't seem to be an application of this rule. I saw a lot of bargaining, of reference back to last year's budget, and incremental changes in it. If the word "marginal" was ever spoken, I missed it. Moreover, which participants would support which items was quite predictable. . . . I could see a clear connection between people's positions on budget matters and the values and beliefs that prevailed in their sub-organizations.
>
> I brought back to my friends and teachers in economics two gifts, which I ultimately called "organizational identification" and "bounded rationality." (1999, 112).

I would not object to having my whole scientific output described as largely a gloss—a rather elaborate gloss, to be sure—[on these two ideas]. (1996a, 88)

Bounded rationality and organizational identification (which is today seen as a consequence of bounded rationality) won acceptance in political science, with its emerging empiricist orientation, but they were largely ignored in the more theoretical discipline of economics. Or, as Simon puts it, economists "mostly ignored [bounded rationality] and went on counting the angels on the heads of neoclassical pins" (1999, 113). Indeed, Simon spent a great deal of time and energy attacking the abstract and rarefied economic decision-making models. Much of his attack was negative—showing how the model did not comport with how people really made decisions. But he also developed what he termed a "procedural" model of rationality, based on the psychological process of reasoning. He saw as particularly important the need to explain how people conduct incomplete searches and make trade-offs between values: "Since the organism, like those of the real world, has neither the senses nor the wits to discover an 'optimal' path—even assuming the concept of optimal to be clearly defined—we are concerned only with finding a choice mechanism that will lead it to pursue a 'satisficing' path that will permit satisfaction at some specified level of all of its needs" (Simon 1957, 270–71).

Simon elaborated on his "satisficing" organism over the years, but its fundamental characteristics did not change They include

1. Limitation on the organism's ability to plan long behavior sequences, a limitation imposed by the bounded cognitive ability of the organism as well as the complexity of the environment in which it operates;
2. The tendency to set aspiration levels for each of the multiple goals that the organism faces;
3. The tendency to operate on goals sequentially rather than simultaneously because of the "bottleneck of short-term memory";
4. "Satisficing" rather than optimizing search behavior.

An alternative "satisfices" (the word Simon coined to define "good enough") if it meets aspirations along all dimensions (attributes). If no such alternative is found, a search is undertaken for new alternatives. Meanwhile, aspirations along one or more dimensions drift down gradually until a satisfactory new alternative is found or some existing alternative satisfices (Simon 1996b, 30).

In detailing the general requirements of an organism operating under bounded (as contrasted with comprehensive) rationality, Simon notes the following requisites: a way of focusing attention, a mechanism for

Box 3.1:   Behaviorism and Behavioralism

Behaviorism in psychology and behavioralism in political science were distinctly different scientific philosophies. Behaviorist psychology, which developed in American psychology during the early part of the twentieth century, emphasized the laboratory study of the connection between stimulus objects and the responses of laboratory subjects, usually animals. Reacting against European psychologists' free-flowing interpretations of patients' self-reports, behaviorist psychology distrusted reports of cognition on the part of subjects, treating them as epiphenomena. It was thought to be unscientific to rely on them. Psychological behaviorism reached its high point in the 1950s under the leadership of B. F. Skinner. Behaviorism retreated under the onslaught of findings from cognitive science that showed the independent influence of thought processes on behavior.

Today laboratory psychologists rely on "process tracing," or "thinking aloud protocols," in which subjects report the process by which they are reaching a decision. This is a far cry indeed from the refusal of behaviorist psychologists to consider the "thoughts in one's head."

Behavior*al*ism in political science was similarly rooted in the observation of behavior, but there the similarities end. Behavioral political scientists believed (and continue to believe) that the study of politics and government ought to be based on systematic observation, including the self-reports of thought and action by voters, public officials, and other political actors. The social survey became the prime instrument of study of public opinion and voting behavior—and it relies completely on self-reporting.

Political science at the turn of the century consisted of the empirical and normative study of government. Empirical studies concentrated on collecting information on government forms and performance. Normative analyses were concerned with good government and the use of public power. When Herbert Simon arrived as an undergraduate at the University of Chicago in 1933, there was revolution—academic revolution—in the air (Simon 1996a). Under the leadership of the chair of the political science department, Charles Merriam, the behavioral revolution was underway. Merriam insisted that political science ought to focus on behavior—the behavior of voters, candidates, and public officials. And scientific methods ought to be used to analyze this behavior—mathematics, statistics, quantitative observation in general. But Merriam did not eschew the normative bases of political science (as latter-day behavioralists tried to do). He saw the scientific study of politics as the foundation for human progress through the use of governmental power.

Merriam and his troops profoundly transformed political science, and Simon was profoundly influenced by the behavioral revolution. He insisted—and continues to insist—that models of human choice be grounded in rigorous observation rather than the mathematical speculation characteristic of theoretical economics.

generating alternatives, a capacity for acquiring facts about the environment, and a modest capacity for drawing inferences from these facts (1983, 20–22).

The behavioral theory of choice was an early demarcation of the points at which we should expect human cognitive architecture to show through in performing adaptive tasks. The paradigm was laid out: to study situations in which goals are clear and there exists a clearly optimal solution, but where environments are complex enough to reveal the contours of human thought patterns.

Problem Solving and Intended Rationality

Bounded rationality and the behavioral theory of choice were born in organization theory and public administration, but they could not be fully tested there. It was too difficult to isolate those components of choice that were caused by the individual's limitations and those imposed by the structure of the organization. An experimental program was necessary, and psychology was the right discipline for those experiments.

Psychological experimentation in the 1950s and 1960s remained under the grip of behaviorism, whose key thesis was response conditioning. Organisms learned stimulus-response associations via the rewards they received from the responses they produced. Only anticipated consequences mattered. This approach ignored the role of the cognitive architecture of the organism, it ignored the goal-directed nature of much human activity, and it failed to incorporate how organisms make choices among goals.

In the late 1950s, Herbert Simon, teaming with computer scientist Allen Newell, had become fascinated with the potential of the digital computer to simulate human thought. Programming computers to mimic thought meant "getting inside the head" of the thinker; as a consequence, artificial intelligence had a great impact on cognitive psychology. Simultaneously, Newell and Simon initiated a program of experimentation into human problem solving, a program that stressed observation of the process of solving a problem, usually one that, while difficult, had a theoretical optimum solution path. Process tracing was controversial; behaviorist psychologists viewed it as "unscientific" because it relied on introspection. Nevertheless, the technique proved extraordinarily useful, and is now standard laboratory practice.

Problem solving falls within the intendendly rational band of human activity. Psychological problem-solving experiments have demonstrated that even when human behavior is intendedly rational, oftentimes an optimal solution path is not followed. If behavior is fully rational, and hence adaptive, then it would be completely determined by the nature of the goals facing the decision maker and the characteristics of the environment (Simon 1979).

The goal of such experiments is fixed and clear: solving the problem. Problem-solving experiments have the advantage of prespecifying a task environment, allowing the experimenter to observe how subjects respond in situations where an optimal path exists but may be very difficult to ascertain. Experimenters have used chess playing and cryptarithmetic (where letters stand for numbers and subjects must solve equations accordingly) to create task environments. In these experiments, "motivation is not in question and emotion is not aroused," so rational, conscious, focused thought can be brought to bear on the task at hand. Nevertheless, experimenters have found a considerable chasm between predicted rational behavior and laboratory observations. "The explanation must lie inside the subject: in limits of his ability to determine what the optimal behavior is, or to execute it if he can determine it" (Newell and Simon 1972, 52, 55).

Phases of Decision Making

Problem solving and decision making are close kin. Indeed, if we think of them in terms of people having a preference for solving a particular problem, they become identical. Both problem solving and decision making involve four distinct phases: (1) attending to the problem, (2) generating a problem-space representation, (3) generating alternatives, and (4) choosing from the alternatives (Simon 1977). Human cognitive limits may affect the process at each of these stages. But only a few aspects of human cognition are candidates for affecting the process.

Working, or short-term, memory. The number of elements or symbols that can be actively manipulated by a human problem solver is severely limited.

Calculational ability. Constructing a problem space, generating alternatives, and comparing solutions can involve vast manipulations.

Knowledge. The construction of problem spaces and solution sets can be extremely inefficient without a proper knowledge base (the preparation-deliberation trade-off).

Retrieval from long-term memory. Unlike working memory, long-term memory has virtually infinite capacity. However, even when a subject has the expertise to solve a problem, he may have trouble accessing the proper solution.

We now turn to each of the four phases of decision making to indicate how cognitive limitations may affect the outcomes of a decision.

Attention

To solve a problem or make a decision, a person must allocate attention to the matter. This stage is far more crucial in the real world than in laboratory experiments—so crucial that its importance can be missed in the laboratory. Experimenters work mightily to ensure that subjects attend to the proper aspects of the environment—how else can one know what stimulus causes what behavior? The problem even plagues psychophysics, the study of how people sense such stimuli as light and sound. As experimental psychophysicist S. S. Stevens noted, "attention must focus on one aspect or attribute, to the neglect of many other aspects that could be attended to" (1975, 54). Psychophysical experiments are simple in design compared to those in cognitive or social psychology or economics.

Problem-Space Representation

Problems must be represented symbolically and accessed in short-term memory if they are to be solved. Basically the problem solver must "focus on the particular features that are relevant to the problem, then [build] a problem-space containing these features but omitting the irrelevant ones" (Simon 1996b, 109). Objective problem spaces (perhaps as defined by an objective observer) may be transformed by a decision maker in trying to solve the problem at hand in a way not anticipated by the objective observer. Allen Newell has written that "[i]n complex situations . . . there is great uncertainty over what information is entering into [judgment]. . . . If only the task environment were appropriately described, the nature of the judgment would be clear. That is, the judgmental law is quite secondary, and amounts to doing the obvious with the information finally selected" (1968, 13).

In their studies of problem solving, Newell and Simon (1972, 848–67) developed a theory of problem-space representation. They listed six sources for the determination of a problem-space representation by their experimental subjects: (1) the task instructions read to the subject; (2) previous experience with the same or nearly identical tasks; (3) previous experience with tasks that are recognized as analogous; (4) general-purpose stored programs in long-term memory capable of being used on a variety of tasks; (5) stored programs in long-term memory that combine current information from the environment with internally stored information; (6) the course of problem solving itself, which can augment or modify the problem space as the problem is worked on.

In real-world decision making, of course, experimental task instructions are not relevant. But instructions about the task from others are an important source of input on problem representation. Otherwise the Newell-Simon list is completely general.

Problem-space representations are related to preferences, because we have to understand what it is we want in order to pursue goals. To understand problem-space representation, we may return to the decision matrix presented in figure 2.1 in chapter 2. Recall that the matrix displayed the choice alternatives and the attributes against which the alternatives were judged together. Viewing preference structures from a problem-solving perspective involves two processes: the first is how information is structured and the second is what information is selected. The structure of the problem space is simply the set of attributes used in describing the process. The second process is selection: what attributes are seen as relevant to the problem situation?

As an analysis of a decision-making situation proceeds, the decision maker receives information from the environment. This adds a dynamic to preferences analogous to problem solving. Information can cause the restructuring of the alternative space—another alternative is discovered in the search process. But the search process can also uncover a previously unattended attribute that is suddenly viewed as relevant. That introduction of a new attribute can radically restructure the understanding of a problem, and hence can radically alter one's preferences for outcomes.

In many cases, problem spaces cannot be defined without reference to solutions. Computer scientists refer to a problem as "well defined" if "there is a test which can be applied to a proposed solution" (McCarthy 1956, 177). So a well-defined problem is one in which there is a solution. Naming the solution set in effect identifies the problem.

The deliberation-preparation trade-off ensures that any decision maker will harbor many prepackaged solutions to the multiple tasks facing him or her. In modern life, task environments are often complex and problem spaces can be ill defined. Indeed, in democratic political systems, there can be a cacophony of competing claims for the definition of public problems. Where problem spaces are ill defined, solutions are prepackaged, and there exists cognitive and emotional (and in politics, often financial) identification with solutions, the solutions can start to define the problem. That is, one can understand the problem only by reference to the solution. This facet of problem solving serves as the basis for an entire theory of how organizations decide what problems to work on (Cohen, March, and Olsen 1972; Kingdon 1996).

Representation-Hungry Problems

Is the construction of problem spaces necessary for problem-solving activity? Philosopher Andy Clark notes that many findings from cognitive science have led to the conclusion that "we must go beyond the passive image of the organism perceiving the world and recognize the way our actions may be continuously responsive to worldly events which are at the same time continuously responsive to our actions" (1997, 171). Humans, like all organisms, are immersed in complex systems of reciprocal causation that require continuous modulation with the environment (Clark uses the example of a jazz quartet).

Box 3.2:   What Makes the French Happy?

A French poll a number of years ago was commissioned to ascertain the subjective factors in happiness. When asked about the factors leading to happiness, people mentioned first, a relationship with "another person" and second "the full realization of one's own potential." In last place was "to be in good health." But when asked about the things that caused unhappiness, the first-place mention was "not being in good health."

The simple restatement of the same problem (most of us would assume that happiness and unhappiness are just opposite ends of the same problem) has caused what psychologists Daniel Kahneman and Amos Tversky call a "preference reversal." The preference ordering is reversed depending on where one anchors the problem (at happiness or unhappiness). This preference reversal is clearly due to problem-space representation and in particular information selectivity. In responding to the question on happiness, it is most likely that most respondents simply assumed good health or just never thought of it at all (that is, the alternative "good health" just didn't enter into working memory at all). But the question on unhappiness primed the respondents to include the lack of good health, hence inducing the preference reversal (Piattelli-Palmarini 1994, 7–8).

The necessity of continuous responsiveness and immediate action means that much of human action must occur in the cognitive band. The need for continuous modulation suggests cognitive structures that are decentralized, quasi-independent, and not monitored by a central representational and computational system. Clark, however, notes a class of problems that humans solve that he terms "representation-hungry" problems. These are problems characterized by either (1) thoughts that involve "potential outcomes of imagined actions" or (2) selective responses to wildly varying states of affairs, states "that are unified at some rather abstract level, but whose physical correlates have little in common" (167). These are the kinds of problems that require intended rationality and problem-space construction.

The distinction between problems requiring continuous reciprocal interaction with the environment and representation-hungry problems mirrors Newell's time scale for human action. This key distinction, whatever we term it, is fundamental to understanding human behavior in complex, artificial systems such as polities and economies.

Generating Alternatives

Once we understand a situation by generating an adequate problem representation, how do we come up with a solution? There are only two places to find alternatives: the external world (via search procedures) or our own memory, where we have stored strategies (or some combination of the two).

Early rational theorists blithely ignored search costs; search was simply assumed away. One of Herbert Simon's major criticisms of the assumption of economic rationality was that real-world actors never seemed to search for the optimal solution to a problem. Rather they "satisficed"—just found one that was good enough.

Economists retorted that no rational actor would engage in a comprehensive search for most decisions. The reason is that information entails a cost—in particular, a time cost. So the extensiveness of the search should be related to how important the choice is to the decision maker. For the typical voter, it is rational to do no search. For a major life change, extensive search would be in order.

A rational approach would require explicit and conscious cost calculations comparing the value of a search and the likely benefits of the decision. If these calculations are not done, then the process of decision making cannot be fully rational. While it is often claimed that decision makers spend more time and energy searching where the issue is important to them, there is little empirical evidence to support the proposition (I know of none). In the real world, important decisions often require rapid response to changing circumstances.

It does seem clear that for many decisions most people make no explicit cost-of-search calculations. We tend to rely on heuristics. These heuristics are important to conserve cognitive resources in a complex world; as a consequence, they are unavoidable parts of decision making. They may, however, lead to less than optimal decision making. For example, by relying on our political party to guide our vote choice, most of us don't make the explicit calculation that party voting is an informational shortcut for what we really want—issue payoffs. We don't because we actually *like* our party—we identify with it—and want it to win.

If we become emotionally involved in an organization—if we identify with it—and leaders of that organization do not deliver the individual payoffs that we would like, what do we do? Most of us would prefer to ignore the discordant information rather than bring it explicitly into a cost-benefit calculation. At some point, of course, we may feel misused by the organization and reverse our loyalties to it. As a consequence of our identifications with an organization, we delay in abandoning it, but when we abandon it, we do so wholeheartedly. Organizational identification causes a "drag" on adaptive, fully rational behavior, making it more epi-sodic and disjointed than it otherwise would be. In this manner cognitive heuristics and emotional arousal can act to limit adaptation.

Choice

Once alternatives are generated, the decision maker decides between the possibilities. A major problem in evaluating alternatives is that if the alter-native set is at all large, a solution-by-solution comparison becomes impractical.

Filtering

Many observers of decision making in practice claim that people go through a two-stage process in coming to a final choice. The first stage is a filtering or editing phase, in which people determine whether an alter-native is a feasible one. In the language of psychologists Lee Roy Beach and Terrence Mitchell (1998), the first issue is whether an alternative is to be admitted to the "choice set" as a reasonable alternative. Part of filtering involves framing, in which long-term memory is probed to ascertain the relevant factors characterizing the decision. Once the decision is charac-terized, admissibility to the choice set depends on a comparison between the alternative and the decision maker's values or principles, and his or her goals. Beach points out that many decisions that might maximize one's goals, or plans for the future, are rejected because they are inconsistent with principles—"they are just not right." One might treat these as deci-sional constraints, but that seems to underestimate their key importance in the decision-making process.

In the second stage, the best alternative is selected. In the approach of Beach and Mitchell, and of Payne and his colleagues (Payne, Bettman, and Johnson 1993), people use a range of decision-making strategies depend-ing on the nature of the task and the environment in which the task takes place. As is the case for all empirical decision researchers, these psycholo-gists are struck by how often a search for proper frames or alternatives is not seriously conducted. Indeed, Beach and Mitchell (1998) suggest that in many situations only one alternative is explored, on an up-or-down basis, and this choice is contextually determined. Oftentimes the choice is the status quo.

Comparing Incommensurate Attributes

As we noted in chapter 2, people have considerable trouble in making decisions when the attributes that characterize that decision are incom-mensurate. Samuel Popkin writes: "People have a general aversion to making trade-offs and instead search for a way to make their choices one-dimensional" (1993, 371). While it is doubtless true that people would like to avoid trade-offs, it is also the case that the basic cognitive architecture we have inherited makes trade-offs difficult. As Howard Margolis (1987) notes, the choice between "jumping" or "checking" is fundamental to human behavior (and very probably adaptive). The necessity of deciding whether to jump or check would tend to operate against the ability to make smooth, indifference-curve trade-offs. Instead of making the easy, compensatory trade-offs of consumer choice theory, we often use "noncompensatory strategies." Three main noncompensatory strategies have been isolated by decision-making researchers.

Satisficing. In picking a "good enough," or alternative people set aspiration levels on each dimension or attribute. "Aspiration levels provide a computational mechanism for satisficing" (Simon 1996a, 30). If an alternative meets aspiration levels along all attributes, it is chosen as "good enough" (but not necessarily best).

Lexicographic strategy. In the lexicographic strategy, the decision maker focuses on only one aspect of a decisional situation, and chooses the alternative that scores highest on the one criterion (see Beach and Mitchell 1978, 441–42). The attributes are simply not combined.

Elimination by aspects. In the process of elimination by aspects, the decision maker first uses a lexicographic strategy but moves to a second aspect when alternative scores tie (Tversky 1972).

These strategies emerge because of the difficulties inherent in combining aspects in an overall utility score. Tversky and his collaborators indicate that "because it is often unclear how to trade one attribute against another, a common procedure for resolving conflict is to select the option that is superior on the more important attribute" (Tversky, Sattath, and Slovic 1988, 372). Noncompensatory approaches have clear effects on critical and important decisions. For example, Mintz (1993) shows how the U.S. decision to attack Iraq in the Gulf War was affected by the unwillingness of key decision makers to make trade-offs.

There is evidence that people tend to use a net benefits approach when asked to match each alternative in a decision-making situation with underlying standards, but tend toward elimination by aspects (using only the most prominent dimension) when asked to compare alternatives directly. Tversky and his colleagues term this tendency the "prominence hypothesis" (Tversky, Sattath, and Slovic, 1988, 372). The price system in a capitalistic economy allows a comparison with an underlying standard, probably pushing people toward a net benefits approach. Where metrics are not available, as in politics, people may rely on prominence.

Nonequivalence of Gains and Losses

A special problem in evaluating alternatives comes about because people do not treat gains and losses from decisions similarly. In effect, we dread losses more than we value gains. In the expected utility framework, gains and losses should be valued similarly. Experiments indicate that in fact we evaluate losses more severely than we evaluate gains (Kahneman and Tversky 1983). A major consequence of this phenomenon is that people's choices are sensitive to the reference point that distinguishes gains from losses. Think of the different consequences for your feelings about a stock you bought a year ago that lost 20 percent yesterday but has gained 80 percent since the purchase. Now consider those feelings if you bought the stock day before yesterday. Rationally, we should be indifferent between these two reference points. Most of us are not.

Heuristic Decision Making

Heuristic decision making uses "rules of thumb" to simplify a complex problem. Heuristics affect every stage of the decision-making process: attentiveness, problem-space representation, alternative generation, and choice.

Sometimes these strategies are conscious. We decide not to go to the bother of finding out everything about candidates in an election, for example. We know that our vote will count little in the outcome of the election. There are costs to finding out many things we would want to know about the candidates. So we decide just to vote for the Republican. Or to vote for the candidate our union has endorsed. Or to take the daily newspaper into the booth to vote for the all those judicial candidates that nobody knows very much about. Or to vote for or against the incumbent.

It is almost never fully rational to collect full information about a candidate in an election—"rational ignorance," as some political scientists have put it. A decision is rational or adaptive to the extent that the heuristics we use lead to the same choice as a full-information decision would. If heuristics lead to differences in decisional outcomes, then we have another incidence of bounded rationality showing through in our decision making.

For the most part, heuristics are "spontaneous" strategies. We seldom go through a cost-benefit analysis to try to think through whether our heuristic strategies will yield the same choice as if we had collected the appropriate full information. Heuristics are part of our genetic or social inheritances. So the key question is whether our inherited tendencies toward intuitive and spontaneous strategies will mislead us (in comparison to rational and adaptive behavior). The answer from laboratory and observational studies is a resounding yes. But studies that explicitly compare behaviors in the real world with rational strategies have not played a prominent part of social science, so the key question of the deviation between fully adaptive behavior and bounded rationality has not been answered.

A number of cognitive heuristics have been described by researchers (Mondak 1994). It remains to be seen how many laboratory-induced effects operate to affect real-world decision making. Feedback has the potential for error-correcting, as does moving from the cognitive to the rational band of thought. Three general heuristic modes are likely to be important in social settings in any case: reasoning by analogy, trial and error, and social cueing. In reasoning by analogy, we see (or think we see) that a current problem is like one we have solved before. We tend to reason that, if our problem-space representation is similar to that of a past problem, then the past solution will probably work too.

There is generally considerable trial and error in problem solving. Often that trial and error is anticipatory—we rule out a path to a solution because we find a reason that it won't work. Often we consult with others, who may encourage or discourage us in the path we propose. In politics, the "trial balloon" is an explicit policy proposal that tests the political reaction before implementation. In campaigns, polls and focus groups are designed to assess the reaction of a candidate's proposed position on an issue.

So human problem solving has more than a superficial resemblance to Darwinian natural selection. Trial and error in the generation of alternatives in decision making can proceed much more rapidly than pure random generation of the alternatives because of the ability of humans to try out solutions hypothetically or in limited situations. The more reversible a solution path, the more likely it will be abandoned in the face of contrary information.

This suggests that organizational arrangements that allow for trial and error and reversibility are likely to be more adaptive than those requiring conformity and central direction. It has often been noted that state and local governments in the United States serve as "laboratories of democracy" through their trial-and-error approach to public policy adoption. Similarly, a competitive economic sector with many firms is more likely to generate useful products (and many not-so-useful ones) than a monopolistic or oligopolistic one.

There is, however, a competing tendency that can offset the flexibility of trial-and-error problem solving. That is the tendency of people to identify, both cognitively and emotionally, with the means of solving a problem rather than the goal, or end. Sociologists of organizations speak of "goal displacement"—a circumstance that occurs when people value the organization and its procedures more than the goals that the organization is trying to accomplish. These goals may seem very distant to people, whereas their immediate work environment provides structure and direct (often nonmonetary) incentives. Identification with the means implies that it will be harder to abandon an inadequate solution than would otherwise be the case—a major cause of bounded rationality showing through in adaptive decision making.

Social cueing occurs when a decision maker observes and follows the cues of another person (or group) who shares the decision maker's values. This process has been observed in mass voting behavior (Lupia 1994), in legislatures (Matthews 1960), and in market behavior (Lux 1995). While the issue is far from settled, there is considerable evidence that social cueing will lead to appropriate behavior in many cases, particularly in stable environments. In rapidly changing environments, however, emotional arousal can cause many to engage in less than optimal behavior.

It is important for us to appreciate that heuristic strategies are *not* the key limitation on our decision-making capacity. They are strategies, and as such are potentially infinite—at least if they are inherited socially or learned. So the study of heuristic decision making must be based in observation. I stress this seemingly obvious implication because some economists and political scientists have tried to "model" bounded rationality through listing heuristics (Sargent 1993; Rubinstein 1998; Lupia and McCubbins 1998).

Arousing Emotion: Setting Priorities or Enjoying Utility?

Much analysis in political science, and virtually all in economics, proceeds as if human emotion is irrelevant to substance and process in decision making. When emotion is integrated, it is treated mostly as either an end state—the payoff of pain or pleasure from a choice—or as an impediment to rational decision making. Emotion can be either of these, of course. But emotional states are more bound up with the thought process. As E. O. Wilson writes, "Without the stimulus and guidance of emotion, rational thought slows and disintegrates" (1998, 113). Work by neurologists such as Antonio and Hanna Damasio at the University of Iowa Medical School shows that damage to regions of the brain responsible for emotional arousal also results in defects in reasoning and decision making (Damasio 1994, 1999). Of course most people making decisions in modern economies and polities don't have partially destroyed brains. But the findings seem too strong for social scientists to ignore: emotion and reason are intertwined.

The question is, So what? Our standard here is adaptive behavior, and it may be quite irrelevant if there is no connection between emotional states and what our choices would be under the strictures of rationality. Indeed, there are differences. In the first place, emotions are critical in the selection of information for a decision. Emotions function to select "particular things in our environments as the focus of our attention" (Simon 1983, 29). Emotions highlight what is important; they are critical in setting priorities. More than that, they are critical in problem-space representation. Emotions act as the gateway to our short-term memories. Herbert Simon says that we cannot be rational about things we do not *attend* to. Modern cognitive science indicates that we cannot be rational about things we do not *feel* about. Of course, we may also be less than rational when it comes to our feelings. Moreover, both feeling and cognitive attention are linked to behavior—one cannot fully account for actions without incorporating an affective component. For example, both cognition and emotion are linked to the direction of voting (Granberg and Brown 1989; Marcus and Rahn 1990).

Emotional states of arousal are not diffuse; there are distinct types of emotion: fear, anxiety, elation. Our feelings direct our attention, but they do more as well. The kinds of feelings we experience direct our behaviors into different paths—including search behavior.

Three political scientists, Michael MacKuen, George Marcus, and Russell Neuman, have shown how this works in the case of deciding how to vote. Using data from national surveys, these scholars find that people use different modes of political judgment depending on their emotional reactions to the political environment. When calm, they rely on habitual cues such as partisanship; however when anxious, they examine the candidates' issue appeals, reconsider their own standing preferences and vote accordingly (MacKuen, Neuman, and Marcus 1997, 17).

Political scientists have understood for many years that voters maintain what V. O. Key called a "standing decision" to continue to vote for their party. But in some circumstances, they change that decision. The research program of MacKuen, Marcus, and Neuman, which involves experimentation as well as survey analysis, is directed toward understanding both stasis and change in the vote. Critical to their analysis is the "emotional surveillance system" that selects or highlights those aspects of the environment that are deemed important by the voter.

It is clear why political campaigns seem always to "play to our emotions." In order to change a voter's standing (and mostly unexamined) decision, an appeal to the voter must rouse emotions. Since anxiety seems to be the factor that is causally related to reconsideration, it is natural that campaign managers would try to arouse anxiety.

Problem-Solving in Complex, Dynamic Environments

Human decision makers do not respond to static, controlled environments. Inputs are dynamic, and people must decide, over and over again, what part of the environment is relevant to their goals. Oftentimes, they receive too much information from many diverse sources. The bottlenecks of short-term memory and attention mean that all of the environment cannot be monitored simultaneously. Parts must remain unattended, and those aspects that are relevant must be combined in a manner that bears on future strategies.

The limits of short-term memory mean that human decision makers will have to shift from one focus to another episodically. A shift in focus of attention is exactly that: a shift. Even if relevant environmental conditions have changed in a smooth and continuous fashion, a decision maker's problem-solving abilities must shift discontinuously to apprehend the now relevant conditions.

One may wonder why attentional mechanisms and limited short-term memory would evolve even in a Stone Age brain. Wouldn't it make more sense if a more comprehensively rational mechanism had emerged? There are two answers to this. First, evolutionary solutions are always based on past solutions. It is generally more efficient for an organism to modify an existing structure than to develop whole new ones. Second, a critically important facet of attentional mechanisms is to screen out irrelevant stimuli. If an organism could not "pay inattention," it could not concentrate on food gathering, or mating, or whatever the necessary task. As a direct consequence of the need to pay inattention, organisms can quickly become habituated to a stimulus. Like the boy who cried wolf, a signal may no longer have the capacity to elicit the normal response.

Howard Margolis (1987) has developed a theory of cognition based on pattern recognition (what we call problem representation here) and the decisions that follow a recognition. Independently, artificial intelligence researchers have also emphasized "pattern completion and associative memory" (Clark 1997, 67) in human thought. Any situation facing a decision maker can be a threat, an opportunity, or irrelevant. In response, an organism can take one of two responses: jumping (responding) or checking (taking a closer look). Two other processes are involved in deciding what action to take: priming (a predisposition to make certain jumps) or inhibiting (refusing to make certain jumps). What action to take depends primarily on what pattern has been recognized. The fundamental decision facing any organism is to decide between jumping too soon and checking too long. The severe consequences of a decision to avoid a threatening situation compared to the benefits derived from a felicitous situation may well account for the differential evaluation of gains and losses found in decision-making experiments.

It is easy to see how pattern recognition is adaptive in an evolutionary sense. Organisms jumping too quickly could use too much energy; those checking too long could get eaten. Again, however, epigenetic rules and prepared learning play the key part. If a pattern is categorized by the organism as threatening, it is primed via evolution for "fight or flight." But the predisposition can be inhibited and other responses conditioned (through operant conditioning or anticipatory learning). As a consequence, the relationship between our genetic inheritances and goal-oriented or adaptive behavior is complex. To some extent, however, these predispositions may limit adaptability in present decision-making situations. In particular, they can cause us to over- or underreact to task environments.

Public Problem Solving

President Calvin Coolidge is alleged to have commented that there are only two kinds of problems that governments face: those that solve themselves and those that can't be solved. Public problems are hard problems: by the time government gets around to examining them, the easy solutions have all been used up. A hard problem is one that has lots of underlying attributes, such that any attempt to address one attribute invariably affects others. So it is difficult to achieve consensus on the nature of the problem and on the effectiveness of proposed solutions since different solutions (including Coolidge's favorite, doing nothing) address different problem-space attributes. Indeed, one aspect of public problem solving is that it often occurs in the absence of a full consensus.

Attentional dynamics and problem-space representation are critical processes in politics, and a great deal of research has focused on the notion that public problems must be defined in order for them to be solved (Rochefort and Cobb 1994). Generally, problems as complex as those debated by modern governments are only partially understood, are driven by alleged solutions to the problem, and are path dependent (each step in the process adds constraints, so that the history of attempts to solve the problem affect current opportunities to solve it). It is not always clear which aspects of a public problem are relevant; moreover, different political actors may benefit from different kinds of problem representations. Open democratic systems allow a great deal of dialogue over collective problem representation, in effect recognizing that problem representation is a fallible process.

The limits of human attention and short-term memory bring into sharp question the notion that better decisions come from "more information." A large amount of unorganized information can just confuse a problem-space representation. Indeed, "more information" has two meanings. The first is more information about alternatives. The second is more information about attributes. We even have different terms for the two processes. We "search" for more information on alternatives (including devising new alternatives). But we "recognize" the relevance *of* attributes or factors that were previously ignored. Indeed, decisions are most influenced by the introduction into the problem space of attributes previously not included. Most political campaigns are concerned mostly about calling voters' attention to factors they may have omitted in calculating candidate desirability.

Moreover, the definition of problems is strongly affected by what aspects of a problem people attend to. How people understand a problem is affected by the attentiveness they give to the attributes that characterize that problem (Baumgartner and Jones 1993; Jones 1994). Because much of policymaking takes place out of the public limelight, aspects of attentiveness may be manipulated in ways that foster prevailing understandings of problem-space construction (Cobb and Ross 1997).

Low-Information Rationality

If consumers are not comprehensively rational, then it is possible that they can be deceived and will suffer. If voters are not comprehensively rational, it is possible that the collectivity will suffer. We now turn to a key question of democratic governance: the performance of electorates. If voters are not supremely rational and fully informed (and they are not), then does democracy suffer? Can heuristic decision making with attention-allocation based on emotion substitute for fully informed voting?

Political scientists studying voting behavior and public opinion have been at pains to show how adaptive decision making can emerge from the use of heuristics, whether or not those heuristics are conscious choices to limit information costs. As Lupia (1994) puts it, does a voter have to be an encyclopedia to make reasoned choices in elections, or will low-information shortcuts do?

This issue has an important history in political science. Roughly speaking, modern-day political science inherited two diverging conceptions of the voter in democratic societies. On the one hand, the older voting-behavior literature, grounded in the sociology and social psychology of the day, viewed voters as pawns of social location or their limited cognitive makeups. Two schools of thought on voting developed. For the sociologists of the Columbia school, the causes of voting behavior were found in groups. The vote was dictated by one's social position. For the social psychologists, the Michigan school, attitudes were critical. Political attitudes were viewed as a mix of cognition and affect (thought and emotion) toward political objects, and were linked to behavior (albeit perhaps in complex ways). Neither "school" offered much that would help one understand the voter as a decision maker, rational or otherwise.

Much of the work in these schools was directed at debunking the "myth" of the informed voter that, supposedly, was a prerequisite for enlightened democratic politics. The voter had been examined empirically, and had been found wanting. Whatever the intent of the original investigators, we end up with a picture of a cognitively crippled voter. The voter was a prisoner of his social group and attitudes transferred from parent to child in a process of political socialization. The crippled voter was thus generally unable to organize and understand the political world around him, and reliant on a more educated and informed politicized elite to pass on cues about what to do in the voting booth.

A second conception of the democratic voter was diametrically opposed to this pessimistic view. Born in economics and offered to political scientists in Anthony Downs's *An Economic Theory of Democracy* in 1957, the rational voter maximized utility subject to constraint. Downs spent much of his book trying to explain why voters were not supremely informed in politics. Voters were just as uninformed as the survey researchers had documented, but for very different reasons. Voters were not cognitively crippled; they were rationally ignorant. Given the low probability that they could influence election outcomes, and hence reap rewards from their actions, voters had very low incentives for informing themselves. As a consequence, it was rational for them to rely on political parties to field candidates and offer voters cues about their candidates' policy positions.

In the meantime, a new approach to understanding voters has emerged. Voters are neither pawns of social forces nor their own "hardwired" attitudes, nor or they powerful calculating and utility-maximizing machines. They are cognitively limited, perhaps, but by no means cognitively crippled. They are boundedly rational.

The Early Voting Studies

The study of voting behavior was transformed by the advent of the scientific mass survey in the 1930s and early 1940s. Prior to the extensive use of survey instruments, most voting studies had explored the association between demographic characteristics of geographic areas, such as counties or census tracts, and their voting patterns. Then sociologists Paul Lazarsfeld, Bernard Berelson, and Hazel Gaudet (1944) published their analyses of the repeated surveys they conducted in Erie County, Pennsylvania, on voter choice in the 1940 presidential election. Lazarsfeld thought that campaigns proceeded much as the selling of products did, and he initially postulated a "consumer preference" model. But the data dictated a different view, the role of group affiliations in voting choice. Rather than campaigns generating images and information that affected the course of tentative voting choices throughout the election period, it seemed that voters made up their minds early in a campaign, based on group affiliations, and stuck with these choices. The exception was the "cross-pressured" voter: one whose group affiliations did not all predict the same candidate choice.

During the 1950s, the center of academic survey research moved from Columbia University to the University of Michigan and shifted emphasis from group identity and sociology to the concept of attitude and social psychology. The Michigan researchers were more interested in the "immediate determinants" of voting behavior—attitudes and perceptual organization—than in factors such as group identification that were thought to determine attitudes (these sociological factors were "further back in the causal funnel," in the language of the Michigan researchers). The Michigan researchers produced three major books, cumulating in the classic *The American Voter* (Campbell et al. 1960), and numerous articles during the 1950s and 1960s. The scholars at Michigan not only emphasized social psychology and survey research, they also promoted the use of sophisticated methodological techniques in the analysis of political and social information. In all three respects, the Michigan school had major and lasting impacts on the development of political science. Because of the undeniable importance of party identification, the Michigan approach continues to anchor the study of boting (Miller and Shanks 1996).

The careful picture of the American voter offered by the Michigan scholars was not a pretty one. Public opinion scholars Michael Gant and Norman Luttbeg write: *"The American Voter* concluded that most citizens restricted their political involvement to the one act of voting, and this act was influenced largely by almost blind allegiance to party affiliation. Thus the voter was understood as an uninvolved, dependent creature: this was not the rational citizen that theorists had envisioned populating a democracy."

The picture of the voter as a captive of his virtually unchanging attitudes received some criticism at the time, and was modified in various ways by the Michigan researchers themselves. Much effort was expended on explaining why voters chose candidates from the opposing party, if party allegiance was so central. A whole theory of elections stressed the "normal" vote and deviations from it, in which "normal" votes occurred when people voted their party identifications. "Deviating elections" occurred when voters deviated from these identifications for a single election, because of "short-term forces"; and "realigning elections" occurred when people shifted allegiances.

There was also considerable study of the stratification of cognitive complexity in the electorate, where cognitive complexity was viewed as the ability to impose consistency on attitude-elements within the perceptual map of the voter. Only the most sophisticated voters, it was claimed, were able to impose consistency by harboring an internally coherent political ideology that imposed order on a complex and confusing political world (Converse 1964).

Only one major political scientist, V. O. Key, Jr., rose to the task of challenging what was fast becoming the prevailing orthodoxy. In *The Responsible Electorate* (1966), published posthumously and completed by Milton Cummings, Key claimed that "voters are not fools." Key's effort was noteworthy in two ways: it was the last major effort to provide a "boundedly rational" view of voters until quite recently, and it was almost completely ignored by students of mass political behavior. Rather, much effort was expended in trying to show why the Michigan studies may have been time-bound, particularly in the low emphasis given to issues in the model (Gant and Luttbeg 1991, 21). No serious thought was given to the voter model itself.

The New Bounded Rationality in Voting Studies

By the early 1990s, a different perspective on the voter in democratic societies was clearly emerging. Rather than being captives of group identifications and almost permanent attitudes, voters were active decision makers, responding to the dynamics of politics, policy, and external events. This view was championed by scholars interested in the course of the campaign itself—that is, the manner in which candidates and parties presented themselves to voters. While voters were not fools, they could be fooled.

In his *The Reasoning Voter*, Samuel Popkin provides a view of the voter based on low-information rationality: "The term *low information rationality*—popularly known as 'gut' reasoning—best describes the kind of practical thinking about government and politics in which people actually engage. It is a method of combining, in an economical way, learning and information from past experiences, daily life, the media, and political campaigns" (Popkin 1991, 7).

About the same time as Popkin was propounding his analysis, Sniderman, Brody, and Tetlock began their volume of studies—pointedly entitled *Reasoning and Choice* (1991)—objecting to what they term the "minimalist model" of public opinion. Like all opinion researchers before them, Sniderman and his colleagues were struck by the low information levels of the typical voter, and they also believe that many opinions are volatile and superficial. But they also see some opinions as strongly based in conviction, and they think, following Simon, that citizens compensate for low information by judgmental heuristics and reasoning shortcuts. "Heuristics are judgmental short-cuts, efficient ways to organize and simplify political choices, efficient in the double sense of requiring relatively little information to execute, yet yielding dependable answers even to complex problems of choice" (1991, 19).

Heuristics come in the form of decision rules, which vary by the extent of information people have. Instead of a stratification of the electorate based in "belief systems" and ideology, stratification is based on the use and sophistication of decision rules and is governed by the extensiveness of information voters hold. Information, unlike group identifications, levels of education, or presocialized attitudes, is not fixed throughout one's lifetime. As a consequence, the flow of information and how voters process that information has become a central concern of students of mass behavior (Zaller 1992).

As positive as this development is, there has been a little too much faith in the ability of heuristic reasoning to overcome cognitive limits. The literature doubtless demonstrates that in some places in some times heuristics can be compensatory, but it has not directed effort at finding and analyzing the deviations from good decision making, deviations that continually emerge from laboratory studies.

An Epigenetic Model of Choice

Most human behavior is adaptive; as Allen Newell said thirty years ago, if we could just get the task environment right, we could predict most human action. We are concerned both with those human characteristics that lead us to approximate the fully adaptive decision and with those that limit us from doing so.

The aspects of human decision making we have concentrated on in this chapter are process (or procedural) limitations. That is, they affect how we go about making decisions, but they do not directly affect the substance of the decisions we make. Virtually all process limitations are inherited genetically rather than socially. They may be overcome, because they are inherited as prepared learning rather than inevitable hardwiring. But they exert strong influences on our decision-making capacities.

Almost all of the important bounds to adaptive decision making in modern formal institutions are intimately connected to short-term memory. Short-term memory is the key bottleneck through which decision making must flow. Since our short-term memories are so severely limited, we have developed spontaneous heuristic strategies, which we have either inherited genetically, socially, or learned in the past, to prioritize what we think about.

Short-term memory limits force a heuristic approach on three key facets of decision making. They are (1) selecting information from the environment, (2) weighting its importance, and (3) retrieving solutions from our long-term memories. These are the keys to understanding deviations from optimality in the structured decision-making situations that formal institutions present us with. These process limits can be overcome—much in the way that a memory expert overcomes (or compensates for) his or her short-term memory limitations. Most memory experts have no greater short-term memory capacity than the rest of us. They have learned "chunking" strategies—to treat things to be memorized for easy retrieval from long-term memory as associated "chunks" rather than independent bits of information (Simon 1996b, 64).

There is, however, a major caveat to this picture of our limited adaptability, and that is the adaptability of formal institutions themselves. If they are appropriately adaptive, then institutions expand our capacities to solve problems, essentially aiding us in overcoming our behavioral limitations. When ill, we consult physicians, who may consult experts (or turn to computerized "expert systems" to help them diagnose our problem and design a treatment program). Our limitations—in this case the time limits on our abilities to learn modern medicine—are expanded via organization. If it were not for organized medicine, then our adaptability would also be affected by our long-term memory structures.

Human decision makers, however, have developed mechanisms, again either genetically or socially, that compensate for these limitations. One is the surveillance system that is provided by our emotions. Emotions evolved genetically to signal to us what is important to pay attention to. They are, in effect, a compensatory mechanism for our short-term memory limitations, acting to highlight those aspects of the environment that we need to attend to.

Attention is itself adaptable, because otherwise we would be overwhelmed by irrelevant stimuli. Attention and emotion, hand in hand, compensate for what we clearly do *not* have: a comprehensively rational mechanism for sorting the relevant from the irrelevant and weighting the relevant aspects properly.

One of the most important limitations of the rational decision-making model is its failure to address the question of the construction of the problem and solution sets. How do people decide on what alternatives to consider, and how do they decide what attributes are relevant to the choice? Even if the choice can be understood as rational cost-benefit calculation or some cost-saving heuristics in lieu of that approach, we still cannot understand choice. We cannot do so because we have no idea of how the choice set was established in the first place.

In this chapter, we have surveyed those aspects of decision making that result from genetic limits on human abilities to make fully adaptive decisions. Deviations from rational adaptation are linked directly to our biological inheritances. We can understand the processes of decision making only if we understand the architecture of human cognition.

The key concepts here are working or short-term memory, attention and emotion, and storage and retrieval from long-term memory. An epigenetic model of choice—one more directly related to human biology—need not devolve into an examination of synapses and brain scans. The processes that cause us to deviate from rational adaptation are straightforward, although their ramifications are far-reaching.

We must think of a decision maker as continually adjusting to an external environment, consisting of a sometimes stable, sometimes changing and complex set of circumstances, and an internal environment, consisting of needs, emotions, and short- and long-term memories. Needs are translated into goals that mediate between the constraints and opportunities of the external environment. Emotions and memory constitute the procedural constraints on adaptation to the external environment—affecting goal attainment given the external environment.

I am somewhat loath to term this internal environment of decision making "limits." It constitutes limits only in comparison to rational adaptation. Given our genetic inheritances, emotions are key motivators and critical aids to setting priorities. Pattern matching is key to retrieval from long-term memory. Both are critical in screening for admissibility to the choice set. They don't just "get in the way" of more rational decision making. In an epigenetic model of choice, decision making cannot exist without them.

CHAPTER 4

Human Information Processing

Man tends to react by either overestimation or neglect.
—BENOIT MANDELBROT

HUMANS, BEING adaptive creatures, craft strategies that allow them to avoid problems, achieve goals, and otherwise operate in a complex and dynamic environment in a productive manner. But as a consequence of a cognitive architecture that evolved in a very different environment from today's, certain limits to adaptation to the current decision-making environment consistently emerge. Isolating and assessing these lapses is a critical challenge to modern social science.

We have seen in the previous two chapters that models capturing comprehensively rational decision making can serve as a standard from which to assess these lapses. To assess these deviations, we need a solid model of what would be rational given the structure of decision making, a real-world measure of actual behavior, and a theoretical reason for expecting the observed deviation. In the previous chapters, we have sketched the key aspects of rational decision making and indicated some of the myriad empirical findings that fail to comport with the rational model. In this and the next chapter, we explore in more detail those aspects of the human cognitive architecture that interfere with comprehensively rational adaptation.

In this chapter, we focus on information processing as the mechanism that connects the human mind with its environment. Adaptive decision makers update their strategies in light of the information they receive from the environment. If people were completely rational, they would act on relevant information from the environment and incorporate it into their decisions in a seamless fashion. The human mind, however, will not allow the seamless translation of information into decision. Humans do not take action in direct proportion to incoming information. They distort it. This distortion stems from the manner in which the mind operates.

Sources of Information Distortion

There are three primary sources for this distortion. The first is that an incoming signal from a single source is altered as it is processed. Human sensory systems are disproportionately responsive to a signal in certain ranges of the signal. Threshold and habituation effects cause humans to be exquisitely responsive to certain ranges of light intensity, sound, electric shock, and so forth. Similarly, predisposition and habituation may cause us to ignore social information in certain ranges.

The second source of information distortion comes from how decision makers combine diverse sources of information. If a decision, say a legislative vote or buying a stock, is keyed to multiple streams of information, what aspects of this complexity are chosen, and how are they combined? What aspects of the environment do we attend to? I refer to this issue as the "implicit indicator problem" and treat it in detail in chapter 7.

The final source of information distortion comes from how humans construct a problem space for the problems they face. Political scientists and sociologists have noted that there is seldom a one-to-one correspondence between objective indicators of a public problem like crime and the perception of that problem. The match between a more or less objective situation and how people perceive it is critical to decision making. Here I focus on reasonably well understood task environments—in effect, holding the task environment constant in order to study the relative importance of rational adaptation and human cognitive architecture in decision-making situations.[1] This limits, but does not eliminate, the divergence between problem-space construction and the objective task environment.

Decoding and Interpreting Signals

Information processing involves the decoding of signals from the decision maker's external environment. A decision occurs when a person takes action to operate on the external environment in response to the signal that he or she has decoded.

The decoding process is not an objective process by which a signal sent is a signal recovered. Human sensory and cognitive interpretation transforms the signal (not just decoding it), and that transformation affects the choices that a decision maker pursues. But the extent of this distortion is in question. If humans are intendedly rational, then they will minimize to the extent possible the distortion. So the study of information processing is in part the study of the deviation of responses generated by decision makers in comparison to what would be generated *if humans were in fact proportionate information processors.*

Information processing becomes communication when both a sender and a receiver are considered. If humans were proportionate decision

---

1. In this regard I adopt the stance of psychologists studying problem-solving behavior in the laboratory. There the task is carefully described to the subject; nevertheless subjects must augment the problem space via knowledge, etc. See Newell and Simon 1972.

makers, then the only issues in communication would involve the intent of the sender of the information and the "noise" in the channel that transmits the signal. A sender might try to influence a receiver by withholding information or by deliberately distorting the information that is transmitted. And the signal might be attenuated in the transmission process. But there would be no issue of the distortion of information once it is received.

We may distinguish between approaches to information in decision making that assume the infallibility of the receiver (and hence proportionate information processing) and those that assume that the receiver is fallible (ignoring or distorting the received information selectively). The former approach may be termed "information theory"; the latter "information processing."

Information Theory and Information Processing

Nowhere do comprehensive and bounded rationality differ more than in the treatment of information. Rational actor theories of decision making require no theory of decision makers, because all behavior is explained in terms of messages (incentives and deterrents) from the environment (Simon 1979). Similarly, rational actor theories of information need a theory of signals and a theory of senders, but have no need of a theory of receivers. Modern rational choice theorists have developed an approach to the interchange of information that they term "signaling theory." In modern signaling theory, information is costly and noisy. One actor, the sender, has information that the other actor, the receiver, wants. The sender may or may not have an incentive to supply correct information. If the sender does transmit the information, the signal will reduce the variance (noise) affecting the receiver's view of the world. That will allow the receiver to make better choices.

This approach to information interchange has no role for the cognitive architecture of the receiver of the information. The approach is impoverished at best and misleading at worst. It can, however, serve as a standard for the transmission of information, against which real-world communication can be judged.

In essence, rational actor approaches to information depend, knowingly or not, on a theory of information developed by Shannon and Weaver (1949). In this view, information transmission is a problem of coding and decoding a signal that is transmitted across a noisy medium (fig. 4.1). There is no problem of attention or interpretation; transmission is a problem in engineering. Information is uncertainty reduction (Pierce 1980; Young 1987).

Information theory was applied with great success to technical issues in

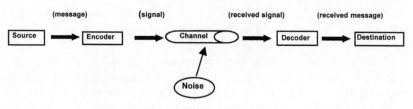

Figure 4.1   Information Theory
Source: Shannon and Weaver 1949

the transmission of messages. "Information theory" was a catchy term, but it had a precise and technical meaning. As a consequence, the notion was useful for technical purposes but was less helpful in the study of the communication of knowledge and meaning. Paul Young notes that information theory "has nothing to do with meaning . . . it is associated with uncertainty—that is, with the prior state of knowledge of the receiver; each bit of information reduces uncertainty . . . more prior uncertainty, more information. . . . Communication theory is an engineering theory through and through, not a theory of knowledge" (1987, 6–7).

Regardless of Young's caveat, a considerable number of studies of human institutions proceed as if Shannon and Weaver's information theory has been adopted as standard. For example, in game theory the assumption of imperfect information in a world where decision makers are comprehensively rational concentrates on information as uncertainty reduction. In "signaling games," information is sent and received by rational actors; if information is received, it reduces uncertainty. But this offers the opportunity of the sender to withhold or distort information; the entire analysis centers on the incentives necessary to induce senders to pass on correct information. In effect, these studies assume that communication may involve uncertainty, but not issues of interpretation. Rational actors may try to manipulate one another, but they never seem to misunderstand one another.

Information processing assumes, not rational actors, but boundedly rational ones. As a consequence, the cognitive limits in communication are studied, with special attention to the receiver. The receiver must attend to and interpret incoming information. Oftentimes the problem for the receiver is not that he or she lacks information; often the issue is information overload. The scarce resource is not information; it is attention (Simon 1996b).

In essence, one needs a theory of the receiver in order to understand his or her response to a signal. Key aspects of communication are the usual suspects discussed in the previous two chapters: attention and short-term memory and the construction of a problem space (in the case of communication, a common frame of reference).

Rational choice analyses of communication processes can serve as a standard of comparison. It is possible in theory to compare the expectations from fully rational and hence adaptive communication processes with controlled observations and assess the magnitude of the deviation. Deviations accounted for by attention and problem-space construction must be assigned to the domain of bounded rationality. Deviations due to "noise" in the communication channel, however, are not problematic from the rational choice perspective. Bounded rationality implies systematic distortions in information processing.

Information-Processing Approach to Cognition

The key to a comparison of expectations and controlled observations is the notion of disproportionate information processing. The issues concern the extent to which our cognitive architecture affects our perception and interpretation of objective information coming from the environment. Our brains operate on stimuli coming from the environment. Both perceptual and cognitive processes are involved. Our sense processes transform stimuli from what we know, thanks to scientific theory, to be objective. A second-order transformation occurs when we think consciously about the (now transformed) stimuli that we receive from the environment.

Allen Newell and Herbert Simon (1972) brought the information-processing approach into psychology in the 1960s, integrating their concerns with artificial intelligence and human problem solving. During the era of psychological behaviorism, in which behavior was thought to consist of learned associations between stimulus and response, information processing was at first not well received. Not only did humanists resent the human-machine analogy, but behaviorists objected on the grounds that it was unnecessary to be so unscientific and subjective as to try to "get inside the heads" of people.

As behaviorism waned under the onslaught of laboratory findings (including the notion of prepared learning) and the availability of new approaches to the study of thought patterns, the information-processing approach became the foundation for the emerging field of cognitive psychology. In Newell and Simon's approach, information processing was critical to understanding human problem-solving behavior. For them, information processing critically involved symbol manipulation. Symbol manipulation was the key concept linking artificial and human thought patterns.

The key components postulated by Newell and Simon for an informa-

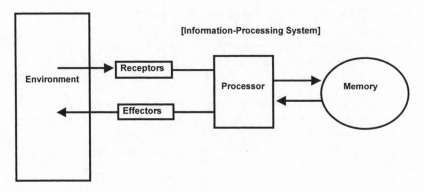

Figure 4.2   Information Processing
Source: Newell and Simon 1972, 20

tion-processing system (IPS) are detailed in figure 4.2. Fundamental conceptions of information processing in cognitive psychology have changed little since then (see Hinsz, Tindale, and Vollrath 1997).

An IPS consists of "receptors" that receive inputs from the environment, a "symbol structure," consisting of "tokens" or symbols and relationships between the symbols, a "memory" or storage capacity, a "processor" with a limited short-term memory that manipulates the symbols, and "effectors" that act on the environment as a result of the symbol manipulation. Newell and Simon's IPS models key elements of human thought, and raise in particular the issues of interpretation or translation of inputs into symbols, and of serial processing.

Serial processing, which is one-at-a-time sequential processing of inputs, is a key link between computers and human thought. Limits of short-term memory mean that, like the serial computer, we are serial processors, at least when it comes to conscious decision making. Our senses may receive inputs in parallel, bringing in a vast array of stimuli, but we can attend to and process consciously only limited bits at a time.

Simon (1989, xii) has detailed the basic principles of an information-processing approach to human cognition. The basic elements are as follows:

1. There is limited short-term memory and essentially unlimited long-term memory.
2. Long-term memory is associative and indexed, and includes "a feature-extracting front-end"; a recognition or indexing system that uses these features to access long-term memory; a semantic memory consisting of a myriad of nodes linked by directed associations" (164).

3. Problem solving consists of generating a problem representation and then engaging in selective or heuristic search.
4. Knowledge is stored in both schemas and productions.
5. Learning occurs via new schemas, new productions, and new connections between them.

The major difference between information theory as applied to human decision making and information processing is that in the latter the information or signal stream is transformed. That is, the decision maker is unable to reproduce with high fidelity the signals on which he or she bases decisions.

Getting Cognitive Architecture to Show Itself

People adapt to whatever situation they face with considerable rapidity. For cognitive scientists, this is an aggravation, because it makes the study of human cognitive architecture more difficult. As Simon has put the issue, "The 'built in' foundations of the human control structure are particularly elusive since they are so richly overlaid by the task-specific strategies that people discover or quickly learn" (1989, xii). Thus, to the extent that we adapt to a task-specific strategy, we compensate for the distortion of information that is produced by our cognitive architectures.

Students of human perception face the same issue. Roger Shepard writes that "for every situation, our perceptual system automatically applies its previously successful and now thoroughly entrenched methods of processing" (1990, 5). Only where our perceptual systems can be confused, as happens in the case of perceptual illusions, can scientists get some idea of the psychological effects of the biology of perception.

Mapping the human cognitive structure is difficult because we adapt so readily to the tasks that confront us. On the other hand, in many decision-making situations, lapses and lags in adaptation are critical to decision-making outcomes.

Transforming an Input Stream

There are several key points in the processing of information in which an objective input stream can be transformed.

The recognition of sensation. The classical study of psychophysics is based on the notion of a systematic transformation between the physical function—light intensity, sound, pressure, etc.—and the psychological recognition of that function.

The extraction of features. Human perceptual systems are based in the ability to parse salient features from the environment—those features that are critical to survival. Features—relevant objects in the environment—

are disjoint entities, and moving from one to another cannot be a smooth process.

Attention and short-term memory. The "bottleneck of attention" is fundamental to the transformation of inputs, because one cannot make decisions from information that is not within short-term memory at the instant of decision. If relevant facets of the environment are unattended to, then they cannot influence decision.

Paying inattention. Decision and action require a method of filtering out irrelevant information that would otherwise distract the decision maker.

Pattern recognition. Long-term memory, which is practically infinite, is accessed only via short-term memory. We must bring to bear past experiences and learning consciously to make a knowledgeable decision. We do this via pattern recognition—we match patterns extracted from the environment with patterns from long-term memory. Easily matching patterns generally make for easy decisions. Nonmatching patterns generally cause further study of the environment.

Combining diverse input streams. In a complex environment, decision makers must monitor many diverse sources of information. They must employ some way of combining these diverse sources that both allows the use of these diverse sources but also pays heed to the limits of short-term memory.

Each of these facets of information processing causes a modification of an "objective" signal from the environment and causes the organism to behave differently from a hypothetical decision maker responding only to "the facts."

Perception

Perceptual processes are not particularly important in understanding social decision making. On the other hand, aspects of the perceptual system are keys to understanding human cognitive architecture and can illuminate the general principle of information distortion that is fundamental to the argument of this chapter.

Francis Crick (1994, 26) notes three key principles of vision relevant to the issue of information distortion: (1) you are easily deceived by your visual system; (2) the visual information provided by your eyes can be ambiguous; (3) seeing is a constructive process.

A simple, well-understood example can show how supposedly objective stimuli are modified in the perceptual process. We view the world in color, but color is a mental construct. E. O. Wilson puts the point this way: "Color does not exist in nature. At least, it does not exist in nature in the form we think we see. Visible light consists of continuously varying wave length, with no intrinsic color in it. Color vision is imposed on this variation by the photosensitive cone cells of the retina and the connecting nerve cells of the brain" (1998, 160).

Not only do our senses impose colors on light waves, but we also automatically break continuous wave forms into discrete categories based on wavelength. The color spectrum is quite arbitrary. It is only one of many possible color spectra (cut points on the continuous visible range of light waves) that could have potentially emerged through evolution. Colors are perceived in three dimensions (lightness, hue, and saturation), even though light can vary in an unlimited number of dimensions (Shepard 1992).

Color vision is not a simple decoding of a signal, as might be implied by an unthinking application of information theory to color vision. There is no color to be transmitted! Only light waves. Color and its organization is a construct of the mind. This construction is universal: color is perceived similarly by people with normal vision in all cultures (Shepard 1992).

Most, if not all, stimuli received by our senses are transformed in some manner from their objective existences. Psychophysics is the study of the relationship between perceived sensations and the stimuli that provoke those sensations. For example, we perceive not only color in light waves, but also intensity of waves. Laboratory studies have repeatedly shown that for almost all stimulus continua, perceived sensation is nonproportionate to the magnitude of the stimulus (See box 4.1).

Perception becomes more interesting when several stimulus continua are combined in forming one's impression of the world. In psychophysical experiments, subjects must be carefully instructed about what stimulus to pay attention to (Stevens 1975, 74). The reason is that we do not generally react to one stimulus at a time. In the real perceptual world, we combine several stimulus continua in forming our impressions of the world. How we combine diverse sources of information is a key issue in information processing.

People employ "representational spaces" to organize the complex perceptual information bombarding them. These representational spaces, like color vision, seem to be invariant across cultures, but they do not reproduce an objective physical world. Invariance comes from the fact that people everywhere have evolved to perceive an invariant set of physical laws. The distortion of the representational space in relation to those physical laws comes from evolution: organisms construct representational spaces based on what is useful for survival and reproduction (Gibson 1979; Shepard 1990). Perceptual systems, then, are feature extracting, with the features that are extracted based both on evolutionary utility and physical laws. These facets of perception seem to affect categorization of higher-order object groupings (Shepard 1992; Gazzaniga 1998).

Attention governs the perceptual features we extract. Findings from studies of the perception of objects involving more than one stimulus

Box 4.1: The Psychophysical Function

The psychophysical function is the term given to the relationship between a stimulus magnitude and a perceived sensation. Many laboratory studies have been conducted in which subjects give direct estimates of the magnitude of the sensation, using either numbers or squeezing a hand dynamometer. These studies indicate that the psychophysical function is a power law regardless of the stimulus continuum (Stevens 1975). This means that the relation between a stimulus, S, and a sensation, P, can be described as

$$P = S^b,$$

where the exponent, b, is different depending on the stimulus continuum. The curve is concave downward if b is less than 1 (as, for example, with the intensity of light), and is concave upward if b is greater than 1 (as, for example, with electric shock). In the graph below, the solid line represents a psychophysical function with b greater than 1 (about 1.5). In this case, our sensations become heightened as the intensity of the stimulus grows. It is also possible that we become less sensitive as the intensity grows. In either case, our sensations do not reproduce the stimulus magnitudes in a proportionate fashion. We respond differently depending on where we are on the stimulus continuum.

Economists use a form of this phenomenon in the concept of declining marginal utility. We have less use for a good (even money) as we acquire more of it. This would correspond to a psychophysical function with an exponent of less than 1.

The graph below depicts a psychophysical function for an exponent of greater than unity.

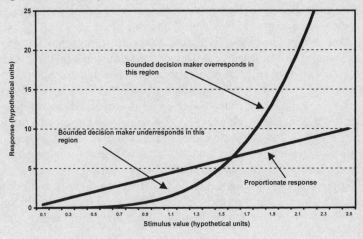

dimension indicate that people tend to attend to one dimension to the exclusion of others (Shepard 1964). We return to the important topic of combining diverse sources of information in chapter 7.

Information Updating

Information processing implies that one's beliefs about the world are updated on the receipt of messages from the environment. Recall Margolis's studies of pattern recognition and its implications for choice. Pattern recognition leads to a choice: check, then explore more, or jump, make a move. The decision to check or jump is fundamentally episodic. It involves continuing with the current behavior, supported by the current pattern. But what happens when new information is available that suggests a new pattern? Now the situation is ambiguous. Should the decision maker adopt a new strategy?

In certain risky situations (that is, when the outcomes of a decision are probabilistic, and the probabilities of the outcomes are known, as in the case of gambling at a roulette wheel), statisticians can tell us when we should and when we shouldn't. The key tool is Bayes's theorem.

Here is an experiment performed by psychologists in the 1960s (Edwards 1968): Two bowls contain 1,000 poker chips each. Bowl 1 contains 700 red and 300 blue, while bowl 2 contains 300 red and 700 blue. I toss a fair coin to decide which to draw from. Then I draw chips randomly from the bowl chosen (which you don't know), replacing each chip after I draw it. Doing this twelve times, I get 8 reds and 4 blues. What is the probability that I have drawn these from bowl 1?

It turns out that Bayes's theorem yields the answer that the probability is .97. It is almost certain that the chips were sampled from bowl 1. But, in the experiments, very few people came anywhere close to that number (the typical estimates were between .7 and .8). These experiments caused Ward Edwards to write that "[a]n abundance of research has shown that human beings are conservative processors of fallible information" (1968, 17). It looks as if the subjects underappreciated the new information.

But wait! Here is another experiment: You are a member of a jury. A taxi driver working for the Blue Cab Company is accused of a hit-and-run accident at night. The prosecutor has one witness, who says the taxi was blue. At the trial, it is established that of the two taxi companies in town, the Blue Cab Company has all blue cabs and the Green Cab Company has all green ones. Of all the cabs on the road the night, 15 percent are blue and 85 percent green. The witness has been given vision tests in conditions similar to those the night of the accident. She can distinguish a blue taxi from a green one 80 percent of the time. What is the probability that the taxi is really blue?

Box 4.2: Bayes's Theorem

Bayes's theorem is a straightforward extension of probability theory that shows how new information should be used (rationally) to update existing beliefs.

Suppose that

D = new information;

H_A = a hypothesis;

$P(H_A)$ = the probability of the hypothesis before the new information is observed (the "prior probability");

$P(D|H_A)$ = the probability that the new information would occur if the hypothesis is true;

$P(H_A|D)$ = the probability that the hypothesis is true after the new information is observed (the "posterior probability");

$P(D)$ = the probability that the new information would occur in any case.

If we have observed the new information, Bayes's theorem allows us to calculate directly the posterior probability, which is what we are interested in:

$$P(H_A|D) = P(D|H_A) P(H_A) / P(D).$$

To illustrate, let us solve the taxi problem set out above. H_A is the prosecutor's contention that the taxi is blue. D is the witness's contention that she observed a blue taxi. The prior probabilities are

$P(H_A)$ = .15 (that is, the cab was blue before we got the new information);

$P(H_{notA})$ = .85 (that is, the cab was green [not blue] before we got the new information).

Calculating $P(D)$ is tricky. We do it by noting a result from basic probability theory that an event may be broken down into the mutually exclusive intersections of the event and the prior probabilities.

$$P(D) = P(H_A|D) + P(H_{notA}|D)$$
$$= P(D|H_A) P(H_A) + P(D|H_{notA}) P(D_{notA})$$
$$= (.8)(.15) + (.2)(.85)$$
$$= .12 + .17 = .29.$$

Now by straightforward substitution

$$P(H_A|D) = .12/.29 = .41.$$

If this seems surprising, think of it this way. We have changed our evaluation from the prior estimate that the taxi was blue from 15 percent to more than 40 percent based on the testimony of a sole fallible witness.

This experiment and others like it were performed by Amos Tversky and Daniel Kahneman, and most of their subjects estimated that the probability of the taxi being blue is considerably greater than 50 percent, but less than 80 percent. Bayes's theorem calculates the proper probability at 41 percent (see Piattelli-Palmarini 1994, 83–84).

Now this result seems the opposite of the conclusion reached by the earlier researchers into how people use information to update their beliefs. In this experiment, people seemed *too willing* to accept a conclusion based on new information!

In each of these two cases, the resolution has to do with "framing." Framing, as developed by Kahneman and Tversky, has to do with how people set a baseline for judging subsequent behavior. The very posing of the problems above has implicitly set a baseline for judging the situation. In the first case, the one with two bowls, the statement of the problem has drawn us to focus our baseline on the prior probability, and we underappreciate the new information. In the second case, we have implicitly been drawn to the new information as a kind of base rate, and the background or prior probability is ignored or discounted. Attentional processes cause us to focus on only part of a complex problem (as, indeed, is required for problem solving, given our short-term memory limitations). As a consequence, we are misled.

These kinds of "tricks" are known as "cognitive illusions." Massimo Piattelli-Palmarini explains that experiments on how people make decisions under risk and uncertainty deviates substantially from the correct decision (precisely calculated by the laws of probability).

> Deep within ourselves we have some *anomalous* systems of mental representation that lead us, for instance, to beliefs about probabilities and fair wagers. When we behave according to those beliefs, we *inevitably* become the prey of situations in which we lose under *every* conceivable state of affairs. Yet, the mere fact that we intuitively come to see the situation as anomalous is not sufficient to set us right. It requires thought . . . *and* on well-constructed theories that can ultimately and persuasively gain our assent. That is how rationality is fostered. (1994, 14)

Bayesian updating in everyday decision making would involve extensive calculations on estimated probabilities. People normally don't do this, of course, but they clearly update their beliefs in the face of incoming information. Exactly how they update in real-life situations has not been extensively studied by social scientists, but laboratory results suggest that they do not update in conformance to Bayes's rule—the fully rational standard.

Cognitive illusions can be overcome by learning. But overcoming them does not come naturally, and we often fall back into them even when we have learned better. In this regard, cognitive illusions resemble perceptual illusions.

Party Identification as Bayesian Update

The tendency of people to fall prey to cognitive illusions must not distract us from the basic principle of adaptation. People, being intendedly rational, do in fact update their belief systems in the face of new information.

Let us take political party identification. Party identification is a special case of organizational identification—cognitive and emotive orientations toward one's preferred party. In early conceptions, party identification was seen as remarkably stable among those Americans who identified with a party. People learned their party affiliations early, and held them throughout life, unless major events or a particularly attractive candidate or significant issue caused them to rethink those affiliations. When voters did deviate from their primary party identification, it was usually a temporary departure, and they almost always returned to the fold in later elections.

More recently, some political scientists have conceived party identification as a kind of "online tally" of party performances and promises. The "standing decision" to support a party, forged in the past, is updated according to information that the voter receives in the present. There is considerable evidence that party identification in the electorate in fact changes with new information (Gerber and Green 1999). It is difficult to see the relatively slow realignment of attachments to American parties that has occurred since the 1960s in any other light than some sort of learning/ updating process.

Because party identification is both emotive and cognitive, and because voters selectively attend to politics (Iyengar 1990), a straightforward Bayesian updating process is highly unlikely. It will be difficult for people to drop such identifications, even if Bayes's rule implies that they ought to do so. On the other hand, it would be inconceivable that voters would simply ignore the implications of party performance and promises for their standing party choices. If your party generates a sub-par performance in office, and if it tends to adopt platforms that run counter to your policy preferences, you, like most of us, would give the party the benefit of the doubt for a while, then shift allegiances. This is a classic case of bounds on rationality (emotional identifications) showing through to limit adaptive efficiency.

Political Information Processing

In political science, the information-processing approach has mostly been concentrated on the study of voting behavior. Information processing in political science has allowed scholars to transcend the old refrain about the limited knowledge that citizens have about politics and government, and to focus on just how they process what information they have (Lodge and Stroh 1993; Lodge, McGraw, and Stroh 1989). While rational choice scholars have isolated the cost of information as a key limitation on comprehensive rationality, students of political psychology have explored the processes by which people make voting decisions. Information processing is firmly rooted in theories of bounded rationality, which, as we noted in chapter 3, has supplanted the older attitudinally based voting research of an earlier era.

Findings from political psychology emphasize the following facets of human decision making: our short-term memory is limited; much of our political information processing is impression-based; our feature extraction is based on the salience of attributes; and our emotions set priorities for political choice.

Short-Term Memory and Impression-Based Processing

Lodge, McGraw, and Stroh (1989) see short-term memory as the key technical limitation on more comprehensive rationality in voting. They see the limited capacity of short-term memory, the serial nature of attention, and the slow fixation rate required to transfer information to long-term memory as the technical bases of bounded rationality.

Their model of the voting decision, the "online processing" model, hypothesizes that voters don't weigh all attributes and report an overall evaluation. Rather, people keep an online tally—basically on whether the things they have observed in the past about a candidate are positive or negative. These evaluations are essentially impressions, and new information either contributes to or detracts from the overall positive or negative impression. Information flows by the voter, and he or she doesn't really explore the information in much depth. Online processing is a direct consequence of attentional allocation. It posits a direct link between attention and judgment without any intervening deeper mental processing (Lodge 1995, 114).

Impression-based processing may be distinguished from memory-based processing (Anderson 1983; Lodge and Stroh 1993). Memory-based processing is thoughtful; it emerges when people use long-term memory to analyze a situation. It is knowledge based. Impression-based processing is automatic, driven by the tendency of people not to allocate the time necessary to proceed to memory-based processing.

One interesting yet mostly unexplored issue is how people move back and forth between impression- and memory-based processing. The process is probably governed by emotions. For example, there is some evidence that negative advertising in political campaigns has the ability to shift people from impression processing to memory processing (A. Simon 1999).

If we return to Newell's temporal hierarchy, discussed in chapter 3, we can see that memory-based processing falls into the rational band of behavior, while impression formation falls into the cognitive band. The time one allocates for a task is the critical determinant of processing level. The more limited the time available, the more likely the behavior will fall into the cognitive band. Behaviors that fall into the cognitive band are more affected by human cognitive architecture than are behaviors that fall into the intendedly rational band. Behaviors that fall into the intendedly rational band reflect the task environment more faithfully.

Feature Extraction and Attention

Feature extraction may fall into either the cognitive band or the intendedly rational band of behavior. Cognitively, we are continually aware of our surroundings—continually monitoring them even when we don't think about them. Occasionally we feel the need to study the environment more closely—to think about certain facets of it. The movement between the cognitive band and the intendedly rational band is governed by attentional mechanisms. Since we have some control over attention, we in effect decide whether to move from the cognitive to the rational band. On the other hand, attention is seriously limited, and most of the time we must process most incoming information at the level of impressions.

While we often deliberately decide where to allocate our attention, that is not the whole story. Our attentional processes are very much affected by emotional arousal. A state of anxiety is likely to cause us to move from the cognitive band toward the intendedly rational band. As a consequence, emotions are fundamental in setting priorities.

Let us return to the basic decision matrix discussed in chapter 2 (see table 2.1). There we characterized alternatives considered in the decisional process by a set of attributes. A candidate for public office, for example, can be characterized by such attributes as his or her party affiliation, ideology, positions on issues, leadership potential, communication skills, and a variety of other attributes. Feature extraction for social decision making is the isolation of the attributes that characterize a situation. In interpreting a problem, people implicitly weight these attributes; indeed, because of short-term memory limitations, they often exclude many potentially relevant attributes from decisional calculations (Jones 1994). This has the consequence of implicitly underspecifying the task environment. In the language of problem solving, the person has constructed a problem space that is not completely representative of the problem. If the task environment is dynamic, and the excluded attributes become more important, adaptive decision makers will at some point bring them into the problem space. This leads to a disjointed or episodic change in decision-making outcomes as the decision maker reevaluates the situation in light of the new facets. Once the problem space has been reconstructed, decision makers tend to put the processing of information back on the automatic pilot of impression formation.

Any conscious decisional process falls into the intendedly rational band of behavior. People construct a problem representation (a "model," even if implicit), and engage in search. Simply because behavior falls into the intendedly rational band and is under the full conscious control of the decision maker does not mean that the expected benefits model of choice will be used. Because people are poor at making trade-offs, they will tend to opt for decision-making strategies that avoid such trade-offs. They may satisfice by setting aspiration levels on each attribute, choosing the strategy that meets the aspiration level on each attribute, or they may choose based on attribute prominence.

Information Processing on Two Bands

Information processing differs fundamentally depending on the time available for the task. At the cognitive level, behavior is basically automatic. The cognitive band produces "a system that engages in knowledge search but it does not engage in problem search" (Newell 1990, 139). There is no time to reevaluate the problem space; it is in essence fixed for the duration of the behavior. When candidates are evaluated online, voters do not reconsider the problem facing them. They just take note of the valence of the information—positive or negative—and "add" it to the tally that represents their impression of the candidate.

The intendedly rational band produces an attribute-based processing system, because it requires the construction of a problem space. The problem space consists of features or attributes that characterize the task at hand. The process of choice involves (1) generating the alternatives to be evaluated and (2) comparing the relative desirability of the alternatives that have been derived.

Figure 4.3 indicates the different paths toward choice in the cognitive and rational bands. In the cognitive band, where time for decision is constrained, people make choices based on previously formed impressions. They may update their impressions based on incoming information, in a process described well by the "online tally" model. No time is allocated for rethinking the situation; the problem space is not searched, and responses come directly from the Gestalt-like impression.

If more time is allocated, however, the mechanisms of the intendedly

Cognitive Band:

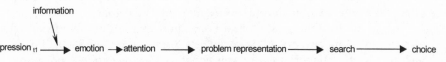

Figure 4.3   Information Processing on Two Time Scales

rational band come into play. An explicit problem space is constructed: What do I want? What is the current political situation? What attributes of these candidates are relevant for my choice? Public opinion scholar Wendy Rahn (1995) notes that the simple process of comparing candidates can cause the voter to move toward an attribute-based judgment system (and therefore toward the intendedly rational band). The observation may be more general: in competitive elections attentional processes associated with campaigns cause people to move from impression formation and online tallies characteristic of the cognitive band to the attribute-based processing characteristic of the intendedly rational band.

Attentional Misers

How do some acts get processed at the cognitive-band level while others get processed at the intentional level? Sometimes, there is no choice: the time available for the act requires action, if it is to occur at all, in the cognitive band. In other cases, there is "choice"—in the sense that it would be possible to bring the item up to the rational band. Time for analysis could be made available. But often time is not allocated.

Social psychologists see humans as "cognitive misers" (Fiske and Taylor 1991) who strive to relieve demands on cognitive capacities. ("Cognitive capacities" here means conscious thought. Newell's reference to the cognitive band of behavior was meant to distinguish it from the biological level. This can lead to some confusion, since the notion of cognitive miser refers to behavior on the intendedly rational band.) Again the bottleneck of attention comes into play. Humans must find mechanisms to relieve stress on the serial processing capacity of short-term memory. Thorngate (1988) asks us to think of attention as a kind of a scarce good, to be allocated to the most worthy aims. Two consequences flow from this. First, the organism must have some way of paying inattention: ignoring irrelevant stimuli in the environment. Organisms quickly become habituated to benign stimuli.

Second, the movement of activities from the rational band to the cognitive band through learning and practice can have enormous advantages in protecting the organism's attentive capacities. The less one has to search the problem space, the less the demands on attentive capacities, and the more the organism can devote toward more essential goals.

As we noted above, emotions serve as indicators of misallocations of attentional capacity. Social psychologists Susan Fiske and Shelly Taylor write: "In effect, emotions are alarm signals consisting of *interruption and arousal,* and they divert people from pursuing one goal and point them toward pursuing another goal that has meanwhile increased in importance" (1991, 443). In politics, as elsewhere in life, emotional arousal may cause a shift from the cognitive band of information processing to the intendedly rational band.

Communication, Context, and Frames

One of the most important effects of human cognitive architecture on information processing involves the role of context. Because we must rely on patterns of attention and inattention in our interactions with our environment—because our survey of inputs into our decision-making processes is not comprehensive—how we understand a problem (and even whether there is a problem) is an active process. Decision makers actively construct depictions of the task environment; they are not passive recipients of information. When presented with a complex situation, we focus on certain attributes to the exclusion of others. Determining what factors are relevant is fundamental to the understanding of a decision-making context.

Any communication has the ability to "evoke a context": that is, it can cue us to what factors are relevant to the decision we must make. Communications scholar Shanto Iyengar notes the "exquisite sensitivity to contextual cues" exhibited by people in responding to messages from the mass media (1991, 11). We have prior knowledge of contexts because we have previously learned about them. The well-known "aha" phenomenon, the felling we get when we experience a flash of recognition, comes about when a problem we face matches a pattern we know. We have retrieved from long-term memory a pattern, or set of relevant attributes, that allow us to understand a decision-making situation.

Much of political information transmission involves highlighting—making more salient—those aspects of the political situation that the voter may be currently ignoring. Feature extraction, attribute-based processing, and the limits of short-term memory all contribute to the phenomenon of "framing." Framing has a somewhat different usage in political communication studies than in the prospect theory of Kahneman and Tversky discussed above. Framing—famous in recent political dialogue as the purview of campaign "spin doctors"—is the phenomenon of directing attention to one attribute in a complex problem space. Short-term memory limitations tend then to limit considerations of other attributes. Much of the influence of the media in politics has to do with the communication of frames of reference (Iyengar 1991; Iyengar and Kinder 1987). Much of politics involves framing, and hence is understood as attribute-based information processing (Jones 1996).

The major issue in the study of frames of reference involves the dimensionality of the frame. A frame may be thought of as the attribute space that organizes our choices, as detailed in table 2.1 in chapter 2. If the frame is one-dimensional (that is, one attribute characterizes the message), then the only issue in understanding has to do with signal noise. If the receiver's frame of reference is multidimensional, then the concept of noise reduction is not enough to explain the receiver's response. Sender and receiver may use different attributes to understand the message. The sender may also try to influence how the receiver's perception of how salient the attributes that structure the decision-making design are (Jones 1996). This is a question of framing and has been important in studies of media influence in politics.

This process of pattern matching is episodic and disjointed—and, indeed, we *feel* the disjunction when we recognize the relevance of new factors in a decision. Pattern matching, a consequence of the necessity of dealing with limited short-term memory, is why an information theory approach for understanding the transmission of messages is inadequate.

Finally, the institutional structure can counteract the tendency of people to form biased frames of reference. In open democracies, if one problem space is constructed for voters by one candidate, a second candidate may put forward a second frame of reference. In effect, democracy offers competing understandings of a problem space. It also provides a mechanism for allocating attention to the panoply of problems that face a citizenry. Too often we focus on the competing solutions to public problems that candidates and parties offer, ignoring its role in prioritizing problems and offering competing understandings of them.

Informational Shortcuts and Rational Electorates

There is little doubt that modern electorates in the United States and other democracies are generally ill-informed about the particulars of the policymaking process. Since the advent of scientific polling, scholars again and again have demonstrated conclusively that, by the standards of the ideal democratic citizen, "the voter falls far short" (Berelson, Lazarsfeld, and McPhee 1954, 308).

It is possible that an electorate operating mostly at the cognitive band of impression formation, rather than at the intendedly rational band with choices following some kind of search process, is quite adequate for the conduct of democracy. As Larry Bartels states the problem, the idea is that "a 'rational,' 'reasoning' public must simply be adept at using the bits and pieces of information at its disposal to mimic the choices it would make *if* citizens were fully informed" (1996, 195).

Two lines of thought have been proposed. The first argues that voters using cues and "informational shortcuts" perform pretty much as would a fully rational electorate. By employing such social heuristics as following the lead of opinion leaders who are more knowledgeable, adopting a standing decision to support one party, and making a choice based on retrospective evaluations of the economy, voters supposedly can perform individually on a par with a fully informed citizen. Indeed, there is both survey and experimental evidence that people can approximate their (hypothetical) fully informed voting choice by mimicking the behavior of trusted sources (Lupia 1994; Lupia and McCubbins 1998).

The second line of thought postulates that, even if voters are information cripples individually, in the aggregate electorates perform satisfactorily. The keystone of the arch bridging the limited information levels of the typical voter and collective electoral rationality hinges on the assumption that the errors voters make because of their heuristics are random, and hence in effect cancel one another out. In 1785, the French mathematician and social scientist Condorcet proved his "jury theorem": that the probability of a correct collective decision goes up as the size of the group increases. Unfortunately, this proof hinges critically on the assumption of random errors of judgment. Bartels notes that a far more likely occurrence is for errors to be nonrandom: "If one uninformed voter is inappropriately swayed by a rhetorical flourish in a televised debate or advertisement, another may be equally swayed in the opposite direction; but it seems more likely that the second 'error' would reinforce rather than mitigate the first" (1996, 199).

Using the accumulating surveys of voters begun at the University of Michigan in the 1950s, Bartels has developed a technique that adjusts the voting choices of groups of voters based on their demographic characteristics to the choice of their most informed members. Bartels found that voters clearly performed better than chance, but "significantly less well than they would with complete information, despite the availability of cues and shortcuts." The study, which covered presidential elections from

1972 through 1992, indicated that Democrats (more than 2 percent) and incumbents (more than 5 percent) benefited from the divergence of the typical voter from the highly informed ideal.

In a study using a similar approach, Althaus (1998) has shown that poll results misestimate the policy preferences of a hypothetical fully informed public. If the entire public were as informed as its most informed members, then the distribution of policy opinions reported in systematic polls would differ by a considerable amount.

The final word has not been written in this debate. Political scientists have moved toward a "bounded rationality" view of the voter, one in which a variety of procedurally rational heuristic devices are used to make a low-information electoral choice. A key issue, as yet unresolved, is the performance of electorates given these limitations. In any case, the matter is clearly one that will be resolved through empirical means rather than abstract argumentation.

Here, again, Newell's time scale is relevant. If time is allocated to the task, then it is probable that the behavior of the voter will move toward that implied by the highly informed ideal. It may be rational for voters to pay inattention to politics, allowing candidates, groups, and parties to capture their attention via emotional appeals. Emotional arousal can push cognitive processing from the cognitive band, where impression formation dominates, to the intendedly rational band, where search is important. On the other hand, there may be important deviations between a fully informed voter employing intendedly rational search processes and one implicitly relying on the impression-formation mechanisms of the cognitive band. Finally, the correspondence may be conditional: it is likely that some electoral situations will evoke more search behavior than others.[2]

Finally, it is possible that the sporadic attentiveness to information will cause less correspondence rather than more, because of the "correlated errors" problem that probably affects the Condorcet jury theorem.[3] In any case, it will result in episodic and disjointed change in the function relating the availability of information to the voter's response to it.

Information Distortion

We began this chapter concentrating on the issue of disproportionate information processing—the extent to which supposedly objective "bits" of information are transformed by the human mind as they are processed.

---

2. Bartels's study (1996) indicates absolute aggregate deviations from a fully informed electorate of between 1.71 percent (in 1972) and 5.62 percent (in 1980).

3. This problem can affect outcomes even under the assumptions of rational mimicking.

How extensively are decision-making responses to information flows distorted—how do they differ from a fully adaptive response to the incoming information? Rational models of communication assume a common frame of reference for both sender and receiver, and focus on the extent to which a message reduces "noise" or uncertainty. Bounded rationality points to the cognitive architecture of the receiver as a factor in communication.

There exists considerable randomness in the world; we perceive it as uncertainty. Even the most rational decision makers are subject to random errors in their responses to new information. Fully rational decision makers should not, however, commit systematic errors of perception and interpretation. Robert Jervis (1976) argued many years ago that psychological properties of foreign policy decision makers could cause them to deviate from such a random pattern of mistakes. While there exist powerful incentives for political leaders to act rationally, the tendency for human cognitive architectures to affect adaptation to the task environment is not limited to the laboratory or to voters in large elections. There is also a psychology of governing institutions and public policymaking, a point that will occupy our attention in chapter 6.

We can suggest several places where bounded rationality will show through by systematically distorting the information that reaches a decision maker.

Cognitive processing. In all but the most stable environments, information processing on the cognitive band will distort responses more than processing on the intendedly rational band. Impressions are likely to get out of phase and need reconceiving in even gently changing situations.

Inappropriate heuristics. Even if behavior is intendedly rational, the heuristics that are employed in constructing a problem space and searching for alternatives mean that distortion is quite probable.

Attention shifts. The movement between the bands is governed by selective attention, which in turn may be shifted via states of emotional arousal. This means that the shift from the cognitive to the intendedly rational can be abrupt and emotion-laden; as a consequence, impressions are likely to be severely challenged or discarded rapidly as the process of examining the problem space and generating alternatives proceeds.

Search strategies. Because the impression-formation process proceeds without the intervention of intended rationality, the choice of "strategies" is not typically under conscious control. As a consequence, the "decision" to work at the level of impression formation cannot be viewed as a strategy to hold the costs of information down. On the other hand, the choice of search strategies at the level of intended rationality may or may not be conscious strategies for containing search and information costs.

Short-term memory. The limits of short-term memory dictate that only a limited number of attributes will be used to construct a problem space. Trade-offs between attributes are difficult, and people tend to focus on one attribute at a time in processing information. Underlying the bounded rationality approach to decision making is the notion that, given time to work on a problem and the incentives to do so, people will adapt to the task environment. They are cognitive misers, all right, but not because they are so cognitively limited. They are misers for two reasons. One is rational: all resources must be allocated economically, and that includes cognitive effort. The second is that they are bound by their evolved cognitive architectures to do so. Attentional dynamics and the preparation-deliberation trade-off make certain that, in some task environments, bounded rationality will show through.

CHAPTER 5

A Social Species: Substantive
Limits on Adaptive Choice

In 1962, William Riker published *The Theory of Political Coalitions,* his elegant analysis of political behavior in formal group decision-making situations, such as committees or legislative bodies. In many situations, committees must decide how to share a divisible good. A "divisible good" is simply one that can be broken up in any number of ways. The good could be streetlights that must be allocated to neighborhoods by a city council, or highway projects to congressional districts, or dollars to any number of worthy projects. Riker assumed that each member of the decision-making body had one vote, and that a plurality was necessary for a proposal to win.

If decision makers are rational in such situations, they will form "minimum winning coalitions," Riker reasoned. That is, rational legislators will find a way to divide the good up in such a way that the winning coalition will share all of the benefits while totally excluding the losers. He called this phenomenon the "size principle." In this strategy, each member of the winning coalition will maximize his or her part of the spoils. Any sharing with the minority will dilute the benefits gained by the majority.

Many political scientists have spent a great amount of effort searching for the predicted minimum winning coalition, with mixed results at best. In the real world of democratic politics and government, there just seems to be too much cooperation. Moreover, oftentimes participants seem to cooperate with the "wrong" others. In an early study of coalition formation in parliamentary democracies, Axelrod (1970) showed that parties tend to form coalitions based on ideological similarity rather than on the size of the governing coalition.

Rational Cooperation

Why might rational actors overcooperate? Political scientists have uncovered all sorts of reasons that minimum winning coalitions might not form on any given vote in a committee or legislature. The vote might not be on something divisible. It might be on something that is not excludable from the minority, such as would be the case in voting for an increase in

Social Security benefits in Congress (Social Security recipients can live in any district). A second reason can be found in the structure of our political institutions. The requirement in American national government for multiple decision-making centers (both houses of Congress and the president) often leads to larger-than-desirable coalitions to overcome potential rejection by other centers (Thompson 1979; Hammond and Miller 1987).

Even on divisible goods, rational legislators might not form minimum coalitions, because of "the shadow of the future" (Axelrod 1984). If actors realize that they are in a long-term relationship with one another, and each actor benefits from the interchange, then cooperation may emerge voluntarily. Indeed, the emergence of cooperation in such situations has been proved analytically (Taylor 1976, 1987) and simulated with computers (Axelrod 1984). That is, if people know that they will be interacting with others over a long period of play, then they are more likely to use strategies that involve offers of cooperation in the rational hope that such offers will be reciprocated, making both parties better off. This sort of cooperation is rationally based—it is a reasoned response to the task environment. If, for example, legislators do not form minimum winning coalitions, but rather party-based coalitions, then a reason could be the shadow of the future—the prospective division of the spoils in latter legislation.

Rational cooperation is uncoerced cooperation. The extent of uncoerced cooperation among individuals is serious business. Political theorist Michael Taylor writes, "[T]he most persuasive justification of the state is founded on the argument that, without it, people would not successfully cooperate in realizing their common interests" (1987, 1). Many theorists believe that whole reason we have government is based on the lack of cooperation among individuals.

These theorists do not mean that people are evil. Rather, they think we are entirely rational. Fully rational individuals will not cooperate in the production of public goods. A "public good" is one that all of us may use whether or not we have contributed to its provision. The classic case is the lighthouse: all ships may use its beacon whether or not their owners have paid to build it. The traditional analysis argues that government must coerce people (via taxes, for example) to provide such public goods; else they will not be supplied. If, however, there is sufficient rational cooperation, the need for governmental coercion will be lessened. If there is nonrational cooperation—"overcooperation" from the perspective of self-centered rationality—the implications for governance can be vast.

Theoretical models based on interactions between individuals are known collectively as "game theory." Decision makers must anticipate and react to the strategies employed by others. The classic analysis of public or collective goods is the prisoners' dilemma game. The prisoners' dilemma, or PD, shows how completely rational individuals can be led to take action that is not optimal. Repeated-play PDs, however, yield considerable cooperative behavior (See box 5.1).

Rationally selfish people can have good reason to cooperate with one another. Game theorists and computer modelers have shown that cooperative behavior will occur where interactions are likely to continue. The

---

Box 5.1:   Prisoners' Dilemma and Its Supergame

The famous prisoners' dilemma (PD) game is used to study collective action problems. Its story line concerns two prisoners offered a deal: Confess and you go free but your partner gets life. If both of you keep quiet, you both get a short sentence.

The PD game can be interpreted as a game between "me" and "all others." There are two strategies (x and y) and $\{x,y\}$ means "I choose x; all others choose y." $\{C,D\}$ means "I cooperate; all others defect." Then the payoff (fitness function) may be specified as the following rank order:

1. $\{D,C\}$
2. $\{C,C\}$
3. $\{D,D\}$
4. $\{C,D\}$

The best thing for me is to defect and to let "all others" provide the benefits. Second best is if I cooperate along with you. The worst thing in the PD game is for me to cooperate and for you to defect. Problem is, I don't trust you. So I better defect first. With both players thinking this way, each "rats" on the other, so both get life (that is, the collective good is not produced). (For a discussion, see Elster 1979.)

If, however, the PD game is played repeatedly, in a "supergame," then cooperative behavior does emerge. "If each player's discount rate is sufficiently low [that is, they place at least some value on the future], the outcome will be mutual cooperation throughout the supergame" (Taylor 1987, 81). Rational actors can produce cooperation if they are locked in extended games with each other.

Most social situations, however, are n-person supergames. As Taylor suggests, cooperative behavior can emerge in such situations (at least where modeled as an iterated prisoners' dilemma, but it is more fragile than the robust results from the two-person supergame.

question we address for the rest of this chapter is whether such rational cooperation is enough to explain human cooperative behavior. If we discount rational cooperation, do people still overcooperate? If we are to study behavior that is overly cooperative, we will have to factor out cooperation that is based on rational calculation, and then see what is left.

Divide the Dollar

Suppose you are a member of a group of eleven people picked randomly off the street. The group has just been awarded $100. You must divide the money, and then you will depart, more than likely never seeing one another again. You, as leader, must divide the spoils, but you will need to get at least a majority of the group to support your decision. How do you divide the money?

The rational choice perspective on decision making makes a very specific prediction. By Riker's size principle, you should divide the spoils with only five other people, thus forming a majority minimum–winning coalition of six. Within the coalition, you should offer only the barest minimum to the other participants, taking the rest yourself. That will maximize your returns, as it should for a good economic decision maker. The payoff matrix, as it is termed, would look like this:

Yourself (1)	Rest of the Winning	Losing Coalition (5)
$95	Coalition (5)	$0
	$5	

This game, or a variant of it, has been played in laboratories many times. The inevitable result is that leaders give away too much of the spoils. They generally don't divide the results up equally, but they do share too much (Thaler 1988). Remember that this is a one-shot game; there is no repeated play. The leader won't see these people again. (Repeated play and knowing the participants cause leaders to share even more.)

It is likely that norms of cooperativeness and fairness play an important role in the "divide the dollar" (or the similar "dictator") game (Miller and Oppenheimer 1982). Most people would say it is quite fair for a leader to get more. And maybe even that a winning coalition ought to share the spoils. But for the "participating" members of the winning coalition to be treated so shabbily seems unjust.

Here we have our first instance of a "substantive limit" on rationality that detracts from the likelihood that human decision makers will make fully adaptive decisions. In comparison to the models of consumer and voter choice that anchor our understandings of adaptive behavior, leaders in the "divide the dollar" game have "blown it." They have failed to maximize their self-interest. Bounded rationality is showing through.

In comparison to the process limitations detailed in chapter 3, however, the limitations here are not because the leader couldn't do the calculations necessary or couldn't attend to the relevant factors. In the simplest form of this game, the ultimatum game consisting of only two players (proposer and responder), the same results hold. The typical offer to the responder is 30–40 percent of the total. Even when the responder can't reject the offer—the "dictator" game—the proposer offers more than predicted (Camerer and Thaler 1995; Güth and Teitz 1990).

These games—which are not affected by the size of the reward but do seem to be affected somewhat by cultural differences—illustrate major deviations from strict self-centered rationality. Heuristic decision making may take over, but this is not a heuristic that serves as an informational shortcut. The heuristics at work here are not the procedural limits of chapter 3. I term these, and other heuristics like them, "substantive," because they directly affect the decisional outcome.

Auxiliary Assumptions

One may object that the division of spoils in "divide the dollar" games is perfectly rational, since rationality affects means and not goals. We have, in effect, postulated a selfish end. But as political scientists Lupia and McCubbins state, "Rationality requires only the feeling of pain or pleasure; it does not restrict the source of such feelings to material concerns for one's self" (1998, 23). But this kind of instrumental rationalism fails completely to yield a prediction in the "divide the dollar" game! The leader could decide to give all the money to others or to keep all of it to himself. All divisions would be rational. Similarly, all divisions of the spoils in legislative coalitions would be equally rational. An assumption of instrumental rationality alone can never yield output predictions. All behaviors are consistent with such a "thin" concept of rationality, rendering the concept scientifically useless.

We need an auxiliary assumption to be able to formulate a prediction. In this case, the (unstated) assumption is one of self-interest. This problem plagues all applications of rational choice analysis: they must use empirical assumptions, such as material self-interest, to proceed (Simon 1985).

There is really nothing wrong with this, so long as we are conscious of what is happening. In the "divide the dollar" game, the empirical assumption is that the leader will maximize material self-interest. If the assumption is wrong, then the model is wrong. And the only way to know for sure is through empirical study of the motives of the participants.

Sociotropic Voting

"Overcooperation" does not seem to be a quirk of the artificial environment of the laboratory. Confirming evidence comes from large-scale voting studies. For a very long time we've known that economic conditions affect voting direction. The link is so consistent that the connection between voting for president and the economic circumstances of the country serves as the major variable in models that predict presidential voting outcomes prior to elections.

Traditionally, it was assumed that when people felt threatened by the economy, they voted against incumbents. In the 1970s, however, Donald Kinder and Rod Kiewiet (1979) analyzed voting patterns and perceptions of economic conditions in the large-scale surveys conducted by the Survey Research Center at the University of Michigan. Their findings were surprising: economic conditions affect the vote only when voters see a national economic problem, not when they see only an individual one. Such voting was termed "sociotropic." Further research showed that, indeed, personal circumstance mattered in the vote, but not as much as their perceptions of the economic state of the nation (regardless of their personal economic circumstances) (Kiewiet 1983). The "fully selfish" economic model of voting in democracies is thus not wrong; it simply misses the point. People do vote for self-centered reasons. But they also vote for cooperative solutions to collective problems.

In the 1970s, economist William Nordhaus was sure that democratic political systems were just not capable of controlling inflation, because democratically elected politicians would continually offer too much inflation in order to gain lower unemployment. Nordhaus wrote that "a perfect democracy with retrospective evaluation of parties will make decisions biased against future generations" (1975, 190). In a generally similar vein, economists Allen Meltzer and Scott Richard were sure that democracy would redistribute income from those of average means to those of lesser means, and this massive redistributive coalition would never be denied. Even if voters were quite limited cognitively, the result would hold: "A voter need only choose the candidate who promises net benefits; majority rule does the rest" (1978, 116).

Neither of these predictions came true—either in the United States or in any developed democracy. Inflation is under control (brought under control in the 1980s by driving up the unemployment rate, with the tacit support of democratically elected politicians). With a set of politically engineered agreements to rein in the ballooning deficit, federal government growth, in real dollars, has barely budged since the late 1980s. We of course can't say just what combination of factors led to this outcome, but sociotropic voting and education of voters by political elites are the major suspects.

Social Influence and Information Cascades

Whole communities suddenly fix their minds upon one object,
and go mad in its pursuit.

  —Charles Mackay, *Extraordinary Delusions and the Madness of Crowds*

Who are you going to believe: me or your own eyes?

  —Groucho Marx

Not only are people, in general, too cooperative for their own good, they are also too susceptible to social influence—in comparison to what they ought to be were they pursuing pure self-interest. In the 1950s, psychologist Solomon Asch (1952) did experiments in which most individuals, faced with uniform opinions concerning the relative length of lines, would agree with the objectively wrong answer, and then deny that they were at all influenced by others. Much additional research has supported this human susceptibility to social influence.

Why do humans so readily take the "advice" of others? Why do fads sweep through a population, only to quickly die out? Why do some stocks become "hot"? Why do presidential candidates spend so much time in Iowa? Why do men march off to war?

Economist David Hirshleifer (1995) and his colleagues show mathematically how easy it is to generate what they call an "information cascade." A decision maker in effect has two sources of information. The first is his or her direct observation. The second is the decision maker's observations of what other people are doing. Even if the decision maker relies more on his own judgment, in a crowd that judgment will quickly be overwhelmed by the opinions of others, even if each opinion is not strongly weighted. If every decision maker is pursuing such a strategy, then the mathematical consequences are information cascades: crowd behavior in which fadlike behavior is easy to trigger and which quickly die out. The cascade is extremely sensitive to the behaviors of those "first in line."

The consequences of information cascades can be severe. To fool all of the people, you need only to fool the first few in line—the rest will follow. On the other hand, we learn to distinguish between credible and less-than-credible sources for our information—in effect, pushing them to the front of the line. As a consequence, visible, credible sources have considerable influence in triggering and stopping cascades.

Why Conformity?

The mathematical economists have demonstrated wonderfully the consequences of a couple of simple assumptions on collective behavior. But they have not solved the question of why people discount their own observations in favor of the observations of others—why they treat others' advice as data on a par with their own observations.[1] The severity of the consequences of following the advice of others to the exclusion of one's own observations would suggest that cascades would either not occur or be quite limited in their effects. There are four possible explanations for uncritical crowd behavior:

1. Conscious heuristics: People do a cost-benefit calculation and decide that the search behavior necessary to garner the proper information is not worth it. Cascades result from low-payoff decisions.
2. Process limitations on adaptation: Being prisoners of their bounded rationality, people unthinkingly apply heuristics to escape these limitations.
3. Unrecognized rewards: People receive direct rewards for conforming.
4. Substantive limitations on rationality: People have inherited a propensity to conform.

Points 1 and 2 can be ruled out. We have no evidence that, in general, people consciously employ shortcuts for low-payoff decisions. Certainly the economists who are quickest to claim that heuristics substitute for search have not conducted the process-based observations necessary to provide support for this hypothesis. Moreover, the heuristics approach fails to explain why people in small groups will, in the laboratory, engage in the kind of conformist behavior demonstrated in the Asch experiments and many others. The issues are clear, and one needs no cognitive heuristics to sort them out. As we shall see later, fads are in evidence in such supposedly rational activities as markets for securities.

Number 3 is a more interesting problem. We do receive rewards for conformity: the approval of our peers (who may have self-interest in our conformity); glory when we march off to war; a sense of belonging. Such rewards, however, are dependent on motivation. Why do men want the glory that supposedly accompanies war, especially in the face of the horrors that any combat veteran will attest to? Why do we seem to have a need to belong, to feel part of a group, to identify with an organization?

---

1. If there are many participants in an information cascade, then even a high weight for one's own observation may be overwhelmed by the observations of others. However, experiments by psychologists show that conformity emerges in quite small groups. Common observation suggests that conformity is higher in small groups than in large aggregations.

An instrumental positivist may say that we have no business, as social scientists, examining the motives of people. But the question goes to the heart of rationality itself. This brings us to point 4, an inherited propensity to conform.

A Problem in Genetics

Modern evolutionary biology has pretty well accepted that genetics will not produce altruists in any species, because they will survive at lower rates, and hence reproduce at lower rates. Even if glory or honor motivates men, these motives are not sustainable unless they contribute to individual, not group, fitness. (Groups don't have genes.) Over many generations, glory as a motive would die out, overwhelmed by a selfish desire to live and reproduce. We should not observe fitness-sacrificing behavior in situations where evolution has had time to excise it.

"Selfish genes" may motivate individuals to sacrifice for offspring, and even for nieces and nephews and other kin, because to do so can act to maximize the individual's genetic material in the next generation. Following the framing of the problem in 1964 by William Hamilton, biologists have shown that the greater the degree of relatedness, the more likely the cooperative behavior. (Hinde 1991; Dugatin 1999).

In human societies, however, we observe more fitness-sacrificing behavior than can be accounted for by such kin altruism. The only answer for the continuing appeal of so-called altruistic motives is that some other factor offers even more evolutionary advantage.

Humans, like all primates but orangutans, are social animals. Our species did not exist in an individualistic, Hobbesean world, suddenly making a conscious choice to avoid chaos by a social contract. We were always a social species; there is no archeological evidence of a "pre-group" life for humans or their ancestors (Caporeal et al. 1989; Caporeal 1997). It must be the case that the fitness of individuals is advanced by social interaction.

The key mechanism is social learning—learning from other humans. As Herbert Simon writes:

> Docility (or instructability) brings with it a very large bonus in fitness, for the docile individual can learn not to touch stoves without first being burned. For a creature of bounded rationality, reason joined with docility in a benign social environment can achieve a much higher level of fitness than the unaided reason of the loner. . . . Docile persons are more than compensated for their altruism by the knowledge and skills they acquire. (1997, 202)

Simon's notion of docility is powerful indeed. First, it offers the possibility of a genetic basis for social learning and conformity. Second, it suggests that evolutionary trade-offs—contradictory demands on adaptation—can exist. Docility and immediate self-interest in a decision-making situation may present a conflict—and a felt emotional tension—to an individual. Finally, it offers a genetic trait that is clearly capable of being exploited by those who have managed to avoid the full implications of docility (Simon 1990, 1993). This could happen genetically, through errors in transmission. More likely, however, docility is a type of prepared learning—it can be overcome with effort. All of us can learn not to be docile, even if we will tend to fall back into the pattern without conscious monitoring.

Conformity is inherited. It is inherited *socially*, because social norms develop that reinforce conformity—glory prestige, pride in the group, patriotism. There are powerful social sanctions to violating such norms, and powerful rewards for those who conform. It is inherited *genetically* because social learning provides such an evolutionary advantage to the individual. But conformity can be exploited by others, and indeed it is regularly exploited—by political leaders, by con artists, by business leaders demanding "loyalty" to the firm. The continual resolution of the tension between self-interested, individually adaptive behavior and conformity to the norms of the organization is a drama played out every day in every human situation.

Finally, note that the nonconscious use of heuristics (point 2 above) implies an evolutionary base, but here social evolution and individual learning are dominant. Solutions that worked in the past may be directly applied to current problems, obviating search. Such behavior can lead to efficient problem solving in stable environments, but in changing ones the results can be nonoptimal, or even disastrous. In a study of financing arrangements for public-private partnerships, Lynn Bachelor and I showed how the uncritical use of an earlier model cost the City of Detroit literally millions of dollars in property acquisition and relocation costs, because targets of the policy had learned the potential for manipulation from the earlier application (Jones and Bachelor 1993).

Sociality

Instructability links human genetics to social learning. With this concept, there is no need to worry about group selection, a concept that has disturbed evolutionary biologists because groups can't be subject to natural selection, since they don't have genes. Early humans, however, gained all sorts of advantages from group life, and group life became an important component of the environment that exerted selection pressures on cognitive and emotional development (Caporeal 1997). Sociality may explain the tendency of people in experimental situations to "cooperate in the absence of selfish incentives" (Caporeal et al. 1989, 683). Using what they term a "subtraction technique," Caporeal, Dawes, Orbell, and van de Kragt report laboratory experiments in which they eliminate self-centered explanations for cooperative behavior, leading to the conclusion that such cooperation cannot be explained (at least without resort to very contorted reasoning) by selfish incentives alone.

If the sociality hypothesis is correct, then evolutionary processes have generated dispositions among humans to be simultaneously self-centered and cooperative. Cooperation should show through in situations where fully rational adaptive behavior would predict consequence-oriented maximization. Cooperative dispositions can explain the paradox of voting, the tendency of people to treat others' observations on a par with their own in information cascades, the willingness of people to contribute to charities anonymously, and a host of otherwise inexplicable "other directed" behaviors.

Values

Niccolo Machiavelli wrote in *The Prince* that "in the actions of all men, and especially of princes, where there is no court to appeal to, one looks to the end." In Machiavelli's theory of decision making, only goals matter. On the other hand, psychologist Lee Roy Beach and Terrence Mitchell (1998) see values—one's sense of right and wrong—as a critical screening factor in admissibility to the choice set, the options that are considered viable. Values and goals, in Beach and Mitchell's theory, occupy coequal positions in the decision-making process. Options are seriously considered only when they are goal related and they do not violate one's values.

Goals are key to adaptive behavior. As a consequence, they fit easily into a model of decision making stressing either comprehensive or bounded rationality. But what about values? They are not individually adaptive. That is, they do not aid the individual in the pursuit of his or her goals. They may be collectively adaptive, however. If they are, one must question where they come from.

We've already noted that many of the altruistic motives in evidence in human populations cannot be justified in evolutionary theory. The individual adaptive advantage of social learning must outweigh the maladaptive consequences of non-kin altruism. If so, then the very existence of values, which for the most part regulate the quality of interactions between individuals, may be related to the evolutionary adaptive value of social learning for the individual.

In any case, values, whatever their source, do affect current decision making. Like all of the limitations on adaptability, they can be set aside, as Machiavelli advised his prince to do. But except for the most ruthless sociopath, setting aside values seems to be a difficult process for most humans.

The Moral Sense

Value judgments seem to pervade human decision making. Even when we are acting in a supremely selfish fashion, we seem to desire to construct nonselfish motives for our behavior. Why do humans feel it necessary to discuss motives in terms of collective as opposed to (or in addition to) self-centered motives?

In the mid-1970s, psychologist Donald T. Campbell (1975) argued that human moral codes had adaptive value. Treading a similar path, James Q. Wilson, in his address to the American Political Science Association in 1993, announced a theory of the development of human morality that was based on genetics. The key notion of the theory, more fully developed in *The Moral Sense*, is that morality has adaptive value for individual humans, and hence has been selected for (in a Darwinian sense). As a consequence, a moral sense—comprising sympathy, fairness, self-control, and duty—is an important facet of daily decision making in the lives of modern-day humans.

A moral sense, of course, is not determinative in any given decision. Wilson writes that "sentiments are not the sole determinants of action; circumstances—the rewards, penalties, and rituals of daily life—constrain or subvert the operation of the moral sense" (1993, 24). The self-centeredly rational individual can be in conflict with the moral sense, and the various moral senses may be in conflict with one another.

But where does this inherited moral sense come from? In Wilson's thinking, it all stems from sociability. "The mechanism underlying human moral conduct is the desire for attachment or affiliation" (127). Humans are *prepared* to be sociable—prepared to learn sociability "before they learn what sociability is all about" (125). He argues that the four fundamental moral senses all stem from the desire for sociability. It causes us to care what others think of us, and to be sensitive to the moral judgments of others. In Wilson's theory, whole moral systems are filtered through sociability.

But why would sociability be so critical for human behavior? Wilson finds the answer in the dependency of the human child after birth. Parents who are attached to their children will raise more children, hence gaining an evolutionary advantage. Such an advantage could have been preprogrammed in humans, but then it would have detracted from the great adaptive advantage of consciousness. Large, complex human brains are able to think consequentially and generalize observations beyond stimulus-response correlations. Any preprogrammed hardwiring would conflict with the adaptive flexibility of such a system.

The evolutionary solution, according to Wilson, is to preprogram only a disposition to attachment. "Attachment, thus triggered, is the mechanism out of which sociability emerges, and sociability, in turn, is the state in which moral understandings are shaped" (128).

Wilson's argument is persuasive, but he has a different aim than I do here. He wants to explain how pervasive moral discourse is in everyday life—a pervasiveness that is reflected in the findings of Beach and Mitchell on the intrusion of value judgments in even the most practical of decision-making tasks in the laboratory. For our purposes, it is enough to note that sociability can lead us to nonrational cooperation. We are prepared to cooperate.

Nonrational cooperation has two powerful likely genetic bases—instructability and attachment. People are disposed or prepared to cooperate because this disposition has adaptive value for the individual person. The instructable or docile person will learn faster than the recalcitrant one, at least in benign and stable social environments. Sociable people will additionally gain selective advantage by being attached to their children, hence producing more viable offspring.

Rationality Traps

If we had a society of completely rational individuals, then several "rationality traps" would plague human interactions—traps that can be avoided only with considerable effort. These traps also emerge in societies composed of intendedly rational individuals, but they are far less severe. Let us lay out these traps that a fully rational analysis has uncovered:

Collective action and free riding. A "collective" or "public good" is something that, once produced, may be enjoyed by all, even if they did not aid in the production of the good or help pay for it. The classic example is a lighthouse, but many goods and services have this characteristic. For example, sociologists and political scientists have analyzed social movements from this perspective (Chong 1991). The problem is that rational individuals, knowing they can't be excluded, will just wait until the good is produced, and then enjoy it. If everybody is rational, then everybody will wait, and collective goods will not be produced.[2] The solution to such "social dilemmas," as they are sometimes called, is to construct rewards and punishments that will encourage people to contribute to the

---

2. Actually they will be underproduced, since there are very few pure public goods, and if enough people are benefited more than the cost they will have to pay, then some goods will be supplied.

collective end. Two mechanisms have been suggested. One is public coercion—use government to levy taxes, fund a police force to enforce tax collection, and produce the collective goods. A second is to construct market incentives to cause individuals, freely acting, to provide the collective good. A good example of the latter is the governmentally sponsored market for "pollution permits" as a way to curtail air pollution. In either case, those running the government must somehow decide which among competing imperfect collective goods are worthy of government sponsorship. And, if the governors themselves are basely selfish, then the possibility exists that they will convert public resources to further their own interests.

The principal-agent problem. The principal-agent problem is a delegation problem. You as a principal may employ an accountant or doctor or lawyer. The only reason you hire him or her is that he or she has more knowledge than you. Unfortunately, this asymmetry of knowledge allows the agent to serve his or her own goals rather than yours. Economists analyze labor-management relations using this perspective, and some political scientists have analyzed congressional-bureaucratic oversight patterns this way. The implication of the principal-agent problem is that one has to establish external controls and monitoring arrangements to ensure that agents refrain from cheating.

Rent extraction. If everyone is self-centeredly rational, but only a few get to exercise power, then those in power will inevitably use their positions to "extract rents" from the rest. Because everyone is selfish, all government will involve the misuse of public power.

The exogenous change problem. In a fully rational society, change can come only exogenously, or externally. Basically, everyone has everyone else pretty much figured out—they have "discounted" others' actions—hence only shocks from outside the system can change things. In the next chapter, we'll see how this works when applied to the stock market via the "efficient market thesis."

Mitigation of Social Dilemmas via Bounded Rationality

Collective action problems are mitigated via two important factors. The first is the "shadow of the future" and the second is overcooperation by boundedly rational actors. The "shadow of the future" causes rational actors to behave differently than they would if they were in a one-shot interchange with other individuals. This is fully a consequence of self-centered rationality: in an extended interchange, a second party can inflict punishment in the future for noncooperative behavior.

We've already seen that the evidence strongly suggests that people cooperate nonrationally. That is, in the lab and on the street they tend to cooperate even when they can't expect any present or future rewards. This is very likely a consequence of the evolutionary efficiency of instructability.

The consequence of instructability is to mitigate the effects of collective action problems. If people have within them a tendency to cooperate, and if social rewards such as approval reinforce those tendencies, then social collectives will tend to display more cooperation than would be predicted by strict rationality.

There is a major caveat: no one wants to be the "sucker" left doing all the work in a collectivity. Avoiding the role of the sucker may be a more powerful incentive than maximizing returns. More generally, because people have an inherent tendency to cooperate, and they are endowed with reasoning powers, many will feel a tension when they try to resolve the defection decision. On the one hand, one may want to cooperate. On the other, even a little reasoning shows that defecting will yield more concrete returns.

Principal agent and rent-extraction problems are mitigated both rationally and nonrationally. First, monitoring of behavior and the threat of punishment to modify behavior is the use of rational means to encourage more acceptable behavior. This principle is enshrined, for example, in the tax audit. (Unmonitored, the fully rational tax auditor will extract rents.) The problem, of course, is that any subjective expected utility (SEU) calculator can figure out the amount of corruption that will exceed the costs of getting caught via the monitoring system. There would have to be enormous amounts of monitoring to overcome the temptations of rent extraction.

Two facets of bounded rationality act in real societies to mitigate these tendencies. First, psychologists have shown the power of random, intermittent incentive and deterrent structures in gaining compliance. Because people are very poor in evaluating probabilities, intermittent random rewards or punishments have a powerful effect on our behavior—more powerful than would be expected in a full-blown SEU analysis. I stress that the rewards or punishments must truly be intermittent and not rare, because humans really blow it in evaluating rare events. We may discount their probabilities completely ("this can't happen to me") or become overly sensitive to their potential occurrence (demonstrated, for example, by the not uncommon fear of nuclear power plant disasters or the dangers of air travel). Intermittent reward and punishment systems work with rats, but they are even more powerful in the case of humans, because we communicate. The punishment doesn't have to happen to you to get the message across.

Second, because of the human tendency toward overcooperation, most societies are not "a confederation of cheaters." Most people want to cooperate. A few won't, and they need watching and sanctioning. Indeed, if too many cheat, then the cooperative impulse will be undermined by the "sucker's cost." Finding the right level of monitoring, enough that citizens don't feel like suckers (they are assured that most cheaters get punished) but "Big Brother" does not result, is a key challenge in democratic government.

Note what a difference it makes in how one would construct and justify a government if people are both cooperative and self-centered simultaneously (actually, they will not be both simultaneously, but sequentially—short-term memory limitations dictate that).

The notion that people desire to cooperate so long as others do is enshrined in game theory as the "assurance game" (see box 5.2). Compared to the prisoners' dilemma, people would rather cooperate than free ride. The assurance game essentially builds in the understanding that, if too many people defect, then the rewards may well be paltry for all.

Logically, there is no way to decide whether people are inclined to play

---

Box 5.2:   Assurance Game

The provision of collective goods can resemble an assurance game more than a prisoners' dilemma. In PD games, the players know that they will be better off if the good is produced, but no player wants to be the sucker who does all of the providing. Hence each player must be assured that everyone is contributing a fair share. Change the payoff matrix just a little in the prisoners' dilemma, and the outcome becomes indeterminate:

1. {C,C}
2. {D,C}
3. {D,D}
4. {C,D}

The only difference between the two scenarios is that in the prisoners' dilemma, actors would rather "free ride" (defect while others cooperate) than enter into a completely cooperative arrangement, whereas in the assurance game, actors would rather everyone cooperate than to be a free rider. The payoff ranking of strategies means that people basically want to cooperate {C,C}, but they also want to avoid cooperating while others defect {C,D}. (See Taylor 1987; Elster 1979.)

Unlike the prisoners' dilemma, which has one equilibrium {D,D}, the assurance game has two {C,C} and {D,D}. Players may jointly cooperate, or they may jointly defect.

a prisoners' dilemma or an assurance game. All we can say is that the preference ordering for {C,C} versus {D,C} can determine whether a "social dilemma" (in which the pursuit of individual action leads to suboptimal collective outcomes) emerges. But Simon and Wilson have given us extraordinarily good reasons to expect that most people will prefer to play an assurance game than a prisoners' dilemma. Sociality also offers an explanation why players in repeated games will begin a "tit for tat" strategy with an offer of cooperation rather than a defection.

This does not mean that collective action is easy—it always will be hard (the assurance game has two equilibria, one of which is for all players to defect). Individual self-centered rationality will continually conflict with the disposition to cooperate. Rather, the important lesson is that cooperation comes naturally to humans—it has a genetic base. As a consequence, it is not necessary to focus only on establishing selfish incentives to induce cooperation.

Tragedies of Commons

If people are rational, then they will inevitably destroy a good they hold in common if they are left to their own devices. They overgraze common pastures (as happened in the American West); they overharvest fisheries and timberlands; they degrade lakes and rivers. Garrett Hardin (1968) termed the individually rational but collectively catastrophic degradation of common pool resources the "tragedy of the commons." The reason is clear: in systems in which participants are numerous, withholding participation in the exploitation of the common pool resource will cost the participant without yielding any benefits, since other participants will simply consume the nonparticipant's share. Traditional solutions to the common pool dilemma are twofold: either internalize the benefits and costs or impose external sanctions. Internalization usually means dividing the common pool into individual ownership shares (as could be done with timberlands, for example, or mineral rights). External sanctions means a regulatory regime that specifies use patterns and punishes noncompliance.

In empirical studies of common pool resources, both in controlled laboratory settings and in field observations, where people are allowed to communicate they often find solutions to the problem. They do this even in the absence of central authority or internalized costs and benefits. Derivations from noncooperative game theory predict that communication in the absence of sanctions is "cheap talk" and will not change the dreary outcome. Somehow, people in communication with one another can use cheap talk to get themselves out of a collectively suboptimal situation.

Elinor Ostrom of Indiana University, the leading academic expert in the management of common pool resources, summarizes the experimental evidence as follows:

- When people can't communicate, they overexploit common resources.
- They use heuristic rules of thumb to allocate resources.
- When they communicate, they use the opportunity to understand the problem (construct a problem space) and arrive at a solution.
- The solutions are heuristics also, and not always those that would yield maximum total value from the resource.
- Most people keep their promises (even when they could accrue individual gain by breaking them).
- If agreements are broken, people are willing to use severe sanctions against the perpetrators. (Ostrom 1999, 506–7)

The experimental evidence, backed up by field studies, suggests boundedly rational actors struggling to understand a problem and devise collective solutions to get out of the "rationality trap." Ostrom suggests that rather than assuming that resource users are "norm-free maximizers of immediate gains" (494), a "better foundation for public policy is to assume that humans may not be able to analyze all situations fully but that they will make an effort to solve complex problems through the design of regularized procedures and will be able to draw on inherited capabilities to learn norms of behavior, particularly reciprocity" (507–8).

The work of Ostrom and her colleagues illustrates the value of a behavioral approach to the study of collective action problems (Ostrom 1998). A purely analytical approach based on comprehensive rationality within a framework of noncooperative game theory has yielded predictions that do not comport fully with the behavior of actors in experiments and the field. Public policy solutions based on analysis alone can be misguided.

Do Heuristics Approximate Maximization?

There is strong evidence that heuristic, "gut" rationality does not yield essentially similar outcomes to those predicted by comprehensive rationality. In the common pool resource experiments without communication, subjects should be able to reach a stable equilibrium of overexploitation of the resource. Instead, they are unable to avoid cycles of investment and disinvestment. They seem to adopt a cybernetic strategy in which "they increase their investments in the common pool resource until there is a strong reduction in yield, at which time they tend to reduce their investments. . . . No game-theoretic explanation exists for the pulsing pattern" (Ostrom 1999, 502; see also Ostrom, Gardner, and Walker 1994).

When participants communicate with each other concerning common pool resources, bounded rationality can lead to better collective outcomes than comprehensive rationality, even though game theory predicts no differences. On the other hand, participants generally devise strategies that are less than optimum compared to a solution that could be imposed by "objective analysts."

We met this issue earlier, in the claims that low-information electorates using heuristics produce similar outcomes to electorates that maximize information. Empirical work in both cases casts considerable doubt on this assertion.

A Physical Locale for Moral Reasoning?

Neuroscientific research indicates that there may exist a specific brain locale for moral reasoning. Medical researchers have suspected as much ever since the well-documented case of railway construction worker Phineas Gage, whose brain was partially destroyed in 1848 when an iron pipe was driven by an explosion through his skull and brain. Gage recovered with his memory and intelligence intact. But his social relations deteriorated, as he no longer was trustworthy and seemed unable to make moral calculations.

In a famous computer reconstruction, a medical team at the University of Iowa Medical School identified the probable areas of damage to Gage's brain. The injury seemed to have damaged primarily the ventromedial regions of both frontal lobes, areas that are central to emotional processing. The fact that social decision making was so severely compromised in Gage suggested to the researchers that emotion is fundamental to decision making. Research on other people suffering selectively damaged brains has confirmed this thesis (Damasio 1994).

The discovery of a locus of moral processing in the brain suggests that sociability and morality have a different physical locale than logical and rational thought. There are of course caveats. Seeing what kind of thought patterns remain after parts of the human brain have been destroyed is only thinkable in the case of severe accidents or perhaps after radical surgery performed to save lives. Experimentation in the traditional sense is not possible. Even though there exist locales in the brain specific to moral reasoning, there also exist complex interactive connections that are not fully understood. In particular, the lack of emotional processing also seems to affect logical processing: the setting of priorities is difficult for people with damage to the ventromedial regions. Logic and emotion cannot be neatly separated. But what is ruled out by these observations is some sort of fully rational foundation for the development of norms of behavior.

Conclusions

Something is very wrong with the notion that rational people cooperate only out of selfish motives. In laboratory situations, as in real life, people don't maximize their returns in social interactions. They "overcooperate" in comparison to what is predicted based on adaptive rationality. While it is possible to try to explain such behavior as instrumentally rational by claiming that the nature of preferences doesn't affect the theory, this approach causes rational adaptation to fail as a predictive theory. In a "divide the dollar" game, no predictions can be made unless one adds the auxiliary assumption that people are selfish.

Very probably there is a genetic basis to cooperation. As is the case for many human traits, there is no "gene" for cooperation. Rather, there probably exists a disposition or preparedness to cooperate. This disposition may or may not be realized in any individual human or circumstance. It is driven by the selective advantage given to cooperative individuals because learning is critical to future performance (and hence survivability), and social learning and imitation are the most efficient mechanisms for the transmission of survival tactics. Sociability is also driven by attachment needs caused by the dependency of human children on parents.

These mechanisms mean that substantive limitations on rational decision making will be in evidence even in those institutions that depend fundamentally on individual rational action. Perhaps most important, the tendency toward instructability implies that there will exist considerable monitoring and mimicking in decision making—activity that is not based in conscious cost-benefit calculations but rather in sentiment and intuition.

If citizens are self-centeredly rational, then social interactions devolve to a series of prisoners' dilemma games in which collective goods are underproduced and public power is continually corrupted. All of politics is about the constructing of external incentives and deterrents that will cause the governed to behave properly. But if people are boundedly rational, and find within themselves competing tendencies to cooperate and act selfishly, then social arrangements become infinitely more benign. Elinor Ostrom (1998) calls this behavior "better than rational." Selfish tendencies must be constrained, but only to the point that the typical individual is assured (as in an assurance game) that others are contributing to the commonweal.

PART **II**

ORGANIZATIONS
AND INSTITUTIONS

CHAPTER **6**

The Behavioral Theory of Organizations

O N 19 J UNE 1998, Kathleen Lee-Geist lay dying in the back of her van at a ferry terminal in Anacortes, Washington. Her husband was bringing her back home from treatment for a brain tumor, and offered Washington State Ferry officials a request from hospital officials that Ms. Lee-Geist be given priority loading privileges for health reasons. The official in charge refused, pointing out that rules required that such requests be faxed ahead of time. Ms. Lee-Geist waited five hours for an available ferry. She died the next day.

A Washington State Ferry official defended the employee, while criticizing his decision: "He is the kind of guy who goes by the rules. He's a great employee, but he made a mistake in this instance. Sometimes . . . you have to make a decision from your heart" (*Seattle Post-Intelligencer*, 7 July 1998).

T HE LESSON of this chapter is that human organizations fall prey to canalization of behavior in the same way that human decision makers do. The relationship is not metaphorical; it is *causal*. The canalization of behavior due to human cognitive architecture is the cause of similar canalization in organizations. Nevertheless, organizations allow us to overcome many of our individual limitations—essentially by coordinating the activities of many individuals, each with partial and incomplete knowledge.

So we have what might be called the "paradox of organization": on the one hand, organizations not only limit our adaptability, they make the situation worse by allowing us to adjust to an artificial context. The organization becomes our relevant referent, in effect selecting the attributes that order our decision making. On the other hand, formal organizations, perhaps more than any other human invention, allow us to escape our individual biological limitations.

The Role of Organizations

Formal organizations—parliaments, business organizations, political parties, interest groups—are deliberate constructions by humans. Organizations are abstractions—they are abstract rules that govern the interaction within particular boundaries. An organization is not the individual people that are "in" it. If someone leaves his position in an organization, the organization itself continues to exist. Its rules tell people how decisions are made, how authority is allocated, and how they are to relate to other members of the organization.

Formal organizations exist because they allow people to accomplish things that they otherwise could not accomplish. Formal organizations are a relatively recent creation; for most of the existence of the human species, only informal associations existed. The ability to create abstract specified rules for the interactions of individuals, such as exist in governments, armies, and business firms, came very late in human development.

While many aspects of organization are similar in government and the market, many are unique. Most important, formal organizational rules in the case of the business firm act to lower what are known as decision and transaction costs, whereas in political systems oftentimes rules are established to raise such costs. "Decision costs" are costs associated with coming to a decision. They are lowest when one person in an organization decides a strategy for all. They are highest when everyone in the organization must agree (Dahl 1967). "Transaction costs" are costs associated with making an exchange favored by all parties in the exchange. Costs such as writing contracts and auditing compliance are examples. Third parties, such as governments, can add transaction costs in a manner that detracts from efficient exchange and, as a consequence, economic production (North 1981, 1990).

In the market, and sometimes in government, it is clear that decision and transaction costs ought to be low. Governmental arrangements that interfere with productivity with no other appreciable collective benefit, economists note, ought to be eliminated. Similarly, in public service delivery organizations such as police, fire, and education, "efficiency and economy" are laudable goals.

When public deliberative bodies are making decisions that bind all citizens, however, high decision costs are oftentimes very desirable. Low decision costs imply oligarchy. In the use of public coercion in the cases of police, prison incarceration, or property seizure through eminent domain, minimization of transaction costs is not always desirable. In such cases, a trade-off exists between efficient implementation of policy and the protection of the rights of individuals. The proper trade-off can be very difficult to achieve; it is certainly not a mechanistic exercise. While this should be obvious, it seems to have been missed in many analyses of public organizations.

Organizations and Human Capacities

Organizations allow us to escape our individual limitations to achieve goals. Limits on what individuals acting alone can accomplish stem from both the external environment and from human cognitive and emotional architecture. Organizations are created, emerge, and evolve in response to both opportunities and constraints in both the outer and inner environment of the human mind. This is an arbitrary distinction because in the real world of organizational life the internal and the external interact in complex ways. But the distinction is a useful one, especially given the modern tendency toward a division of scholarly labor in which behavioral scientists study the internal cognitive environment with little appreciation of the adaptation to the external world, and social scientists build models of external factors that ignore human cognitive architectures.

Challenges External to Human Cognition

External challenges are aspects of the environment of decision making that a hypothetically comprehensively rational person interacting with other comprehensively rational people would employ formal organizations to address.

Coordinating diverse activities. People acting in simple self-interest often will not achieve collective ends. In organizational hierarchies, subordinates follow the decisions of supervisors because they gain benefits, often through an employment contract. In hierarchies, however, subordinates have incentives to "shirk"—to substitute their own goals for those of their supervisors. Organizational arrangements can discourage shirking through systems of monitoring and reporting.

The division of labor. It would not be cost-effective for a single individual to try to perform all the tasks necessary to achieve a goal. Organizations allow different people to perform different tasks, and provide the means for coordinating these activities.

Decision and transaction costs. It can be easier for a transaction to take place within the hierarchical framework of a business firm than to contract with an outside party. Organizations can thus act to minimize the costs of doing business (Coase 1990).

Challenges Based in Human Cognition

Internal challenges are the aspects of our internal cognitive architecture that formal organizations either overcome or channel. Cognitive architectures are not invariably limitations to the achievement of collective goals. We noted in chapter 5 how sociality implies overcooperation; this has clear implications for organizational life.

Attention. As we saw in chapter 3, people process stimuli from the environment serially—one at a time—because of attentional limits. Organizations must similarly process decisions serially, but they can in part get around this limitation by delegating authority and allowing subunits to process information in parallel. Different parts of the organization can examine different aspects of the environment, as do legislative committees. Or the organization may build in redundancy, having different parts of the organization do similar things, to lower the probability of making errors (Landau 1969; Bendor 1985; Heimann 1993, 1997).

Trade-offs. Where organizations have multiple goals, they experience trade-off difficulties. Even when they have what looks like a simple and straightforward mission, the trade-off problem can emerge as resources are allocated to tasks. This is most evident when organizations make specific and risky decisions (from NASA deciding to launch a rocket to a social service agency deciding about an individual's eligibility). An agency is subject to two kinds of decision mistakes: "launching" when the launch should have been aborted and "not-launching" when launching should have occurred. Multiple types of errors means that "trade-offs between the errors must be made; and this moves us into the realm of politics" (Heimann 1993, 422).

The preparation-deliberation trade-off and routinization. Humans, like digital computers, must allocate resources between relying on previously stored solutions and searching for a fresh solution. Routines and decision rules, which specify an action given a stimulus, are the organizational method for programming. Rules-based activity in organizations allows easy encoding in organizational memory (including the written records that are a hallmark of organizational life), easy retrieval, and easy transference to new members of the organization. But such activities also require judgment about what situations are governed by what rules. Such judgment is affected by the cognitive capacities of organizational members.

Problem-space construction and solution search. No one actor within an organization will likely be able to construct an appropriate problem space for problems emerging in a changing environment. Most organizations have mechanisms for deliberation so that diverse perspectives and the highlighting of alternative problem structures may be examined. Donald Chisholm notes that "the most difficult task for decision-makers is to comprehend the problems they confront, because alternatives are rarely given, to devise institutional forms that can effectively redress those problems" (1995, 451).

Learning. Organizations learn by "encoding inferences from history into routines that guide behavior" (Levitt and March 1988, 320). May (1992, 1999) distinguishes three forms of organizational learning in the public policymaking process. "Instrumental learning" is learning about the "viability of policy instruments or implementation designs" (1999, 21). "Social learning" involves constructing the problem space, while "political learning" entails lessons about political feasibility and opportunities. Instrumental learning characterizes even the most rational actor, but the latter two types of learning involve cognitive limitations. In particular, social learning illustrates how cognitive capacities of organizational members interact with the nature of the environment. The more complex the organizational environment, the more important social learning is in decision making.

Identification. The capacity of people to engage in abstract thought and the direct connection between emotion and thought lead to the phenomenon of organizational identification. People identify emotionally and cognitively with an abstraction. As a consequence, their connections with an organization go far beyond the strictures of the employment agreement or other contract with the organization. This phenomenon is perhaps most in evidence in the relationship people have with a local sports team—far different than what would be predicted from the simple act of a ticket purchase. Local civic boosterism, nation-state patriotism, and team spirit all stem from the same basic aspects of the human character. The emotional commitment that defines identification is critical in learning the rules and procedures that form the basis of organizational effectiveness.

Overcooperation. The strong role that sociality plays in human nature leads to cooperation within an organizational structure that often goes beyond that required by the employment contract. People may, however, identify with subunits of the organization, sometimes leading to the undermining of overall organizational goals. These facets lead to far less shirking than suggested by the economic models of organization, even taking into account the limited ability to monitor and punish shirking in public sector organizations. A comprehensive study of several public service delivery organizations in the United States by John Brehm and Scott Gates (1997) has documented this "undershirking" quite convincingly.

In sum, an organization comprised of boundedly rational actors will, of necessity, address both internal and external limitations. An organization that is built on comprehensively rational actors will address external limitations alone. We now turn to a discussion of how these abstract principles work in real-world organizations—particularly in government executive agencies and legislative bodies.

Behavioral Analysis of Political Organizations

Although today models based on comprehensive rationality are common in political science, bounded rationality has served as the traditional foundation for political analysis. It is worth examining how this came about. In political science, behavioral analysis refers to the systematic and often quantitative study of political behavior, including the behavior of both citizens and leaders. Behavioral analysis was part of a broader behavioral movement in political science. The behavioral movement, which may be traced to the school of political analysis that flourished at the University of Chicago in the 1920s and 1930s, emphasized the scientific and quantitative study of politics. The study of behavioral foundations of politics was a major component of this general approach (Eulau 1963).

The direct study of political behavior affected two areas of political science most strongly: the analysis of voting and the study of policymaking institutions, mostly within an American setting. The two arenas of study were only tenuously linked, however, probably because of the focus of much behavioral political science on a distinction between "mass" and "elite" behavior rather than more general models of decision making. Earlier in this book, I reviewed the development of voter decision models. Here I focus on organizational behavior.

Most progress was made in the study of bureaucracy. While the study of legislatures became increasingly behavioral, based in observation and analysis, it was not strongly informed by theory. Major observational studies, such as Matthews's analysis (1960) of the role of informal norms on the lawmaking process, were important contributions, but on the whole the behavioral study of legislatures failed to link legislative activities with policy outcomes in a convincing manner.

A major aim of the decision-making studies of public bureaucracies was to link observed outcomes of public agencies with models of decision making and choice within the organization. These studies were strongly influenced by intellectual and practical developments in the study of the business firm, as well as by the sociological study of organizations. Approaches based in abstract organization theory and in decision making coexisted with more traditional analyses of organizations, which included such topics as political and administrative spheres of influence, and formal internal processes of public agencies. Indeed, Herbert Simon (1947) announced his decision-making approach via an attack on the maxims of the traditional administrative approach. Simon's behavioral study of organizations was a "type specimen" of the behavioral movement in political science, which sought to replace the description of formal organizational procedures in government organizations with rigorous scientific observation and measurement.[1]

At Carnegie-Mellon University, under the intellectual leadership of Simon, Richard Cyert, and Jim March, the behavioral study of organizations flourished during the 1950s and early 1960s. One of the key findings to emerge from the behavioral study of human organizations was the abridgment of the search and choice processes implied by comprehensively rational decision making. Organizations tend to connect an environmental stimulus (a 911 call to a dispatcher or a telephone order to a catalog company) to an automatic response. The automatic connection occurs through "performance programs." Performance programs result in many situations in which a "simple stimulus sets off an elaborate program of activity without any apparent interval of search, problem-solving or choice" (March and Simon 1958, 141). Performance programs are organizational analogues of the preparation part of Newell's preparation-deliberation trade-off. The more an organization off-loads its tasks into performance programs, the less it must engage in expensive search processes in confronting problems.

Performance programs are found in both private and public organizations, and account for a surprising amount of activity in them. Richard Cyert and James March discussed in detail the tendency of private firms to adopt performance programs, or "task performance rules," which reduce uncertainty and promote coordination by members of the firm: "In most of the firms we have studied, price and output decisions were almost as routinized as production line decisions. Although the procedure changed over time and the rules were frequently contingent on external feedback, price and output were fixed by recourse to a number of simple operating rules" (Cyert and March 1963, 104–5).

Oftentimes decision rules are linked, as is the case when a dispatcher in a police department receives a call, classifies it according to the nature of the problem, and responds accordingly by sending aid (Percy 1985). The input and initial decision cause chains of activity; if the initial classification is incorrect, its effects will cascade because of this linkage.

---

1. Perhaps this approach goes too far in downplaying the role of formal rules in organizations. See Hammond 1990.

Organizational Processes and the Environment

"Organizational process models" emphasize the role of internal procedures in the production of organizational outputs. Outputs are not linked simply to informational inputs. Rather, rules, procedures, and other internal processes intervene between demands from the environment and responses generated by an organization and change them so that there is no direct and simple link between environmental demand and organizational product. Organizations, like individuals, are disproportionate information processors.

Programmed decision rules, generally justified because they implement the goals of the organization, can actually interfere with the full realization of the supposed goals of the organization. Businesses respond to profit opportunities, but programming price and output decisions mean that profit is not maximized. Similarly, preprogrammed decision rules in government may interfere with responsiveness to public opinion.[2]

A case in point is public budgeting. Patrick Larkey has said in regard to his study of city budgets that the "insensitivity of the decision-process to the external environment, to demands, was almost total." There was no decision-making mechanism for translating demands into the simple budgeting decision rules that governed the allocation process. Changes in demands and needs offered the proponents of changes in expenditures an opportunity to argue their cases when setting budget "fair shares," but the process was noisy and invited counterclaims that "muddle the implications of any particular claim" (personal communication, April 1998). Larkey (1977) developed an "error-accumulating model" that implied very strong divergence of the decision-making system from environmental inputs. It is, however, unlikely that any system of governance can be insulated from the demands from its environment forever. As a consequence, large budget jumps are likely to occur when enough errors accumulate.

Similar disjointed responses occur within government. Carpenter has studied how federal agencies respond to budget changes, and finds a pattern in which initial budget cuts are ignored but later cuts reinforcing the signal set off cascading cuts in agency performance. "In order to send budget messages to an agency, then, a single budget cut or increase usually will not suffice" (Carpenter 1996, 299).

As we have seen, there is nothing irrational about the use of decision rules and performance programs in formal organizations. By cutting down on information costs and by promoting coordination, they act as

---

2. This may occur deliberately to raise decision costs to avoid premature action. However, many rules are intended, not to raise decision costs, but simply to get a job done.

rational substitutes for full search and choice procedures in repetitive situations. But are such bureaucratic procedures therefore completely adaptive? Quite clearly not. Organizational members not infrequently apply organizational routines when they should be activating problem-solving approaches. And, as we have noted before, members of an organization tend to identify cognitively and emotionally with the set of rules they have learned. Organizational processes can even isolate members from the environment, damping response to it. As a consequence, maladaptive organizational rules can be extraordinarily difficult to change.

Delivering Public Services

During the 1970s, many careful studies of the delivery of public services showed not only that public bureaucracies were subject to task performance rules (certainly no surprise), but that they attain a unique status there. During the Progressive era in the United States, reformers argued that rules for delivering public services and letting public contracts needed to be procedurally fair if they were to be viewed as legitimate. As a consequence, procedurally neutral rules, such as delivering services on demand (not to who paid the most or was the most politically connected) became an important component of public sector reform. The role of procedurally neutral decision rules remains a defining component of public bureaucracies today.

If response to a stimulus was programmed, then the characteristics of the service demander were irrelevant. Only the nature of the problem counted. The bureaucratic rule had taken on new meaning—it was there to promote fairness and limit the discretion of public officials, who might be corrupt. As a consequence of such analyses, task performance rules in public bureaucracies evolved from standardized, time-saving, prepared responses to an essential part of the organization, serving multiple functions.

In the past, of course, there was far less concern about the fairness of service delivery procedures. Indeed, in the political machine cities of the United States, it was expected that a party's supporters would disproportionately enjoy the spoils of elected office. As times changed, demands on the service organization changed. "Good government" reformers demanded that bureaucracies be neutral service providers, delivering services according to general formulae rather than political pressure. One response was an increasing use of task performance rules to ensure procedural fairness.

In the evolution of biological species, it is not uncommon for an adaptation to a previous set of environmental circumstances to be commandeered for new circumstances. Similarly, social organizations can evolve, using existing structures to meet new environmental demands. One

Box 6.1:   Decision Rules and Attention Rules

It has been said that all bureaucracy involves politics, and nowhere is this truer than in the City of Chicago. Demands for responsiveness to neighborhood needs, filtered through the political party apparatus, are quite in keeping with local democracy. But they run afoul of the classic "norm of neutral competence," which dictates that bureaucrats are supposed to leave politics and policymaking to elected officials.

Pressures for fair, impartial service delivery, on the one hand, and responsiveness to the wishes of local politicians for neighborhood benefits on the other, is a classic example of contradictory demands on an organization. Both are not only adaptive, they are well justified by sensible theories of democracy. But the necessity to make trade-offs can cause havoc in the use of task performance rules.

In a study of the Building Department in Chicago, standard task performance rules were not infrequently overridden by a set of attention rules (Jones 1985). Standard operating procedures dictated that service should be allocated according to the severity of the problem. On the other hand, the vast and cumbersome city building code made necessary some street-level allocation of effort. So inspectors oftentimes ignored minor violations, writing up the most critical ones.

Attention rules told inspectors when standard operating procedures were not to be followed. Usually "political heat" had been brought to bear on a particular case. In such situations, the inspector should not simply use standard performance rules, which explicitly tied a situation to a response. Rather, the inspector should use more comprehensive problem-solving techniques in which considerable knowledge of the specifics of the code was required. Someone (the supervisor) had to decide what set of rules were in effect, and communicated the situation to the inspectors (via a simple Post-it note on the file).

consequence of the tendency of task performance rules to evolve to meet new demands in the environment is the problem of what sociologist Gideon Sjoberg called "contradictory functional requirements." Environmental demands can be contradictory, placing considerable stress on an organization as it attempts to forge the proper trade-offs.

These contradictory demands are the organizational analogue of contradictory preferences for the individual. In theory, they are easily resolvable; indifference curves in economics imply smooth trade-offs among valuable things. In practice, organizations have difficulties in achieving trade-offs just as individuals do (indeed, because individuals are the building blocks for organizations, the sources are the same).

One of the most important findings about so-called neutral task performance rules was that they weren't. In quantitative studies of municipal service delivery to urban neighborhoods, political scientists found (1) there
was little evidence of direct discrimination in big city service delivery, but
(2) the task performance rules adopted by an agency had the consequence
of penalizing some neighborhoods at the expense of others. A procedurally neutral decision rule such as using a citizen call to stimulate a government action had substantive consequences. These decision rules delivered
services to those neighborhoods most willing to complain. And complain-
ing has a class bias—given the same objective set of problems, middle-
class citizens are more willing to contact government than lower-income
citizens are (Jones et al. 1977; Coulter 1988).

Political scientists find these sorts of trade-offs all the time in studies of
the policy process. In the case of public service delivery, if one stresses
procedural fairness, the existing task performance rules work adaptively
well. If one stresses substantive fairness, then one must initiate special effort to see that the needs of the noncomplainers are met. Such an allocation would detract from servicing the complainers—except in the most
overfunded agency.

Making Government Budgets

Bounded rationality as a theoretical underpinning for how governing institutions function reached its high point with the studies of government
budgets and service delivery in the 1960s and 1970s. These studies started
with models of decision making featuring "considerations of limited rationality in the face of complexity and uncertainty" (Davis, Dempster, and
Wildavsky 1974, 421).

Aaron Wildavsky's pathbreaking studies saw budgeting as fundamentally organizational, in that it was driven by the necessity of participants
in the budgeting process to establish stable working relationships with
each other and with the external economic and political world (Wildavsky
1964). A decision process was embedded in this system: incremental decision making, in which participants made marginal adjustments using
the principles of "base" and "fair share." Budgeting officials were guided
primarily by the principle of marginal adjustment within the norms of
fairness among budget claimants. Under the normal course of events,
budget bases were not reexamined, and marginal increments or decre-
ments were allocated consensually. Hence the basic budget principle was
one of incrementalism. In a similar vein, Richard Fenno (1966) showed
how incremental budgets derived from a system of shared understandings
and deference that was maintained within congressional appropriations
committees.

The behavioral study of budgeting had the effect of unifying the outputs of the political system with a fairly simple set of behavioral principles within government. If processes were incremental, so should outputs be. The consequence of using such prepared strategies for allocating resources is that the public budgeting system becomes quite removed from the external environment, in particular, from the nature of the problems facing government and the wishes of the public. Organizational dynamics constitute a partially closed system, uncoupled from the external task environment. The system thus performs a great deal of internal adjustment, but is less responsive and adaptive to changes in the external environment.

There are three reasons for boundedly rational policymakers to use incrementalist processes in budgeting. The first involves the relative ease of reversing mistakes following incremental changes. The second concerns the desire of participants to establish stable expectations in a complex and uncertain environment. The third concerns the nature of overlapping, conflicting, and interacting institutions in American politics, which push participants toward compromise.

The incrementalist theory of budgeting was firmly based in bounded rationality and linked processes cleanly with outputs. Nevertheless, it was thoroughly routed. In a rash of theoretical and empirical research, critics noted problems in the models used (Natchez and Bupp 1973; Gist 1982), in the particular measures used (Wanat 1974), in the conceptual clarity of terms (Berry 1990), and in the nature of the underlying decision-making model (Padgett 1980, 1981). The most damaging critique was the simple observation that budgeting is often not incremental. At times, many agencies' budgets did not behave incrementally, rather experiencing large changes.[3] If incremental outcomes were often not in evidence, then it seemed that the simple decision-rule approach of the bounded rationalists must be wrong.

Public Choice and Budget Rationality

Perhaps because of the perceived failure of the incremental model, perhaps for other reasons, budget studies moved away from limited rationality formulations into two distinct directions. The first was a rational choice approach. Public budgeting has been subject to various schemes to make the process "more rational," in the sense of being more controllable by political executives. As a consequence, governments at all levels have tried to

---

3. Davis and his colleagues made provision for such budgetary shifts (Davis, Dempster, and Wildavsky 1974), but that provision was often overlooked. And, in any case, DDW's budget models were nonincremental only with parameter shifts caused by external events—there was no role for endogenous nonincrementalism.

move toward more comprehensive budget planning, and in particular, to-ward unifying budget systems with programs rather than accounting cate-gories. So we have had zero-base budgeting, which requires agencies to justify not just their incremental share, but their entire base in terms of agency missions; program budgeting, which attempts to unify budgeting and program outputs; and other planning-based budgeting schemes.

These attempts were less than successful. They ran afoul of bounds on rationality in organizations. But the first systematic attack on these sys-tems came from rational choice–oriented political economists. As econo-mists found it necessary to relinquish the notion of well-behaved social welfare functions, so political economists were persuaded that nothing in the incentive structure of government would support rational, comprehen-sive budgeting. One major reason was the tendency of agency directors to maximize their own utility functions (oftentimes assessed as the size of the budget of their agencies) rather than maximizing the benefit-cost ratio of the services they provided (Niskannen 1971). This could account for what seemed at the time a steady and inexorable growth in the size of govern-ment. But the approach foundered on the issue of just what was being maximized in complex political institutions, and just how that maximi-zation might be accomplisheds when trade-offs in desired values had to be made (Thurmaier 1995).

A second approach to understanding public budgeting was rigorously empirical, but quite atheoretical. Scholars used the leverage of quantita-tive budget outputs in complex statistical models relating exogenous vari-ables, such as the state of the economy or the nature of public opinion, to budgets (Su, Kamlet, and Mowery 1993). The problem was that budget procedures insulated the process so well from external influences that little of utility emerged from these studies. So neither of the alternative strate-gies has proved particularly useful in understanding public budgeting.

Nevertheless, the major contender for the dominant approach among students of budgets currently is "the standard economic model which holds that spending outcomes are determined by the supply of and the demand for publicly provided goods and services and competition" (Green and Thompson, in press, 2). The clear scientific failure of this approach dic-tates a return to the organizational process models based in bounded rationality.

Bounded Rationality Does Not Imply Incrementalism

Focusing solely on incremental changes caused early behavioral decision theorists to downplay empirical evidence of large-scale change, and it led boundedly rational decision making into a theoretical cul-de-sac. Incre-mentalism did seem to explain much of what happened in the budgetary process, but it had nothing to say about major expenditure changes. And these changes were clearly in evidence in budget data. Bounded rationality, however, does not imply incrementalism. Far from it. The early budget scholars such as Fenno and Wildavsky, focusing on the role of procedures in the normal course of budget behavior, missed the role of attention allocation in the process. When politicians and agency directors direct their attention to particular programs, those programs change.

If the process of attention allocation is added to the earlier approach emphasizing repetitive decisions within an organizational structure, a new picture of budgetary politics emerges. Incrementalism is the rule when most actors are not attending in any detail to a program, but when the program attracts their attention, punctuations (bursts of cuts or increases) occur (Padgett 1980, 1981). This picture has an important role for major punctuations in public budgets, and these punctuations are not directly tied to major disruptions in the environment. They are partially endogenous, or internal, to the process—as an organizational process model would imply.

These punctuations are clearly in evidence in most programs, as we shall see in the chapter 7. If we ignore variability among programs, and focus only on the average program change, punctuations are easily detectable. Changes in the national budget of the United States since the Second World War can be modeled as basically incremental but with two major shifts in the level of commitments to expenditures—one in 1957 and another in 1974 (Jones, Baumgartner, and True 1998; True, in press). These two points bracket a period in which the budget grew at much higher rates than before or since. There are no easy connections between budget growth and gross domestic product, inflation, party control of Congress or the presidency, or the course of public opinion (See fig. 6.1). No obvious external variables explain the observed pattern, but the 1974 punctuation corresponds to the Budget Reform Act of that year.

We do not think that budgets are independent of economic resources, or of party control of Congress and the presidency, or of public opinion. It does seem evident, however, that adjustment to these potentially conflicting demands is anything but smooth. The reason harks back to the dual demands made on intelligent systems, including human formal organizations: one set from the external environment and one set from the internal requirements of the system itself. It is likely that these dual demands will yield punctuations in the responsiveness of the system to environmental change, even when that environmental change is smooth. The situation is even more complex when changes in the environment are

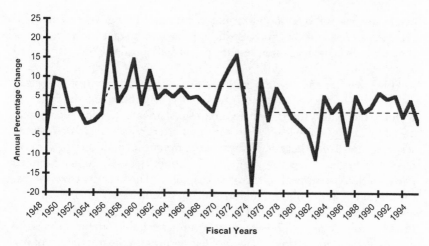

Fiscal Years

Figure 6.1   Incrementalism and Abrupt Change in the U.S. National
               Budget

The figure diagrams the median change in year-to-year percentage change
by discretionary spending subfunction (categorized by the U.S. Office of
Management and Budget). Mandatory spending displays a similar, but less
pronounced, pattern. The line labeled 'predicted' is that predicted by an
estimation model. The radical decline in 1975 was a result of President Nixon's
budget recisions, which were restored the next year.

Source: Jones, Baumgartner, and True 1998

not smooth, but the general principle holds: there is no simple translation
from environmental pressures to budget outputs.

Policy Agendas

To understand how shifts in collective attention affect the course of policymaking, we will need to turn to what political scientists term the "agenda-
setting process." In 1972, Roger Cobb and Charles Elder initiated the scientific study of agenda setting in political science. Following up on even
earlier work by E. E. Schattschneider (1960), Cobb and Elder noted that
much of politics involved deciding what issues get considered seriously by
governments—the agenda for policy action. Politics and consequentially
public policy are attention driven. They distinguished between the "systemic agenda," which refers to the set of issues discussed seriously by
political activists and the mass public more generally, and the "formal
agenda," which is the set of issues considered seriously for action by government. These agenda theorists hypothesized that agendas could be set

externally, via political mobilization, or internally, by governmental officials. As a consequence, an issue did not have to attract the attention of the public at large to gain access to the formal agenda (Cobb, Ross, and Ross 1976).

Policymaking that occurs without broader public interest is termed "subsystem politics." Much of the activity of government in fact falls within such subsystems, where interested private parties work with agency and legislative leaders to make and interpret policy. In democratic systems, however, there is always the temptation for losers in governmental struggles to try to go outside the confines of "systems of limited participation" to appeal to the broader public. This has the effect of disrupting subsystem politics and introducing broader interests into the system (Baumgartner and Jones 1993). When subsystems are disrupted, the broader policymaking bodies must act; broader public attention must be activated. The processing capacity of legislatures is constrained, so only a limited number of issues can be considered in any period of time.

Collective attentiveness is critical for major policy change. At about the same time Cobb and Elder were studying policy agendas, communications scholars Maxwell McCombs and Donald Shaw were studying the issue content of the American mass media (McCombs and Shaw 1972; Shaw and McCombs 1977). They observed that the public agenda typically includes no more than seven issues at one time. They related the public agenda, or those issues capturing public attention, to the media agenda and termed their relationship the "agenda-setting hypothesis." Shaw and McCombs understood that the carrying capacity of the public agenda was related to human attention spans, citing Miller's classic "magic number," but they viewed that correspondence as an "empirical generalization." In the case of collective attention, the driving force was salience on the media agenda.

The correspondence found by the media agenda theorists is not simply an inexplicable empirical generalization. Both procedural and substantive limitations on human rationality and adaptability are responsible for these findings. The connection between human cognitive architecture and the extent of the public agenda are related via short-term memory limits and the allocation of attention.

One important implication of limitations in collective attention spans is that the agenda-setting process cannot involve a smooth transition between the external social and economic problems that governments face and the public policies they produce. If a limited number of issues can occupy public attention at any given time, then the movement of one issue on the agenda must cause a displacement process in which another issue is lost to attention—at least for the time being. This contributes to the disjointed and episodic nature of public policymaking and is not linked to the decision costs imposed by governmental structure.

For instance, President Bush's famous antidrug speech in 1989 establishing a White House "drug czar" took place during a period of declining drug use among Americans (Jones 1994, 106–8). Much of the public and governmental concern on criminal justice policy has occurred as the crime rate declines. Such examples can be cited again and again. Since the problem must capture the attention of governmental officials, and because numerous problems compete for attention on both the systemic and formal agendas, there is no smooth translation of problems into governmental response.

A second consequence of limited collective attention spans is that a "politics of attention" will develop that concentrates on getting people interested in a particular problem that may be ripe for government action. Highlighting those aspects of a situation that imply the need for government action, the politics of attention is about problem representation. For example, Burstein (1998) shows how civil rights groups raised the salience of the issue of discrimination in jobs and translated public support into specific legislation. This kind of political activity develops because there is considerable ambiguity and uncertainty about collective problems. This ambiguity interacts with the participants' cognitive architectures, especially attention structures. Because attention and emotion are inextricably linked, emotion and politics are themselves intertwined.

Ambiguity, Uncertainty, and the Garbage Can

In chapter 2 we noted the fundamental role ambiguity and uncertainty play in the environment of decision making. Ill-structured problem spaces can cause preferences to be ambiguous. This ambiguity often interacts with the cognitive capacities of people, in effect helping to define what they want. What can be accomplished not infrequently affects what we want to accomplish.

Not surprisingly, this individual-level phenomenon has collective consequences. In public life, stating a solution to a problem can, in effect, define the problem, especially where problem spaces are uncertain and ambiguous (Cohen, March, and Olsen 1972; March and Olsen 1976). Ambiguity is not just something that can be dismissed as a random error in decision making. It can fundamentally alter the decision process, even reversing the link between problem and solution. Solutions can search out problems! Cohen, March, and Olsen (1972) claim that much of the connection between solutions and problems is forged by more or less random matings generated when choice opportunities happen to appear. These matings are hostage to the attentional processes in organizations. Problems and solutions can be thought of not as causally but as temporally related. A problem and solution are connected primarily because each has reached the attention of decision makers at approximately the same time. As a consequence, Cohen and his colleagues term their model the "garbage can" model. If this model sounds strange, think of all the new uses computers have been put to in recent years—a technology generating problems which it can then solve.

John Kingdon (1996) has used the garbage can model to study agenda processes in government. Kingdon offers the example of transportation policy, in which interested parties have tried to push their favored solution to emerging problems. Mass transit proponents have tried to attach their solution to urban decay (new stations will stimulate development), urban pollution (more riders will lessen automobile pollution), the energy crisis, and highway gridlock. The motives of politicians pushing urban transit may have been the jobs and business development that enhance their tax bases—quite unrelated to the arguments they have made about the problem-solving capacities of mass transit.

Institutions as Agenda Funnels

Institutions both bind us and free us. They bind us by encouraging us to adapt to an artificial environment. They free us by achieving specialization and coordination. At the highest (and most abstract) level, fairly simple rules in economic and political systems achieve specialization and coordination, both of which are necessary because of the limited rationalities of all participants. In capitalistic markets, specialization occurs across roles, across product lines, and across coordinates—all via the price system. In liberal democracies, specialization also occurs—across voters, politicians, and bureaucrats, as well as across levels of government in decentralized systems. Coordination is achieved via voting, an open discussion of ideas, and specific institutional arrangements (such as the case of the United States Supreme Court, which acts as the arbiter of the federal system).

In both markets and politics, specialization and coordination must also occur intraorganizationally. Elections are critical to democracy, but most action in a democracy is conducted within and between policymaking branches. Many of the processes that have been studied in bureaucracies also are in evidence in legislative bodies, even though they differ fundamentally in their policymaking roles. A major issue in legislatures that is not so important in the formal hierarchies that characterize bureaucracies is how theoretically equal votes are combined into a collective decision.

We may know more about the U.S. Congress than any other single formal organization in the world, given the great amount of scrutiny that it has received from scholars as well as journalists. So it is to Congress that we turn to understand at least some of the most important facets of intraorganizational dynamics in a democratic political system.

The Legislative Division of Labor

For a moment let us take a general, but somewhat arbitrary voting situation in a legislature. Assume that legislators voting on a committee or in the chamber at large vote rationally. That means that in a structured vote they will vote for the proposal that is closest to them in issue space (see chapter 2). Now let us require that the winning candidate or proposal garners a plurality of votes, and that the candidates or proposals are voted on pairwise (as is the case in legislative and most committee voting).

In such situations, it has long been known that there is a winning proposal, that the winner will emerge regardless of how the alternatives are "paired" for voting, and that the winner will emerge regardless of whatever "fair" voting scheme is used. *And the winner is . . .* the proposal that is closest to the median voter. This important finding is known as the "median voter theorem."

There is, however, a caveat. The median voter theorem only holds if the alternatives can be arrayed on one dimension, or attribute. If there are two or more attributes, as depicted in figure 2.2, then all bets are off. In particular, it is quite possible that there will be no clear winner and the winning proposal will be determined by how the proposals are paired for voting. Because the possibility exists for voters to cycle through all the proposals, with each one being beaten by another, this situation is known as "issue cycling" (although it should be termed "proposal cycling"). Cycling gives the leadership of a committee or a legislature great potential power by determining the manner in which proposals are considered (see Fiorina and Shepsle 1989 for a nontechnical review).

Having legislative leadership exercise such agenda-setting power is not the general way, however, that matters are handled. Any multidimensional issue space may be broken into several distinct issues, and voted on one by one. Then there is an equilibrium position on each single issue. And we also know that the winner on each issue will be the median voter. If we can construct a political structure that will cause issues to be broken down one by one, then we will have solved the issue cycling problem. This solution is known as a "structure-induced equilibrium" because structures, rather than voter preferences, cause the equilibrium.

Legislative Committees

The primary example of a structure-induced equilibrium is a legislative committee system. If various committees each handle but one issue, then each can come to an agreement on a winning proposal. But have we just deferred the problem? What happens when all these issues considered by the committees are put back together for voting on the floor? Will issue cycling reemerge? If legislators possess diverse interests, and if they attain membership on committees based on their interests, then a system of deference to committee reports on the floor can ensure that issue-by-issue voting survives.

Unfortunately, we just come back to a set of mutually noninterfering subsystem oligarchies. Majorities don't have to tolerate these little oligarchies. When majorities are aroused to act, they can upset comfortable apple carts. The destruction of these little oligarchies is accomplished through democratic means, but only when majorities become attentive to the issue controlled by the oligarchy (committee/subsystem). In the case of the U.S. Congress, this destruction has been shown to occur empirically (Jones, Baumgartner, and Talbert 1993).

Decentralized democracies give entrepreneurial politicians the means to interfere with and even overturn structure-induced oligarchic subsystems. Note that it is not required that voters (or even congressmen) be informed all the time; just that they become attentive and mobilized occasionally—when a certain tolerance level, or what organizational theorist Chester I. Barnard (1938) called the "zone of indifference," is exceeded.

This sort of system is fundamentally responsive to the limitations on rationality—and in particular short-term memory limits—that characterize human thinking. Most legislators do not attend to all the issues that in theory could preoccupy the legislative process. The division of labor inherent in the committee system allows the legislative body to process far more issues than if the body as a whole were forced to handle each and every issue. Sometimes, however, an issue becomes highly salient, and this mobilization is signaled by heightened attention and emotional states by participants. Then the legislative body may intervene in the business of the committee, or a struggle for jurisdiction over the issue may ensue (King 1997; Jones, Baumgartner, and Talbert 1993).

The legislative committee system allows policymakers to compensate for the limitations on time, attention, and expertise of individual legislators. It is a mechanism that allows legislative bodies to acquire information—encouraging some legislators to specialize in a limited number of issues. But it runs afoul of a classic collective action problem: many legislators will be loath to participate unless they can receive some individual benefits. Better legislation might result, but there will be few suppliers of expertise (King 1997). The inducement to get legislators to specialize is the delegation of some control over the agenda process within their jurisdictions. If, however, the committee becomes too independent of the whole body, it will find that its recommendations to the chamber floor will not be accepted (Krehbiel 1991).

Under the so-called informational model of committee activity, the chamber majority is a passive recipient of proposals from the specializing committee system and decides whether to accept, reject, or modify those proposals. This tells much of the story, but there is more. First, committees have oversight as well as legislative powers, and thus can influence the implementation of legislation without the permission of the chamber. Second, despite the potential difficulties of bypassing a recalcitrant committee, chamber majorities or other committees may simply move legislation directly to the floor. Finally, committees have the opportunity to frame legislative proposals in a manner that attracts the interest of other members. In the 106th Congress (1998–2000), Republican tax committees reframed a generally unpopular tax reduction measure into a series of more popular targeted bills that could be associated with simple election slogans: "End the marriage tax and the death tax!"

It is certain that legislative committee systems did not come into being to solve the issue cycling problem. Legislative committees doubtless emerged to take advantage of the efficiencies of division of labor—to gather information and produce appropriate legislation. Committees and other decentralized arrangements allow organizations to process information partially in parallel rather than just serially (Jones 1994). That is, committees can process business simultaneously, avoiding the bottleneck of legislative floor action until the last minute. This process expands the capacity of the organization, essentially freeing it from agenda attention limits. The cost is that the committee may pursue objectives that contradict the wishes of the legislative body.

The legislative system of delegation and division of expertise results in an institutional "stickiness" in responsiveness to changing policy issues. Again we have an example of a formal organization adjusting both to its external environment and to its internal structure. The result of this dual adaptation is an alternation between periods of quiescence and tolerance of oligarchy and periods of activity and interference with the oligarchy—a punctuated equilibrium of policy change (Baumgartner and Jones 1993; True, Jones, and Baumgartner 1999).

Voting in Congress

The political world is multifaceted. First, issues themselves are complex, involving numerous considerations. Second, there exist many other stimuli that compete with an issue-focused politics—party and group identifications, ideological orientations, individual gain.

No organization can make decisions in a space of high dimensionality. A high-dimensional space is one where each solution to a problem (such as a bill before Congress) may be characterized by many attributes. Democratic organizations have particular difficulties here, because they are based on free discussion and majoritarianism. As a consequence, it is difficult to exclude consideration of a panoply of policy considerations.

There are two main difficulties with high-dimensional decision spaces, where a decision must be reached by a number of interacting individuals (such as a democratic legislature). First, there may be no agreement on the nature of the problem representation. The spaces of different individuals involved in the process may not correspond. Second, even if problem-space representations do correspond, we may face the issue cycling problem: the leadership may be able to manipulate the order of presentation of proposals to achieve an undemocratic result.

All decision-making institutions have mechanisms that reduce the dimensionality of the problem space facing participants. When votes are cast by committees or on the floor of the chamber, complex issues have been simplified. Mostly they have been simplified via the mechanisms of party and ideology. The trick for party leaders in a legislature, according to John Aldrich (1995), is to highlight the party cue such that individual legislators will be the organizing force for their voting behavior.

In parliamentary systems, party is the only cue. Legislators vote against their party leaders only at the peril of being excluded from the party. Of course, such systems can work only if the "back benchers" defer their judgments to those of the party leadership. In essence, the institution has simplified a complex space into a single dimension. Having thus simplified the complex political problem space, the voting decision itself often takes place in Newell's cognitive band (see chapter 4). Most floor votes never reach the rational band—they take place at the level of impression formation.

In the United States, party discipline is high—congressional scholars show that it is the most important explanatory variable in accounting for floor votes—but it is not absolute. Ideology, constituency opinion, and interest group claims occasionally compete for the vote of the American legislator. Ideology and constituency, of course, often correspond to party wishes. Parties are comprised of like-thinking legislators elected from roughly similar constituencies. But there is no doubt that party and ideology are different organizing principles for American legislators. For example, Hager and Talbert (2000) examined the voting records of congressmen who switched from one party to another, finding the voting behavior before the switch to be quite different from the voting pattern afterward.

Some rational choice proponents see ideology as an information shortcut. In this view, ideology is a rational method for dealing with complex political stimuli. In the electorate, it has the advantage of allowing efficient decisions in the face of very low probabilities of influencing the outcome (Downs 1957). In legislatures, where the probability of any one legislator influencing the outcome on a vote is much higher, ideology nevertheless serves to simplify decisions by reducing a complex high-dimensional problem representation to a simple unidimensional one (Hinich and Munger 1994).[4]

Ideology, however, is far more than a rational informational shortcut. People generally identify emotionally as well as cognitively with a political ideology. When they identify with a political ideology—"I am a conservative"—the ideology can serve to motivate them and, in effect, becomes a proximate cause of a decision.

Keith Poole and Howard Rosenthal (1997) have developed a quantitative scaling technique that arrays roll call votes in legislatures in a spatial format, and they have applied that format to roll calls in most U.S. Congresses. This has allowed them to trace the dimensionality of the Congresses throughout American history. Their technique suggests one prominent dimension—organized around party, or a general left-right dimension—but with a secondary dimension occasionally appearing. The second dimension has a strong regional component. It was prominent through much of the middle part of the twentieth century, but has declined in importance in recent Congresses. It is generally associated with the famous "conservative coalition" of Republicans and conservative Democrats.

Critics of the approach of Poole and Rosenthal have suggested that the metric scaling method they use tends to overcollapse complex data into low-dimensional spaces. They also argue that, even within the metric scaling system that Poole and Rosenthal use, there is considerable room for error, pointing to "other factors" that may go into the voting decision.

---

4. Or at least it simplifies a complex situation into a space of lower dimensionality. Hinich and Munger (1994) note that ideology can be multidimensional, as is indicated when we refer to "economic conservatives" and "social conservatives."

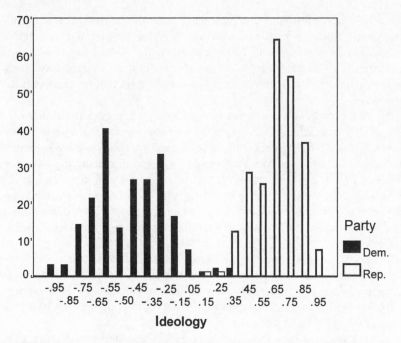

Figure 6.2   Party and Ideology in the U.S. House of Representatives,
                  105th Congress

Source: Calculated by the author from Keith Poole's Web Site (http://
voteview.gsia.cmu.edu/) Jan. 1999

Nevertheless, few political scientists would dispute the contention that
voting decisions are low dimensional in comparison to the complexity of
political stimuli. Somehow the legislative institution is acting to constrict
the problem space.

Figure 6.2 shows how closely the ideological dimension isolated by
Poole and Rosenthal has corresponded in modern Congresses to the partisan orientations of the members. Note how cleanly the ideological dimension cleaves the two parties (conservatism is to the right and is desig-
nated by the positive numbers.) There is practically no ideological overlap
between the parties! Very nearly all Democrats are more liberal than very
nearly all Republicans. This has not always been the case; in the past there
was considerably more overlap.

In the past, political scientists and many analysts of current events argued that the lawmaking process simply reflected the relative "liberalism"
of the legislative bodies. In effect, ideology or party cues served to move
the level of legislative behavior out of the intendedly rational and into the

cognitive band of behavior. So politics was simply about the ideological and party composition of the legislative body. But this view ignores how issues get defined on the basic dimension(s), a facet of politics that Poole and Rosenthal acknowledge (1997, xx). Much of the interesting activity in the lawmaking process involves what issues receive attention and how those featured issues are defined on the low-dimensional voting spaces.

The Debate Space, the Decision Space, and the Outcome Space

The world is complex, but unless we "pay inattention" to parts of it, our decision-making processes will be immobilized. On 22 July 1999, the House of Representatives passed, on a party-line vote, a ten-year plan to reduce income taxes by $792 billion. House Republicans were focused on the standard ideological message: reduce the size of government and allow people to make economic decisions on their own. By happenstance, chairman of the Federal Reserve Board Alan Greenspan was testifying before the House Banking Committee on the same day. Greenspan said, "I'm saying hold off for a while. And I'm saying that because the timing is not right" (Sanger 1999). Greenspan was concerned about the inflationary effect of a tax cut on a full-employment economy. Republicans had conveniently ignored the macroeconomic effects of their proposal, and were furious at Greenspan for highlighting an attribute that they had worked to suppress.

Policy debate generally occurs in a multifaceted "space" in which policy proposals may be characterized by a number of attributes. In the case of the tax cut proposal, at least three major dimensions of discussion emerged: the intrusiveness of the national government, the protection of popular programs (particularly Medicare and education), and the macroeconomic effects of the cut (hardly mentioned in press coverage until Greenspan's testimony). Yet the votes of members in the House can easily be arrayed along a single dimension, left to right. Just how this happens is not yet well studied, but the effects must be a combination of incentives wielded by party leaders relevant to the careers of members and the "bottleneck of attention" so critical in human decision making. In this case, decision makers must deliberately pay inattention to potentially relevant aspects of a complex policymaking situation in order to make the voting choice.

Figure 6.3 illustrates the collapsing of the multifaceted debate space concerning the Republican tax proposal into a single-dimensional decisional space. In the case of the tax cut, the attributes are clearly incommensurate; it is difficult if not impossible to weight the trade-offs between the three attributes. Heuristic strategies dominate such comparisons, and decision makers try to avoid having to make them. Legislators, being

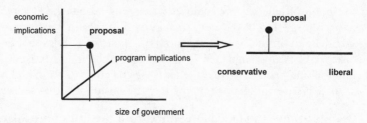

Figure 6.3   A Multifaceted Policy Debate Space Collapsed into a One-
Dimensional Decisional Space

bounded rationalists, tend to focus on one dimension to the exclusion of others. Democrats focused on the program implications of the cut, while Republicans focused on limited government. The chairman of the Federal Reserve talked about macroeconomic implications.

Research has generally supported three conclusions regarding public policymaking. First, the "policy debate space" is multifaceted. For example, a study of the topics addressed in congressional hearings between 1925 and 1990 uncovered four major dimensions: health and safety, economics and class conflict, regulation and debt issues, and urban policy. These dimensions waxed and waned in importance throughout the period, with economics and class conflict dominating until the late 1960s, when a more complex debate space emerged (Jones 1994, 149–54). Talbert and Potoski (2000) show that the bill introduction process is multifaceted.

Second, the "policy decision space" is low dimensional. Many studies have shown that congressional voting occurs in a low-dimensional decision space. Many studies conclude that the space is essentially one-dimensional, dominated by a scale of left to right that is highly correlated with political party (Poole and Rosenthal 1997).

Third, the "outcome space" is multidimensional. If and when the effects of the policy are tabulated, they tend to be multifaceted.

In an important study, Potoski and Talbert (1999) show that the voting patterns of congressmen for domestic programs that are distributed to states and localities fall along a single dimension. But the implementation of the programs, and in particular the distribution of the programs to localities, cannot be ordered along a single dimension. The criteria for distribution are multifaceted.

We lack the critical studies that would explain just how debate spaces and policy decision spaces are related. Clearly they may influence each other in complex ways. To the extent that the decision space is structured by ideology and political party, with their associated cognitive and emotional resonance for members, then the decision space will influence the manner in which legislators construct the debate space. Just as clearly, no decisions can be made in a high-dimensional space; there must be some mechanism to reduce the space to manageable proportions.

Legislatures operate to reduce decision-making complexity in a manner consistent with the limits imposed by individual cognitive capacities. Legislative organization allows a democratic system to do many things individuals, acting alone, cannot, but it also replicates some of the limitations that characterize human cognition. Most important are the serial carrying capacity dictated by the bottleneck of attention and the phenomenon of identification with subgoals (the political party, responsible for organizing legislative activity).

This dynamic involving a shrinking and simplification of the policy space and the substitution of a party-and-ideology space, is supplemented by a system of policy division of labor and deference. Legislative committees develop expertise in policy matters, and there is a tendency for

Box 6.2:   Policy Dimensionality

Psychologists and later political scientists have developed several methods for studying the underlying attributes of a complex policy space. Initial work by psychologists in the 1930s was motivated by the issue of whether a single dimension of general intelligence underlies a series of tasks, such as items on an intelligence test; L. L. Thurstone (1947) generalized the approach that came to be termed "factor analysis." Duncan MacRae (1958) pioneered the use of dimensioning techniques in the study of legislative voting in the 1950s.

A number of other scaling techniques have been developed, and all have a common goal and general method. The goal is to see if a matrix of data that represents the similarities between objects (which could be legislative roll call votes or items on an intelligence test) can be reduced in complexity to one or more ordered variables (termed the "factors," the "attributes," or the "dimensions"). Then the analyst studies how well the matrix of similarities can be reproduced by relying only on the "extracted dimensions."

Similarities may be measured in a number of ways. The common approach for legislative voting is to calculate correlation coefficients between pairs of votes (across the legislators). The resulting correlation between two roll call votes assesses how similar the support coalitions are between the two items.

members in the chamber to defer to the judgments of committees in floor votes. At some periods in American history, Congress has been more characterized by this system of expertise and deference; at others, more characterized by party and ideology. Compared to the recent past, today's Congress is quite polarized along the latter organizing principle.

Modularity

Human organizations are modular—they are composed of subsystems or subassemblies (Simon 1996b) that act both alone as freestanding units and together to form larger wholes. This is true of a single business firm, with its personnel, finance, and production units; it is also true of a democratic legislature, with its committees, party leadership, and floor activity.

What is true of single organizations is true of systems of organizations. Modern democracies consist of national legislatures, executives, and bureaucracies, but also local councils, mayors, and service agencies. Economies consist not only of a multitude of interacting firms, but crosscutting organizations of human activities—trade associations, labor unions, professional societies. A lawyer employed by a firm owes fealty not just to the firm, but to the legal principles of his professional association.

Almost all of the activities within and between organizations occur in the absence of central control. Most coordination occurs without a coordinator. Coordination proceeds with each subassembly following a set of quite simple, generally preprogrammed decision rules. The parts of the entire system are connected via a very limited number of "signals" that stimulate action. To the extent that an organization is tuned to a limited part of its environment, its attention problem ("information overload") is solved, as is the coordination problem. The strategy of subassemblies connected via very simple signals works superbly well in stable complex environments, but, as this book has repeatedly emphasized, can be a disaster in rapidly changing circumstances where a premium is placed on conscious analysis of the task environment.

Is modularity in human organization also in evidence in human thought? There is clear direct evidence of mental modularity (Fodor 1980). The suggestion of organization theorist James March (1994) that we can learn much about human cognition through the study of human organization is now being acted upon (Hutchins 1995). In effect, studies of human organization are field studies of human cognition, and ought to be treated as such. The link between formal organization and human thought is causal, not metaphorical. Through genetics and prepared learning, organisms are tuned to those parts of the environment that are most relevant to their survival. They are exquisitely sensitive to those cues, and have preprogrammed solutions to the repetitive problems they meet. As a consequence, organisms, including humans, can interact with their environments without fully comprehending them, and without spending much (any) cognitive resources on such repetitive problems (Clark 1997). Surely the manner in which we interact in formal organizations reflects this modular mind.

Political Organization and Human Cognitive Limitations

Formal organizations impose heavy constraints on the behavior of participants through formal rules and informal expectations. The payoff for adhering to these constraints is an extension of our adaptive capacities. We accomplish more working together than working separately.

On the other hand, organizations mimic the cognitive limitations of their human occupants. Organizations, like individuals, have attention spans. Organizations, like individuals, prepackage solutions to repetitive problems. Organizations, like humans, have trouble making decisions characterized by multiple attributes. Organizations operate in a modular fashion: subassemblies have limited communication with each other, and then communicate best through simple and easily interpretable signals. As a consequence, organizations disproportionately respond to the information from their environments.

Some aspects of organizational life aid in reducing the disproportionality in response, in particular, the ability to process information in parallel and the ability to call on people with diverse perspectives in constructing a problem space. Other aspects, however, can interfere with proportionate information processing, including the tendency of organization members to identify with subunits and their strict reliance on rules and procedures that do not properly capture the relevant aspects of the task environment.

Legislatures and public bureaucracies simplify decision making for participants. So do business organizations and labor unions and religious bodies. Given human nature this is inevitable, but it lends an interesting disjointed and episodic nature to social and political change, as we see in the next chapter.

CHAPTER 7

Efficient Markets, Efficient Politics, and the Index Problem

BECAUSE OF their cognitive architectures, people do not react in a proportionate manner to information they receive. Because the building blocks of organizations are people, organizations do not produce outputs in a proportionate manner to the information they receive. The cause of the disproportionate response is human biology.

Does this mean that people's decisions and organizational outputs are biased when judged objectively against the information they receive? Bias here means a consistent difference between what is expected based on the information and what people do in their decisions. The answer is no. The reason is that people are not irrational; they are boundedly rational. They adapt. But they adapt imperfectly. The result is a disjointed and episodic adjustment process.

Can we assess this disjointedness in real-world situations? This task is not as easy as the statement of it implies. Outputs from decision making are reasonably easy to obtain, but information flows are devilishly difficult to measure. We can't rely on the reports of decision makers, because they attend imperfectly to the environment. Nor can we rely on, for example, the media when we study government outputs, because the media tend to index government activity rather than monitor the problems that serve as the fodder for public policy (Bennett 1990). We can't rely on our own estimates, because we fall prey to the same selective attention problems that real-world decision makers do.

This chapter develops a method for assessing the extent of disjointedness in information processing that relies on the normal distribution to serve as a standard for assessing input distributions, and then compares output distributions to the normal. (A better name for the familiar bell-curve distribution is the Gaussian, after the mathematician who derived it. As we shall see, in decision-making the normal is definitely not "normal.") We expect output distributions to display two characteristics in comparison to the normal: more stationary values where nothing is changing (because no one is paying attention) and more punctuated, large changes when attention shifts and action is taken.

A Standard

Why would the Gaussian distribution serve as a standard for comparison? The reason has to do with the way in which information is combined. If there are lots of independent sources for the information, and if the many sources are combined additively, as we might construct an index, then the distribution of the index values would be Gaussian. For those unfamiliar with the central limit theorems that justify this, a simple example may help.

Suppose you are hammering a nail into a board. Most of us can hit the nail most of the time, but occasionally we strike glancing blows. Mostly these glancing blows are harmless, and many even help a little in driving the nail in the board. Once in a while, however, we miss the nail entirely, sometimes with tragic results for a nearby thumb.

The nail problem can be understood via the statistical theory of errors. Each strike we make is made up of a single "cause"—our directed hammer blow, plus the additive effect of numerous small factors. These small factors are very numerous, involving variations in how tight we hold the hammer, our concentration level, wind, lighting, the internal state of our retina, and the firing of our nerve endings. Mostly these many "error causes" are not very large, and because they don't generally operate in the same direction, they have a tendency to cancel one another out—at least in part. However, once in a while everything goes wrong, and our "mistake" causes us a sore thumb.

In the nail problem, and many, many like it, the distribution of blows (measured, say, as the distance from the very center of the nail) will approximate the Gaussian distribution. The vast majority of blows, even for us weekend carpenters, fall on or near the center of the nail. As we move away from the center, the number of blows falls, until very far away from the nail almost no blows fall. About the same number of blows fall in any direction from the center; the distribution of blows is symmetrical.

We can prepare a frequency distribution in which the x-axis is the deviation from the center of the nail and the y-axis is the number of blows (fig. 7.1). If we have a look at all the nails we hammer over the course of a building project, then the distribution will come closer and closer to the theoretical normal distribution.

Even a master carpenter will not hit every nail right in the center. But the distribution of blows around the center of the nail will be much tighter—that is, on average much closer to the center of the nail—than for most of us. (Close enough that the master carpenter's thumb is never in danger!) We say that the variance of the distribution of blows for the master carpenter is smaller than the variance for mine. But both sets of blows have the same shape—the normal distribution.

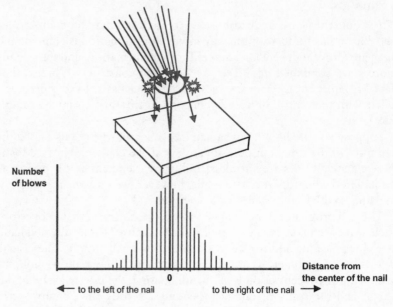

Figure 7.1   The Nail Problem

Now suppose you were buying and selling stock. You still want to hit the nail on the head, but that now means you want to make as much money as you can on the stocks you buy and sell. For any single stock there are lots of small factors that may affect why a stock gains or loses in value. You are now an information processor, combining in your mind the many factors that might affect a stock, deciding whether to buy or sell. If you are a rational market participant, you will nevertheless make some mistakes—because the numerous, minor factors that might affect a stock are not worth trying to assess, even if you could assess them. In effect, your decisions would not invariably hit the nail on the head, but rather would be distributed around the head. Sometimes you would buy too soon, sometimes sell too early, but most of the time you would come close to making a maximum profit on your effort.

The Efficient Market Thesis

You are not the only person buying and selling stocks today, however. You are involved in a complex game involving millions of participants making hundreds of millions of decisions every day. In what economists call an "informationally efficient" market, the price of a stock tomorrow cannot be predicted from the price of a stock today. The reason, as Paul Samuelson put the enigma, is this: "In competitive markets, there is a buyer for every seller. If one could be sure that a price will rise, it would have already risen" (1965, 41).

There will be plenty of price movement in the stock all right. But because all participants are fully rational, they will use up all of the available systematic information. That means they will fully value the stock. The next move of the stock cannot be predicted—it could be up or down. But because the factors that will affect the price of the stock (after it has been bid up or down by investors based on systematic information) are random, the distribution of the changes in a stock's prices—hourly, daily, or yearly—will be normal, and the average change will be zero.

The interesting implication of this, the so-called efficient market thesis, is that you can't make money buying and selling stocks. Money is made, according to the proponents of the efficient market thesis, because markets rise over the long run. Experts trained in this school invariably recommend a buy-and-hold strategy, usually of an index of stocks that reflect the whole market (Malkiel 1996).

The implication of the efficient market thesis is that a stock market (or other asset market, such as bonds) will follow a "random walk." In a random walk, we cannot predict the next step from previous steps. The future series of events is not predictable from the past. If we define the (daily) returns in a stock price as the price on day two minus the price on day one, and we make a frequency distribution of these daily returns over a long period of time, this frequency distribution will approximate a normal distribution—just as in the case of our hammer-and-nail problem. And for the same reasons: the many factors that could affect the price of a stock (or a whole market), when added up, mostly cluster around the average return, with very few changes a long way (either up or down) from the average return.[1]

The efficient market thesis hinges on how markets induce participants to process information. Market participants are single-minded (they

---

1. Financial economists have proposed more complex models of asset market behavior. The most important is the "random walk with drift," which suggests that the stock market drifts upward over time. Other models have been developed in which returns are correlated and hence not normally distributed, but which cannot be exploited by rational actors (see Fama 1970; Campbell, Lo, and MacKinlay 1997). They are not as persuasive behaviorally as the pure form of the model because they are consistent with a system of actors taking unpredictable nonrandom actions. If, for example, market participants react by ignoring most information by occasionally overreacting to it, then the result will be correlated, nonpredictable returns.

want to make money); they are rational. As a surprising consequence, efficient markets, the aggregation of vast numbers of individual exchanges, are random.

One might object that the "news," or "information set" as economists term it, might surprise market participants. But recall that the systematic part of the information set has already been removed, or "discounted," in the previous period's stock price. So if there are sensible expectations about the news, we have basically already discounted it. What about the leftover information? Here is what one proponent of the random walk hypothesis wrote some years ago: "[In efficient markets] the only price changes that would occur are those that result from new information. Since there is no reason to expect that information to be non-random in appearance, the period-to-period price changes of a stock should be random movements, statistically independent of one another" (Cootner 1964, 8).

Failure of the Efficient Market Thesis

For years, specialists in finance have noted that actual returns from stock markets have not fit the predictions from the efficient market thesis. The major problem is that there have been many more large-scale changes than would be predicted based on the random walk model, many more small changes, and far fewer moderate changes. On a day-to-day or week-to-week basis, changes in stock market returns have been mostly very small, but when there has been change, it has been more extreme than the efficient market thesis predicts.

If we plot the values of daily changes against the number of these changes in a "frequency distribution," we get a distribution that has a slender peak and fat tails in comparison to the normal. This is kind of like saying that in our nail problem of figure 7.1 we have hit our thumbs not just once in a very great while, but several times a day! On the other hand, for most of the rest of the time, we have been very close to the center of the nail.

Figure 7.2 represents a frequency distribution of all of the daily changes, in percentages, of the Dow-Jones Industrial Average from its inception in 1896 through 1996. The distribution consists of 27,594 data points arranged in categories. Figure 7.2 also depicts the normal curve that is predicted by the pure form of the efficient market thesis. Note that the distribution exhibits little or no skew; that is, one tail is not significantly larger than the other. The distribution is basically symmetric, but it is nevertheless clearly not normal. The shape of a frequency distribution is known as its "kurtosis." Distributions with slender central peaks and fat tails are known as "leptokurtic," while distributions with flat tops and small tails are called "platykurtic."

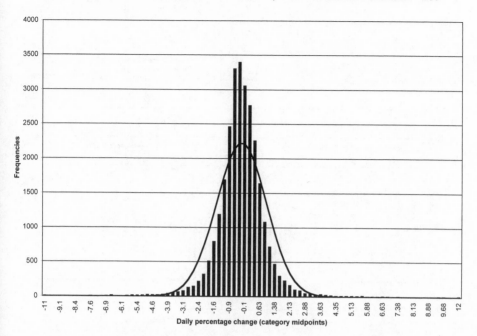

Figure 7.2   Frequency Distribution of Percentage Changes in the Dow-Jones Industrial Average, 1896–1996, Compared to a Normal Distribution with Similar Mean and Variance

The deviations of the DJIA from what is predicted from the efficient market thesis are shown in more detail in figure 7.3, which graphs the differences between the observed frequencies in the categories and the frequencies that would be predicted from the efficient market thesis.

Figure 7.3 shows graphically the excess cases in the center of the distribution and in the tails, and the paucity of cases in the "shoulders" or "wings" of the distribution. There are not an enormous number of cases in the tails of the distribution, but those few cases have great implications for the course of the stock market through time. On almost a thousand days during the first century of the Dow, the daily percentage change exceeded plus or minus 3 percent (622 days on which the DJIA gained 3 percent or more and 356 days on which it lost 3 percent or more).

What is just as striking is the market's seeming inability to make the moderate changes that would damp down the extreme shifts. On what might be thought of as "slow news days," the market barely moves. This is most of the time. On a handful of days, however, the market moves dramatically. What is missing is a more moderate response to changing

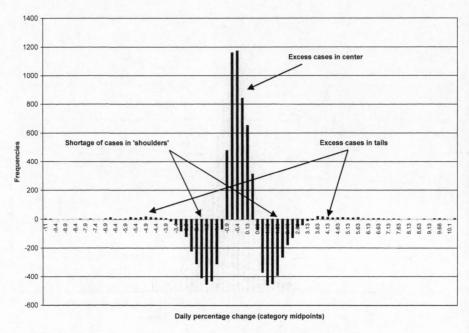

Figure 7.3   Differences between DJIA Actual Frequencies and the
                     Frequencies Predicted from the Efficient Market Thesis

circumstances, represented by the lack of cases in the shoulders of the distribution.

Some Explanations

So what is going on? There are two potential explanations for the deviations of figures 7.2 and 7.3. First, the news relevant to stock market prices does not arrive randomly, and second, market participants are not fully rational.[2]

Measuring the distribution of information that might move the stock market is difficult, but the evidence to date indicates that there is no systematic relationship between the news and major market moves. Whatever initiates such moves is not in the obvious part of the information set, and interviews with participants indicate that new information is not what is driving the change (Shiller 2000). But a considerable body of evidence has accumulated that market participants are not fully rational.

---

2. A third possibility involves complex modeling of the distribution of risk propensity of market participants. See Campbell, Lo, and MacKinlay 1997.

First, economic historians have noted the difficulty of explaining panics and crashes based on fully rational behavior alone (Kindleberger 1996). Second, some evidence comes from economic modeling. Economists have introduced elements of bounded rationality into their models, with considerable success in mimicking leptokurtic results. Thomas Lux (1995, 1998), for example, has introduced two elements of bounded rationality in his market models: emotion and contagion. The result is "sudden bursts of optimism and pessimism" (1998, 160) that correspond to the rapid growth and sudden bursting of financial bubbles. These processes result in the leptokurtic results depicted in figure 7.2.

The third source of evidence comes from experimental economics. Experimental economists have run toy economies in their laboratories, and have observed bubbles and crashes (Smith, Suchanek, and Williams 1988). Studies of the exploitation of common pool resources similarly yield pulses of investment and disinvestment, as we saw in chapter 5 (Ostrom, Gardner, and Walker 1994). Bubbles, crashes, and pulsing levels of activity imply the fat tails (representing the large changes) characteristic of leptokurtic change distributions. The experimentalists have also observed directly leptokurtic distributions in simulated markets (Plott and Sunder 1982).

The simulated markets may not reproduce all the elements of a real stock market, but they have one major advantage: they control for incoming information. We can rule out the notion that the news is arriving according to a leptokurtic distribution, because the distribution is, in effect, under the control of the investigators. Participants in the experimental markets are, in effect, generating all the news themselves, because there is no new information coming into the system. The bubbles, crashes, and leptokurtosis are endogenously generated—by the participants themselves. As a consequence, leptokurtosis in the output distribution cannot be linked to the shape of the input distribution.

The Cecilia Principle

Contagion may be the result of mimicking behavior in information cascades. In chapter 3, we noted that rational actors wishing to lower information costs may follow the lead of trusted sources, and that this can unleash cascading behavior. At the time, we questioned a major assumption of the so-called rational cascades: why would rational individuals treat others' observations on a par with their own, and why would they not recognize immediately what was happening to them in a cascade? Losses from a few days' cascades in asset markets can be extreme, so that it is indeed surprising to encounter a full-rationality model of information cascades that causes everyone to act in such a docile manner.

A little thought should convince one that information cascades cannot occur in efficient markets. The reason is what I term the "Cecilia principle" after a 1960s Paul Simon ballad. Turns out that when the singer comes back to bed after leaving his lover to use the bathroom, "someone's takin' my place."

Efficient markets work according to the Cecilia principle. If information cascades exist, they will not fully utilize available information. This will leave systematic information lying around for the picking, and someone will come in and exploit that information. This is essentially the principle of arbitrage, which exploits differences in the efficiency between two different asset markets. Computers in recent years have allowed increased exploitation of minor differences in market efficiencies.

The exploitation of information inefficiencies via arbitrage strategies pushes markets toward fuller and fuller efficiency in the use of incoming information. In an efficient market, lazy, copycat participants will be driven out (or at least they will give up their profits to more ambitious actors). As a consequence, information cascades would disappear (actually, never exist) in fully efficient markets. The behavior of participants would adjust for them.

Bounded Rationality Showing through in Markets

The theory of efficient markets provides a powerful standard for evaluating human behavior. In theory, there is nothing in the structure of a market to interfere with individual rationality. Markets are the sum of myriad individual decisions, all directed at the same objective: to make money. Systematic information is extracted by participants, leaving only a random residual to observe in the movement of stock prices. This random residual means that stock market returns will be normally distributed.

In the case of leptokurtic results in stock markets, it seems that the disjointed changes are due to the behavior of the participants, not the arrival of information.[3] And that behavior is not based in rational information cost–cutting strategies. Either these strategies are fully efficient, or they are not. If they are, then output distributions will be Gaussian. If they are not, and some participants use these strategies, others will arbitrage and pick up the profits left on the trading room floor. Output distributions will again be Gaussian.

The only explanation left is that participants, individually and collec-

---

3. There is one caveat. Participants may rely on news *reports,* which are themselves governed by the dictates of bounded rationality. In such cases, the news (as observed by participants) will arrive leptokurtically. But if indeed news reports are some sort of selected set of the universe of possible stories, one would question the rationality of relying on them.

tively, are not fully rational. Moreover, the difference between the normal distribution predicted by the efficient market thesis and the observed behavior of markets can be taken as a measure of the extent to which bounded rationality is showing through in that most adaptive of human institutions, asset markets.

The efficient market thesis is a powerful result of theoretical economics. It is not supported by the data. Does that mean the thesis is wrong? In one sense it is: it does not comport with the evidence. In another sense it is not: the distributions we observe are reasonably close to what is predicted. The observed distributions of stock market returns are not, after all, heavily skewed or bimodal, or rectangular. While there are systematic deviations from fully rational (and thus fully adaptive) behavior in markets, this by no means implies that markets are seized by complete irrationality (although they may be for brief, or even extended, periods of time). As a consequence, deviations from normality in markets may be taken as a measure of the extensiveness of bounded rationality showing through.

In the language of chapter 4, we will need to focus on information processing to understand aggregate behavior of stock markets. That is, we will need to take into consideration the process by which people make decisions. People, individually or aggregated in economic institutions, transform information as it comes to them.

The information that people use in the complex decisions of stock and bond markets comes from a diversity of sources. Market participants rely on numerous sources, all of which may contain some errors. As a consequence, we concentrate on how they combine the incoming evidence to make a decision.

Information Processing in Political Institutions

The power of the efficient market thesis can serve as a way to compare political and economic institutions. We have seen that the efficient market thesis makes strong predictions that fail to hold completely. It is possible to compare political institutions in a similar manner, using the efficient market thesis as a standard.

Of course political institutions aren't designed to be informationally efficient. In the United States, James Madison and the rest of the founding fathers deliberately designed a set of institutions that would not be overly sensitive to information, especially changes in public opinion. Political scientists think of political institutions as "sticky" because of their reluctance to move when the flow of information into them changes. The popular notion of "gridlock" embodies this seeming inability of political institutions to change in the face of new information.

On the other hand, democratic governments clearly respond to information. Elections are the mechanisms that enforce that responsiveness. So long as politicians are "ambitious"—so long as they want to retain office or go on to higher elective office—they will have motive to attend to information flows. Moreover, since most judgments of politicians by voters is retrospective—an evaluation of how things have gone while they are in office—elected leaders in a democracy have strong motive to solve problems before they fester and grow. And, because reelection is always an uncertain business, politicians have an incentive to pay attention to all sources of information, including news reports, group claims, public polls, contacts by constituents, etc. A considerable body of empirical evidence indicates that, indeed, public opinion matters in how congressmen vote and what policies governments pursue (Page and Shapiro 1992; Stimson, MacKuen, and Erikson 1995; Wlezien 1995).

There are actually two reasons that political institutions are "sticky." First, the structure of government, in the United States at least, allows a minority to block changes in the status quo. In many situations, it takes extraordinary majorities to change policies. Even if participants were fully rational, there would nevertheless exist a tendency to follow the status quo. These are the institutionally imposed decision costs noted in chapter 6. If, of course, an information flow were powerful enough, change would occur. The classic leptokurtic distribution of a slender peak and fat tails would occur in distributions of public policy outcomes even if participants were fully rational (so long as they had somewhat different policy preferences, as is always the case).

The second reason for us to expect that policy output distributions would be leptokurtic is bounded rationality. Like all of us, policymakers can ignore a change in information for a very long time before taking action, owing to short attention spans, organizational identification, and monitoring the behavior of others. When, however, change occurs, it tends to follow a pattern of alarmed discovery, emotional arousal, and contagion. These are the human factors showing through, just as in markets.

Unfortunately, in politics it is difficult for an objective observer to tell whether a rational institutional explanation or a boundedly rational human explanation accounts for the distribution of policy outputs. Indeed, a combination of both is highly likely. Unlike pure markets, democratic policymaking is not a simple sum of individual decisions. Governments do not just add up individual decisions. They translate individual decisions, weighted in complex ways, into collective ones, binding on members of society. This makes government and politics fundamentally different from markets.

On the other hand, this process offers us some degree of leverage in studying the translation of information into public policy. A sequence of events is necessary to make this translation, not a single, simple act, as in the case of markets. Some of these events are, in theory, more efficient than others. For example, voting is a more direct expression of preferences of citizens than, say, budgetary outputs. Voting is not, of course, a perfect reflection of preferences. In the United States, we normally get to choose between two major party candidates, and our winner-take-all, single-member district system reinforces this tendency. Nevertheless, it is reasonable to view the distribution of election-to-election voting changes as similar to market data—certainly more similar than policy outputs, affected as they are by "sticky" institutions.

Voting and the Absence of Realignments

In the 1950s, political scientist V. O. Key, Jr., set forth the outlines of what became the theory of election realignments. Studying historical voting records, Key noted the existence of what he termed "critical elections" that changed the course of electoral history (Key 1955). Walter Dean Burnham (1970) developed the theory historically, viewing critical elections as fundamental turning points in the development of American public policy. The Michigan school of voting behavior, discussed in chapter 3, contributed by using survey research to study the individual decisions comprised by the aggregate vote (Campbell et al. 1960, 1966).

The Michigan school explained historical election changes in terms of individual behaviors. Voters maintained a "standing commitment" to one party or the other. This standing commitment might deviate in elections where a particularly popular candidate was running, say, General Eisenhower in 1952, but would return to a "normal vote" in the next election. Occasionally, a large segment of voters would be shaken loose from their traditional party identifications. Such large-scale shifts in the party allegiances of voters are termed "realigning elections." These realignments could happen because of a catastrophic event or a change in the election issues, or because of "lurch" as the political system caught up to long-term changes in economics or demographics.[4] This movement of groups of voters from one party to another might reinforce the winning coalition, as it did in 1896, or change completely the dynamics of elections, as in the 1928–32 period.

Realignment theory is firmly based in bounded rationality, particularly organization identification. Indeed, the theory postulates such strong emotional organizational identifications with the parties that they stunt

---

4. It is also possible that voters drifted from one party to another over the course of several elections. The full story is told in Mayer 1995.

the adaptive adjustment process to the extent that major traumatic events are necessary to cause serious election change.

Realignments imply leptokurtic distributions. If we were to plot election-to-election changes over a long period of time, we would expect to see most elections cluster around the center—very little change in the pattern of standing allegiances for most elections. Once in a while, however, a major change would occur, falling in the fat tails. Very few cases would fall in the shoulders, or wings, of the distribution.

There is, however, a second hypothesis. In this approach, parties are the creations of ambitious, election-driven politicians (Aldrich 1995). Politicians play the part of entrepreneurs in market economies, immediately responding to the preferences of voters for "packages" of public policies. This suggests a relatively efficient response to information because of the activities of entrepreneurial politicians. Elections, under the hypothesis that their processes are relatively informationally efficient, would have output distributions similar to the stock market.

There is some observational evidence in support of the Aldrich thesis. First, in the midst of a major shift in the issues underlying partisan divisions in American presidential politics in the 1960s and 1970s, no firm evidence of realignment has occurred. Many novel explanations have been proposed, including the hypothesis that voters—or at least enough voters to influence outcomes—deliberately split their tickets to try to achieve divided government (see Fiorina 1996).

Second, Peter Nardulli (1995) has produced a phenomenally complete analysis of presidential elections since 1824 at the county level. He finds scant evidence of national realignments, but points to a series of "rolling realignments" that are regionally based. Nardulli's evidence is particularly persuasive, because it eliminates increasing sophistication of voters in the postwar years as a potential explanation of the apparent pattern of failed realignment since 1968.

Nardulli's data may be plotted in a frequency distribution similar to the stock market data discussed above. Figure 7.4 represents the distribution for 110,004 observations on election margin swings on U.S. counties for presidential elections from 1824 through 1992.[5]

The lesson of figure 7.4 is that presidential elections look like stock markets. Both are leptokurtic, having more slender central peaks and fatter tails than the corresponding normal distribution. But neither is wildly

---

5. The election data are "pooled" across time and counties. Each of the 110,004 observations is an election margin swing from one election to the next on one county for one election. Election swings are defined so that positive changes are in the direction of the Democrats; negative changes are changes toward the Republicans.

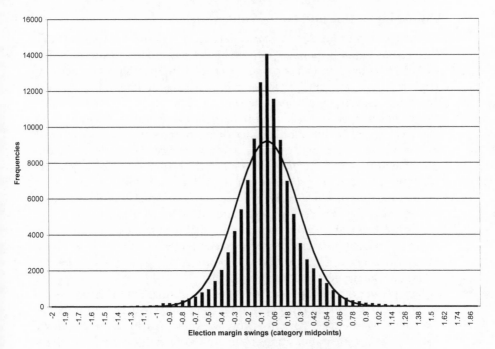

Figure 7.4   Frequency Distribution of Election Margin Changes in
                    County-Level Presidential Elections, 1824–1992, Compared
                    to a Normal Distribution with Similar Mean and Variance

Source: Peter Nardulli, personal communication

pathological in comparison to the normal, either. Elections seem to have
been reasonably efficient as information-processing devices. Elections are
subject to large swings from one party to another, but that is not typical.
Markets are similarly subject to wide swings, but they do not normally
"melt down" instantaneously.

Obviously this is a judgment call, but I read these data as signaling that
these two central institutions of capitalist democracies are not wildly out
of line with what theories of adaptive behavior predict. On the other hand,
we are most certainly observing bounded rationality "showing through."[6]

---

6. Tracy Sulkin and I have plotted distributions of returns from congressional elections,
with far more leptokurtosis in evidence. There are good reasons to expect that congressional
elections will be far "stickier" than presidential elections. This is due both to reelection-
driven politicians trying to ensure their survivability via constituency service, and to the in-
attentiveness of the public to the details of congressional elections (Jones and Sulkin 2000).

Public Budgeting and Policy Subsystems

If we now jump to the end of the sequence of actions that are necessary for producing public policies, we find an entirely different pattern. Political scientists have known for a very long time that much policy activity tends to occupy the limelight for only brief periods of time. When a policy area, such as welfare reform or deregulation, moves out of the limelight, two things happen. First, like all policies, the new policy, assuming one was passed, will be difficult to change owing to the structural "stickiness" of governing institutions. Second, only those directly interested in the policy tend to participate in it, even when the system is completely open. Most of us have neither the time nor the will to participate vigorously in the many arenas in which policy is made. As a consequence, policy is made within policy subsystems. These subsystems are "nearly decomposable"— nearly independent—of the normal policymaking process. They can exist for years without interference from citizens, and with only sporadic interest by the congressional oversight committees of the executive branch's Office of Management and Budget (OMB).

Subsystem politics implies incremental budgeting. But in chapter 6 we saw that the incremental theory of budgeting failed to account for major punctuations in budget patterns. Now we know that these punctuations are associated with mobilizations by interested parties—politicians, interest groups, concerned citizens—to alter the status quo. And since these patterns involve shifts in attentiveness and emotion, they are as much a part of a boundedly rational budget process as incrementalism, with policymaking only by the interested, is.

Because of the limits imposed by the cognitive abilities of political actors and the governmental structures within which they operate, we expect that information processing in public budgeting will be highly inefficient. That means that a frequency distribution of budget changes should deviate very substantially from the standard curve, and it should do so by a wider margin than either elections or markets. Figure 7.5 shows that indeed this is the case.[7]

Unlike the figures presented above, figure 7.5 is a very messy diagram. But we can learn much from it. First, unlike elections and markets, the budget distribution is highly skewed. There are far more large increases than large decreases. In part, this is for a simple technical reason:

---

7. The frequency distribution consists of 2,637 observations of year-to-year changes in percentage changes in inflation-adjusted congressional budget authorizations, pooled across domestic policy subfunctions. A subfunction is a group of governmental functions that are similar, as judged by the U.S. Office of Management and Budget. Domestic subfunctions alone are used to minimize external influences.

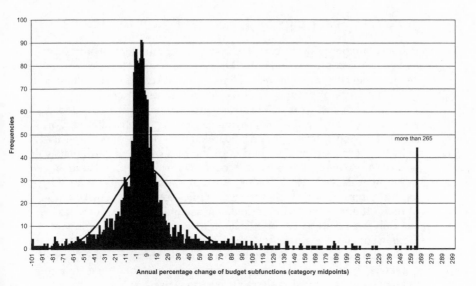

Figure 7.5   Annual Percentage Changes of U.S. National Government
Budget Authority, by Domestic Policy Subfunctions, FY1947–
FY1996

percentage increases are unbounded, whereas percentage decreases are bounded. If the whole budget of an agency is eliminated, the percentage change is −100 percent. In part, the skew reflects the fact that program start-ups usually involve large budget increases over several years. But a simple count indicates that there is more growth than decline in subfunctions. On the other hand, it may surprise many that there are as many program cutbacks as there are. Cutbacks are not an uncommon occurrence.

In the second place, program growth tends to be more abrupt than program cuts. Notice that the "shoulders" of the distribution are not the same. There are more cases in the left side than the right. This means, in effect, that big cuts are more difficult than big increases. This is no surprise, but it is reassuring that our technique of frequency distributions is sensitive to such information.

Agenda Setting in Congress

As part of a comprehensive project on the dynamics of agenda change in the United States, conducted with Frank Baumgartner, I have studied a variety of other frequency distributions that are "in between" elections

Box 7.1:   Complex Systems and Power Functions

Readers familiar with the complex systems literature may be intrigued by the distributions presented in this chapter. If one plots percentage change frequency distributions like the ones presented in this chapter of certain physical phenomena, they are not normal. Rather, they are Paretian (after the great Italian sociologist/economist who developed a model for studying income distributions). Paretian distributions, or power function distributions, are leptokurtic—slender peaks and fat tails. In particular, the distribution of the occurrence of earthquakes (size of the earthquake versus the frequency of occurrence) is Paretian.

Physicist Per Bak (1996) has suggested that such phenomena, including his famous sandpile laboratory example, are "self-organized criticalities." If one drops grains of sand on a sandpile, the pile grows incrementally but is subject to episodic landslides. The Paretian distribution of landslides implies a paucity of modest slides.

Bak thinks that nature (perhaps including human nature) "self-organizes" to the point that the system is generally stable, but is subject to large punctuations when destabilizing forces are strong enough.

Simple tests on our sample budget distribution show that the positive side is Paretian, and unmistakably so. But none of the other policy and market distributions I have studied are Paretian. Actually they are of an intermediate form between the normal and the Paretian—the exponential distribution.[8] I have detailed the reasoning for this finding elsewhere (Jones 1999a, 1999b). It may be a more general aspect of complex systems: LaHerrere and Sornette (1998) report that many of the supposed power distributions are in fact stretched exponentials (a general form of the exponential).

and budgets in the likelihood that the structure of government would affect the outcome. For example, I have studied the year-to-year change in the scheduling of congressional hearings, across a set of content categories reflecting policy activity, in the period 1947 through 1994. Compared to changing agency budgets, scheduling hearings is easy. They of course re-

---

8. It might be objected that the percentage change distributions I use bias the findings away from the Paretian. In many cases, pooled data require percentage change data (or other standardization) because the units are of such different sizes. National government subfunctions are a good example. In any case, the objection can hold only for decreases, and, except for the budget data, all distributions I have studied are exponential.

quire the attention and interest of committee chairs, and they involve the time and energy of staff that could be used productively elsewhere. But the entrepreneurial, ambitious politician will be sensitive to changes in public opinion, and will try to raise the level of attentiveness to policy areas that he or she can influence. Since agenda processes are disjointed, we expect that committee processes will also be disjointed, but in a fashion intermediate between shifting election allegiances, on the one hand, and budget changes, on the other. And, indeed, that is what we do find: a distribution that is more leptokurtic than voting behavior (or markets), but less than budgets. In essence, the flow of information from the environment affects the scheduling of hearings relatively more easily than the modification of budgets. Adaptation to the external environment is more pronounced in scheduling; adaptation to internal demands is relatively less pronounced. Less leptokurtosis is the result.

A good summary measure of changing legislative agendas is the extensiveness of coverage of legislative issues by "inside the beltway" publications. Publications such as the *Congressional Quarterly* monitor and report ongoing legislative activity, essentially following rather than leading legislative activity. Our agendas project has coded the extent of *Quarterly* coverage of nineteen major policy categories for most of the postwar period (Baumgartner, Jones, and MacLeod 1998). If we calculate year-to-year percentage changes within each category, and pool the data across the categories, we observe the characteristic leptokurtic frequency distribution (fig. 7.6). The shift in year-to-year coverage is not smooth, but abrupt, as legislators react to an emerging basket of issues that is substantially different each year. But neither is it as leptokurtic as budgeting.

Immoderation in Politics and Economics

We take away three important lessons from the study of the distribution of political and economic change. First, the distributions are all roughly similar in form—from markets to elections to congressional activity to government budgets.

Second, the standard in adaptive behavior for informationally efficient institutions, the normal distribution, is not met in market data. It is even less in evidence in those political institutions that are not designed to be informationally efficient. In social change data, the normal is not "normal." Leptokurtosis is the norm.

Third is the absence of moderation in processes of economic and political change. Humans, even within institutions that bring forth adaptive, rational behavior, are not very good at smooth responses to external circumstances. In many cases, of course, external events force themselves on

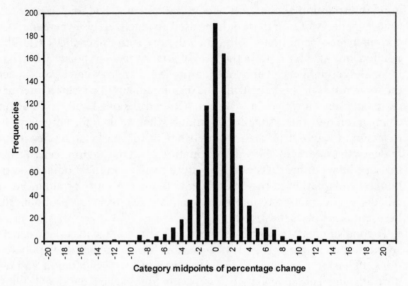

Figure 7.6   Annual Percentage Changes in the Amount of Coverage of
                    Nineteen Policy Issues by *Congressional Quarterly*, 1946–94

people as crises or traumas. But in many cases it can be argued (as second-guessers always do) that the recession, or foreign policy crisis, or the voter revulsion at "policy as usual" should have been foreseen. Information was almost always there; we just failed to attend to it.

As a consequence, we are always shifting attention, in an ongoing juggling act, to those aspects of the environment that are most relevant. In this juggling act, unlike the master juggler, we lose sight of lots of balls. Sometimes it takes dropping one (in an old but apt metaphor) before we attend to it.

There is a direct connection between the limits to individual rational adaptation discussed in earlier chapters and the distributions of collective activities in markets and politics detailed here. The "immoderation" we observe in political and economic change data corresponds to changes in the relative weights of the attributes in the basic decision-making model described in chapter 2. As we recognize the relevance of new factors, our decision-making choices may change, and change abruptly.

We have limited capacity in our short-term or working memory. Yet many, many factors potentially indicate that a change may be in the offing. Monitoring these factors and combining them appropriately to indicate what we should do is a monumental task—given our short-term memory limits. We employ all sorts of aids to calculations, from the "yellow pad" to the digital computer. But we also are influenced by the views of others.

Implicit Indexes and Cybernetic Decision Making

Much of the disjointed nature of organizational outputs comes from the manner in which people combine information from lots of different sources. Organizing information from diverse sources in a useful fashion invariably means index construction—either explicitly or implicitly. An "index" is a combination of factors that constitute a complex phenomenon. In economics, we have stock market indicators, price indicators, leading and lagging indicators, consumer sentiment indicators, and a host of others. In politics, we have presidential approval scores, interest group ratings of legislators, indexes of military strengths of nations, tax burden and effort scores, quality of service scores, and many others. Implicitly, every congressman "keeps tabs" on the pulse of his constituents via polling, newspaper coverage, constituent calls, and meetings at home. We have indicators of religious liberty, of conservative or liberal voting in legislators, of the "livability" of cities, of fitness to be admitted to college. We use these indicators, in the best case, to predict the future.

Sometimes, in structured decision-making situations, we employ a "formula" to combine these diverse sources of information, as is the case for a law school admission committee or a loan officer in a bank. The formula relieves us of the pressure of discretion. But, like all preprogrammed strategies, it can fail to match current circumstances.

The "index problem," however, does not just affect explicit formulas. Everyday life, from crossing the street to buying a home, involves the combination of diverse sources of information. Because of limitations on the ability to comprehend numerous factors at once, we construct "implicit indexes" of the complex world around us. Sometimes these indicators are based on a single factor, sometimes several factors. In any case, over time these indicators change in how they relate to reality. They are also subject to shifts in the salience of their various components in the face of no real change in the aspects of the external world they are supposed to measure. For example, in strategic situations, indexes may be manipulated by actors in order to shift the image held by another—often by directing attention to one component among the many comprised by the index (Jervis 1970, chap. 7).

Let us take the case of the reelection-driven congressman. Douglas Arnold (1990) sees legislators as most concerned with estimating their individual constituency's "potential preferences" on an issue, adjusting their

Box 7.2:   Handling the Senator's Mail

Responding to constituent input is a primary concern of elected politicians. Senator Patty Murray of Washington receives more than five hundred pieces of mail a day, in the form of letters, telephone calls, faxes, and e-mail (almost half are now via the latter source). The manner in which she handles communication is more or less typical of the modern legislator.

This deluge of information must be organized to be useful, and the organization is handled by a set of simple decision rules. Staff and interns screen the incoming mail, and route the constituent mail to an office specialist. The office specialist generally answers the query on behalf of Senator Murray, using a set of form letters generated by a computer program used by most senators (Quorum). If the constituent is raising a specific problem with government, the mail is forwarded to the Seattle office, which specializes in casework.

The D.C. staff keep tabs on the number of contacts on each topic, and on contacts by "VIPs." Once a week a "mail memo" is prepared for the senator, indicating the distribution of contacts and the sources in the case of VIPs (Drewel 1999).

Note that (1) handling correspondence is routinized; (2) specialization of labor characterizes the process; (3) data are summarized in a format useful to the senator in responding to particular concerns and in updating her "implicit index" of constituent concerns.

The process of handling the mail should also illustrate why polling will always be only a part of the modern legislator's implicit index. At their best, poll questions are hypotheticals. Mail involves real people in contact about real problems. On the other hand, mail may be stimulated by interest groups (and staff members make sure legislators know this proportion, where it is evident). The implicit indicator construction process always involves combining diverse information from numerous fallible sources.

voting before the legislative body accordingly. Congressmen are not interested in estimating all potential preferences that constituents might have, only those that may be evoked in a campaign by opponents. In estimating potential preferences, legislators do not usually rely on scientific opinion polling, because of their expense and limitations in estimating what citizens might be interested in, in any given context. "Instead," writes Arnold, legislators use a form of political intuition that comes with experience. They talk with and listen to their constituents, they read their mail, they watch how past issues develop over time, they look for clues about salience and intensity, they consider who might have an incentive to arouse public opinion, they learn from one another and from others' mistakes. . . . [L]egislators need only combine estimates from various sources in order to estimate their own constituents' potential preferences. (1990, 10)

How do decision makers combine the information that they receive and make decisions from it? We break this question into two parts. First, how would a fully rational actor combine and decide? Then how would a boundedly rational actor deviate from this ideal?

Rational Decision Making with Implicit Indicators

In any decision-making situation, a rational decision maker would construct indexes of the diverse information coming in. These indexes would be a weighted sum of the information from the various sources that might have a bearing on future action. A fully rational actor (hypothetically not subject to information costs) would continuously monitor and update this index.

Figure 7.7 illustrates this "implicit indicator" model. Our hypothetical rational decision maker constructs indicators, implicitly or explicitly, to monitor the state of the world he or she faces. The indexes are a combination (usually a weighted average) of several different data sources. In a manner similar to the hypothetical information stream facing the rational

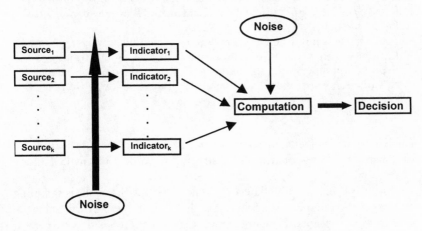

Figure 7.7   Implicit Indicator Model of Decision Making

Box 7.3:   The Central Limit Theorem and Implicit Indicators

The central limit theorem (CLT), the most important theorem in applied statistics, says that the average of a sample of observations drawn from some population is approximately distributed as a normal distribution, under certain conditions. There are many forms of the theorem, and statisticians continue active research on the theorem.

The most basic form of the theorem goes as follows. If we draw a sample from a hypothetically infinite population, then as the sample size goes to infinity, the sample mean is distributed normally with mean equal to the population mean and variance equal to the population variance divided by n, the sample size. Of course we don't ever draw infinite sample sizes in everyday life, so the question becomes how fast the distribution of sample means converges to the normal distribution. It turns out that the convergence is quite rapid. Each of the samples we draw must be from a similar distribution, and they must have finite variances. But the shape of the underlying distribution can be anything!

More specifically, suppose we take a random sample, $X_1, X_2, X_3, \ldots$ X_n, from an infinite population with mean μ and standard deviation σ. Then let us form the sum of these observations. Hypothetically, we could repeat this sampling exercise over and over again. If we did, then the distribution of these sums would approach a normal distribution as the sample size n goes to infinity.

It turns out that the CLT is quite robust with respect to violations of the premises from which it is derived. Samples may be drawn from different distributions; they may be correlated; and they may be weighted (all within limits).

An index is just a sum of observations (oftentimes a weighted sum). Each observation can be seen as a sample of 1 from a distribution of hypothetical observations. If an index is calculated from n of these observations, it can be viewed as a sample analogous to the above.

participant in an efficient market, we may use the implicit indicator theory to construct a "hypothetical input stream" for a decision maker in any institution.

A fully rational actor will make mistakes, because he or she is sampling information from a noisy world. Note that "noise" (error) will enter the system at two points. First, the sources are themselves subject to error; they consist of a signal and noise. Every observation of data is fallible.

There is every reason to believe that the noise is normally distributed, since such measurement error is comprised of numerous small factors (Guilford 1954, 28–29). The central limit theorem tells us that even if these factors are themselves not drawn from normal distributions, they will nevertheless in the limit be normally distributed (See box 7.3).

Second, noise will enter the computational process. The implicit computations are sums of fallible data, but we know that each datum for the index is drawn from normally distributed data. Now if a decision maker is trying to decide on a course of action, he or she must combine the indexes into some measure that will assess (empirically) the probability that action ought to be taken. If the indicators are summed or averaged to indicate the probability that action ought to be taken, then the distribution of action-relevant probabilities ought to be normally distributed— again by the central limit theorem.

The resulting index would form a normal distribution over time for a single decision maker (or, similarly, would form a normal distribution for a number of similarly situated decision makers at one point in time). If the rational decision maker were to adjust his or her decisions directly to the indicator, then the decisions made would follow a normal distribution. In this manner, information from outside the decision maker (or the decision-making institution) would dictate the outputs of decision making.

Bounded Rationality and Implicit Indicators

Bounded actors are disproportionate information processors. What does this mean in the context of index construction for decision making? A boundedly rational actor subject to attention limits would combine only a subset of these indicators, and would update them sporadically rather than continuously (Steinbruner 1974). It is easy to see that under such circumstances a continuously changing input distribution would be transformed into an index that would change either not at all (when not updated) or considerably (when updated). Moreover, because the entire index would be a subset of the diverse objective information flows, the entire system could become seriously biased over time, and would need reconfiguration.

Think again of the overloaded legislator or bond buyer, or any other decision maker in a changing situation. Employing an implicit indictor approach, the decision maker would monitor diverse sources of information from the environment. But short-term memory limitations and the difficulty in making smooth trade-offs between the attributes characterizing a task environment means that not all variables will be monitored all of the time. These facets also mean that the decision maker will tend to gravitate to a "favorite" indicator or two and follow them more closely than others. This may be fine in static environments, but with even a little change, the whole system will increasingly misrepresent the task environment. In the language of problem solving, the construction of the problem space (based on multiple information sources) will not fit, and may fit more poorly over time.

The decision maker is likely to need to add more "favorite" indicators to the index, or to readjust the weights of those in the index. But this updating will be attention driven. The stochastic implication of this model would be leptokurtosis, with clustered outputs when the index was not updated and punctuations when it was, with further punctuations at reconfiguration time.

The implication is this: regardless of the informational input distribution, the output distribution in efficient institutions with boundedly rational actors will be leptokurtic. This is a direct consequence of the fact that humans are disproportionate information processors.

Lepokurtosis in output data has an important implication for decision making. Change data from human institutions have, in comparison to the Gaussian distribution, an excess of cases in the central peak, an excess of cases in the tails of the distribution, but a paucity of cases in the "shoulders," the area between the central peak and the tails. The general substantive interpretation of these results is that change in human institutions tends to be quite conservative—most cases clustered around a central peak—but is subject to occasional quite large punctuations (the tails). On the other hand, moderate change, as represented in the shoulders of the distribution, seem underrepresented—at least in comparison to the Gaussian. It would seem that a hypothetical decision maker would have to be prepared either for virtually no change or a very large change—he or she could not hope for moderate adjustments to changing circumstances (Jones, Baumgartner, and True 1996).

Conclusions

In a complex and noisy world, decision makers must find ways to combine fallible data from numerous sources and act on it. An index, implicit or explicit, is such a combination. Fully rational decision makers using indexes will make mistakes, because the world is noisy and the data are fallible. Even the best of decision makers will make mistakes, but the mistakes are mostly manageable, because the index will be distributed normally. As a consequence, decision makers who maximize will produce normally distributed output distributions. These output distributions will mirror the input distribution. As a consequence, decision makers in informationally efficient institutions, such as pure markets and elections, will produce normally distributed outputs.

Bounded decision makers, however, take the input distribution and transform it. By paying sporadic attention and updating episodically, they produce leptokurtic output distributions. This behavior causes institutions to behave more erratically than they would under our hypothetical fully rational decision makers.

CHAPTER **8**

The Design and Evolution of Formal Institutions

BY ALLOWING people to achieve goals they could not accomplish alone, formal organizations let people escape their biologically imposed limits, but they also reflect many of those limits. In chapters 6 and 7, we examined how the tension between human adaptation to their external environment and adjustment to the internal cognitive architecture leads to disjointed and episodic decision making and organizational outputs. Now we address one final issue: how do organizations adjust over time to this balancing act of human nature? On the one hand, we would expect that, through trial-and-error learning, organizational structures would evolve over time to match the environment better while simultaneously harnessing human thought processes in a more effective fashion. On the other hand, particular facets of human cognition, and particularly the tendency to identify with organizations, suggest that such changes will not be simple and smooth.

At one time, social scientists thought that social systems could be seen as functioning at general equilibrium. The notion of general equilibrium was not viable empirically, and has been replaced by those who analyze social systems within a framework of partial equilibria and those who dispense with the notion of equilibria entirely. The evolution of organizational structure implies that the notion of general equilibrium is not sustainable, but it also implies that the static partial equilibria are but way stations in a more interesting evolutionary process.

Two Great Social Equilibria

At midcentury, social scientists had developed two comfortable notions of market economies and liberal democracies. Systematic thinking, more developed in economics than in political science, laid bare the essentials of open systems—markets and democracies—and showed how they possessed the characteristics of scientific equilibria. Not only was a stable configuration of social forces achieved, but as if by magic, these equilibria fostered the social good. Both were based on bare-bones conceptions of institutions—a few rules that channeled behavior and offered incentives

186

for participants. Both were attempts to emulate physics—economics with its "marginal analysis" that allowed the use of calculus, political science with its "vectors of force" that, in balance, produced public policy.

Economists showed mathematically how capitalist markets achieved a social optimum equilibrium by balancing the self-interested preferences of participants weighted by their ability to pay. Political scientists argued in nonmathematical terms how collective good was achieved by self-interested preferences weighted by the willingness of citizens to participate in interest groups.

Classical marginalist economics has provided the primary paradigm for the discipline of economics for a century. Economists showed analytically that the pure pursuit of self-interest in free and open markets would lead to a dynamic equilibrium in which no one could be made better off without someone else suffering. Markets, it was said (and proved mathematically) were at "Pareto optimum." If everyone were fully rational, then free markets would yield a global equilibrium where no one could be made better off without making someone else worse off.

An immediate objection is that it might be worth it to make a few worse off in order to make lives better for many. The economists pursuing this approach refused to consider such intersubjective comparisons of utility. Maybe we would have a better society if I sacrificed for you, they said, maybe not. But how would we ever know? Only a Supreme Being could weigh the well-being of one individual against another's, choosing to benefit some at the expense of others. Any human choice in this would have to be arbitrary.

But some political scientists have thought that not only can such choices be made, but that they are made every day in government. A school of thought known as "group theory" saw the responsiveness of elected officials to group demands—a contingency enforced by the uncertain nature of upcoming elections—as enforcing just such comparisons. An "equilibrium of interests" was achieved in open, democratic politics, and it automatically prioritized preferences through a kind of self-weighting scheme. Preferences were weighted by the actions taken by groups pursuing interests in the political arena. The more groups committed themselves to political action, the more important their preferences were. Political equilibrium was achieved by the balancing of interests, which themselves were weighted by their (imputed) importance. Liberal democratic politics were at "Truman equilibrium."[1]

---

1. This is my terminology—after Columbia University political scientist David Truman, whose book *The Processes of Government* codified the group theory of politics. As might be expected, group theory never came anywhere as close as neoclassical economics to providing

The End of the Global Equilibrium

Both of these intellectually impressive attempts ultimately failed. They failed for similar reasons: first, people didn't conform to the models, and second, the bare-bones institutions didn't work as they were supposed to.

The development of game theory delivered a hard blow to the notion of Pareto optimim economic equilibrium. The major point of the prisoners' dilemma game is that self-interested maximization is not enough to ensure a socially optimum equilibrium. Today economists accept that many equilibria exist in modern economies, and they analyze how one is chosen over others. And empirical studies in the laboratory continue to pile up evidence that the comprehensive rationality necessary for the mathematical demonstration of equilibrium are simply not met by consumers.

Even harder blows have been struck at group theory. From public choice economist Mancur Olson (1965) came the question of why rational self-interested individuals would join an interest group in the first place. Why wouldn't they just wait until the group had gained its benefits from politics, which they would enjoy too? From political scientists came a barrage of criticism. First, the "Truman equilibrium" was undemocratic, since under its effects only those who had resources could speak in politics. E. E. Schattschneider (1960) penned his famous aphorism that "the pluralist chorus sings with an upper-class accent." Others pointed out that democratic institutions tended to devolve into subsystems, which worked on the principle of mutual noninterference, not balance of interests. Small-scale oligarchies, with the interested holding both power and resources over limited areas of public policy, developed. And the masses, armed only with the vote, sat it out on the sidelines. An equilibrium of sorts existed, but it was an undemocratic one indeed.

Finally, the internal operation of organizations that comprise markets and democracies—the firms, labor unions, interest groups, and public agencies—did not operate according to the simple barebones principles of general equilibrium. One needs to know much about how these formal organizations work to understand how democracies work (Simon 1997c).

These attacks made social scientists perhaps more critical of markets and democracies than these institutions in operation would warrant. Most political scientists today probably agree with Winston Churchill's state-

---

a base for analysis for the discipline—primarily owing to the limited scope of group theory and the empirical demands of the behavioral revolution. On the other hand, the notion of intensity-weighted preferences has had staying power. For example, Richard Hall (1996) has studied the participation of congressmen in committee deliberations as an indicator of the intensity of their policy preferences.

ment that democracy is the worst form of government, except for all the rest. A similar statement likely holds for capitalist economies.

The bottom line: institutional design is more complex than general equilibrium in economics and pluralism in political science have assumed. There doesn't seem to be any fundamental institution that can rely on the simple motives of its participants to ensure the public good. For our purposes, the most important implication of the end of the notion of global equilibrium in economics and politics is the necessity of considering both the fallibility of individuals and the fallibility of the institutions and organizations they create.

Some Definitions

There is some confusion in the use of terms in institutional analyis, and it is worth a clarifying note. The terms "institution," "organization," "structure," "formal rules," "norms," and "informal organization" are not always used consistently. One distinction is that institutions are formal rules and organizations are the set of individuals who broadly agree to operate within the confines of these rules (North 1990). This isn't a perfect definition, since we think of a business firm or a labor union as an organization even if people leave it. Another approach is to use institution in a more general sense: a market is an institution, a government is an institution, but Microsoft, the UAW, and the French Parliament are organizations. Institutions in this sense are collections of organizations. Political scientists, however, often refer to Congress as "an institution." "Legislatures" or "firms" are simply general forms of the class "organization" in this approach.

To add to the confusion, if we define a formal organization in terms of the rules it employs, then rules and organization are confused. Similarly, "structure" generally refers to formal rules, while "norms" refer to informal or unwritten rules. "Informal organization" does invariably refer to those aspects of an organization that emerge from the interaction of people in the organization rather than from the design developed in the formal rules.

In what follows, I shall use the term "institution" in a more general sense than "organization"—institutions are markets and governments, legislatures and firms are organizations. But where we refer to a set of organizations, such as the court system, then again the term institution is appropriate.

Institutions and Choice

At the height of the behavioral revolution, many political scientists thought that they could uncover general principles of political behavior.

Institutions and organizations really didn't matter very much—if treated at all, they were seen as a kind of backdrop, a stage on which political action occurred. But this view ignored an important aspect of political behavior and institutions. Because people are adaptable creatures, the institutions in which they find themselves operating elicit behavior—by the explicit incentives they provide, by the social understandings they promote, and by the subtle cues concerning the right mix of self-centered and cooperative behavior they emit.

Both the hard-line behavioralists and the bare-bones neoinstitutionalists have it wrong, and for somewhat the same reason. They underspecify the role of institutions and organizations in modern political and economic life. People can learn, and so can the organizations they inhabit. People can make better decisions, individually and collectively, because of institutions. And organizations can be designed better if they incorporate sensible concepts of human nature.

We design institutions with a formal structure that is more or less easy to change. Constitutional facets of government—the set of rules that govern the fundamentals of the policy process—are deliberately difficult to change. Yet the set of constitutional rules can (and does in the United States) offer a built-in advantage to the status quo.

Political scientist William Riker was fond of pointing out that political institutions are "congealed preferences." Because the rules of our governing institutions are hard to change, and because these rules make the alteration of the status quo difficult to overturn, we are often stuck with the preferences of majority coalitions from the past, even if majority preferences have changed. Stability is built into American-style power-sharing arrangements. Tom Hammond and Gary Miller (1987) have shown this facet analytically. In parliamentary systems, bureaus are created and rules written in a sometimes deliberate effort to "congeal" policy preferences.

The work of Hammond and Miller shows that public policy can change disjointedly even where preferences of participants in the institution change gradually. Supermajority provisions can cause such episodic updating even with fully rational actors, as we noted in chapter 7.

Formal rules act as incentives for participants to act in certain ways. They channel behavior. In the case of supermajority requirements, the rules ensure a great deal of stability and isolation from the demands of the external environment. Any model of political change must factor in the institutional incentives that are created for participants; these incentives can cause episodic change in policy outputs.

But that is not the whole story. People must learn how to respond to the incentives generated by the rules. This involves time, effort, and mistakes. In the words of Allen Newell, rationality does not come free—even when it is of the intended variety.

Enabling Choice

The English political economist John Stuart Mill argued in his essay *On Liberty* ([1863] 1956) that seemingly irresponsible people would rise to the challenge when allowed full rights of participation. Responsible voters are creations of democracy, not prerequisites for it. Similarly, many economists argue that moving from a bureaucratic service delivery system to a market-oriented one will cause people to make better choices—certainly better choices than the bureaucrats would. Many political scientists—led by Vincent and Elinor Ostrom of the Workshop in Political Theory and Policy Analysis at Indiana University—have made the case that decentralized democratic processes lead to more efficient and effective service delivery systems than centralized, bureaucratic ones.

The theme that runs through a rich literature in political science on democratic design is "enabling choice." The central notion is Mill's: if institutions of governance are designed to facilitate repeated choices by individuals holding diverse interests, identities, and understandings, then better choices will be made—in two senses. First, democratic institutional design can help citizens avoid the rationality traps detailed in the chapter 5. Second, better design can help avoid downward spirals of conflict and other mistakes based in limited rationality. Proper design will encourage individual choice and collective choice to converge.

We might, for analytical purposes, suggest two general positions on the issue of design. One contends that getting the incentives right in a proper institutional design elicits the proper behavior of the participants. The other would be less sanguine about the ability of institutional design to elicit the proper behavior immediately; indeed, it is not clear in an uncertain world just what behavior is required.

Most political theorists would agree on the following points:

• Some degree of coercion is necessary in any society. Even in the most open and free society, rules will be necessary to establish stable expectations of behavior. But rules are a collective good: individuals will have some incentive to defect. Monitoring and enforcing the system of rules is therefore necessary even in a minimalist state.
• Where public coercion exists, there is always the temptation of the governors to exploit the governed. Hence some mechanism of accountability is necessary.

• Liberal democracy, by ensuring regular elections and open criticism, provides that mechanism of accountability.

A minimalist democracy might be enough for many political theorists, especially those adopting a public choice perspective—emphasizing the self-centered calculating rationality of people. But for a bounded rationalist, this may not be enough.

Vincent Ostrom has developed the connection between boundedly rational citizens and institutional design extensively. Ostrom's work is firmly grounded in the genetic and cultural evolution of human cognition. "In some basic sense, all of us are learned ignoramuses" (Ostrom 1997, 148). Human cognitive and emotional capacities adapt to environmental demands through three mechanisms: genetics, culture (where the use of language is key), and learning during the lifetime of an individual organism.

These mechanisms are double-edged swords. Genetic endowments of emotions and sense data are critical in giving an organism feedback about the world, and are hence adaptive. But they also can be at war with civilized, stable societies created and maintained via cultural evolution. Language, the key to culture, is not a simple civilizing device—it has the power to appeal to emotions, encouraging strife between people with different organizational identities (also a consequence of genetic endowments such as limited cognition and the reliance on local knowledge). So there is nothing simple about adaptation—it is filled with the tensions born of incompatibility.

Democratic governance is facilitated when we appreciate fully these aspects of human nature. "When everyone is assumed to be fallible, error proneness can be reduced by the development of error-correcting procedures in the organization of decision-making processes." These error-correcting procedures require openness and the ability to rearrange existing interests in myriad governing arrangements. "Where error correction procedures can be built into the structure of decision-making procedures, we can view such procedures as organizing processes that facilitate learning and create a culture of inquiry" (Ostrom 1997, 147).

A minimalist conception of democracy filled with maximizing actors faces problems of rent extraction and principal agency. The governors must be controlled, and the agents of the governors must be controlled. If elections can control the governors and bureaucratic oversight and proper hierarchical incentives can be instituted, these aims can be achieved. The "overhead model of democracy"—in which a legislature (or legislature and executive) are elected by the people, and these elected officials delegate the operation of government to a professional bureaucracy—would be the preferred method of ensuring accountability.

On the other hand, if people are bounded in their rationality, have trouble figuring out just what their own interests are because of the tension between self-centeredness and cooperation, and fall prey to limited conceptions of the issues of governance, then a more decentralized decision-making system is called for. "Obedience to a system of command and control is ostensibly easier to understand," but it fails to incorporate opportunities for citizens to learn to govern themselves (Ostrom 1997, 147). It also generally fails to incorporate the error-correcting mechanisms built into redundant systems (Landau 1969).

Ostrom's work points to the possibility of establishing institutional frameworks that both appreciate the limits of human nature and elicit better choice making from the inhabitants of those institutions. Work on school choice by Mark Schneider and colleagues (1997) suggests the processes that encourage citizens to make better choices. They studied parents' school choices in two inner-city school districts in New York City. One district allowed parental choice for middle-school children (District 4); the other did not. Schneider and his colleagues looked at parental choice using the decision-matrix discussed above in chapter 2. That is, they saw schools as alternatives, with a series of attributes such as academic achievement, diversity, and safety underlying the alternatives. They determined that (1) in general, parents have very low knowledge about such important attributes as reading scores and school security; and (2) even in the face of this low information, parents who valued a particular attribute (say, diversity) enrolled their children in schools that matched their preferences.

These findings reflect classic low-information rationality in which the structure of choice leads parents to make choices more consistent with their preferences. Schneider and his colleagues' work, and research like it, indicates that institutions may be set up to elicit better choices from people (though of course the converse is also true).

Human Institutions as Incentive Creators

In biological evolution, incentives for change come directly from the environment. Selectivity acts on a random distribution of mutations. The organism has no direct control over selectivity—what is favored and what is not.

The same is not true of human cultural evolution. Conscious creation and modification of institutions changes everything, making the evolution of institutions fundamentally different from biological evolution. The difference is not in the role of trial and error; far from it. Much human problem solving involves trial and error, even if it is goal directed (evolution is not).

A more fundamental difference is the fact that human institutions, which are created, can be designed to evoke particular behaviors out of the participants in those institutions. A major reason that institutional reforms fail to perform as well as expected is that designers do not pay enough attention to how the incentives they create or alter are likely to be received by participants in the institution. This can happen for three reasons. First, there is a misunderstanding of the incentive structure that the institutional reform has created. Second, people, being bounded rationalists, do not respond according to the theory of the designers. Third, people can identify with the old institutions in ways that make them more difficult to change than reformers think (North 1990). In effect, we see the old issue of "bounded rationality showing through" in a different format. Or, put another way, the designers themselves are bounded rationalists.

If institutional designers were omniscient, and if participants in institutions were comprehensively rational, then institutions would not evolve except under the control of the omniscient designers. But human institutional arrangements do not stay fixed; they evolve. They evolve for three reasons. First, they evolve because the rules are changed by designers. Second, they evolve because the institutional environment changes. These two sources of change are exogenous changes. But, third, they evolve because institutional rules are not infrequently ambiguous, and individual participants can, in effect, take advantage of this ambiguity to redefine the institution "on the fly." Usually this happens because institutional participants take advantage of some change that occurs in the institution's environment. They note that an opportunity has occurred, and that, by proper argumentation, they can modify the existing set of rules to their benefit. In so doing, however, they often amplify the effects coming into the organization. Disproportionality in response can affect organizational reform through the mechanisms of attention-arousal and emotional commitment.

Political Jurisdictions

The evolution of political organizations changes the incentives before people in those organizations. As a consequence, organizations change the behavior of participants. There is, however, no designer of change. The change in form just happens, as a consequence of the interactions of members, both within the organization and with those outside of the organization. Because of this evolutionary process, no political organization can be at equilibrium.

Many studies of legislatures and other political organizations have used a framework termed "comparative statics." The idea is that an equilibrium legislature is affected by the exogenous shocks of reforms. The analysis compares how an organization or institution works before and after the new rules are imposed. The failure of such equilibrium analysis comes from the endogenous change that will occur as formal and informal rules evolve in response to actions by members of an organization.

One instance of governmental evolution occurs in changes in political jurisdictions. Political scientists use the term "jurisdiction" in an encompassing manner. It refers to the assignment of authority to territorial units, but it also denotes the kinds of policy issues assigned to institutions. For example, courts and legislatures are assigned jurisdiction in different ways, and the manner in which issues are considered by these two policymaking institutions differ. Similarly, states may share issue jurisdiction with the national government in economic development, education, social welfare, etc., but they cannot coin money or engage in relations with other nations.

The allocation of policymaking authority to jurisdictions has great consequences for the conduct of politics. As public law scholar Roy Flemming writes, "Jurisdiction creates a forum for disputes. By expanding the jurisdiction of a trial court, cases move into or out of the forum, a change proponents hope will favor their interests" (1998, 947–48). Any unit of government—federal agency, state bureau, legislative committee, city council—could be substituted for "trial court." A considerable amount of political energy is expended on the struggle to determine what "forum for disputes" is used in resolving policy conflicts.

Jurisdictions can be ambiguous. Oftentimes this ambiguity is simply reflective of a complex world. A few years ago British beef was banned from sale in European Union nations because of the threat of "mad cow" disease. Is this an agricultural issue, to be dealt with by agricultural officials, or a health issue? Most of us would say in some meaningful sense it is both. If, however, health officials and agricultural officials were predisposed to offer differing policy prescriptions, then the assignment of the issue to one jurisdiction or another could have far-reaching consequences (Jupille 2000).

Moreover, actions tend to have jurisdictional consequences. Courts operate explicitly according to the principle of *stare decisis*—a decision should be allowed to stand in order that people will understand what their rights and obligations are. Similarly, in the broader case of policymaking jurisdictions, decisions serve as formal or informal precedents, guiding the future behaviors of policymakers. Every decision has downstream implications for the very definition of the authority of the institution. But every decision also involves the settling of ambiguity in the assignment of the issue to one class or another in a more or less arbitrary fashion. Clearly the result is that jurisdictions, rather than being clear and fixed, are ambiguous and changing—although that change is likely to come in a punctuation rather than as a continuous response to environmental change (Jones, Baumgartner, and Talbert 1993).

This phenomenon has been most carefully studied for committee jurisdictions in the U.S. Congress. Each house of Congress has attempted sporadic reforms aimed at making clear which committees are supposed to consider which policy areas for legislation, policy problems, and executive committee oversight. The most comprehensive modern attempt at reform was the Legislative Reorganization Act of 1948. The committee system was restructured, and the number of committees reduced.

Nevertheless, committee jurisdictions still tend to wander as entrepreneurial committee chairs try to claim new issues for their committees to consider (King 1997). The problem, moreover, extends beyond this tendency. The environment of congressional policymaking—the economy, social trends, and so on—is continually changing. In particular, new issues (or new understandings of old issues) are presented to the legislature for consideration. Oftentimes these issues, like the British beef issue, span more than one previously established policy jurisdiction. As parliamentarians struggle with the legislative leadership to keep jurisdictions clear, an arbitrariness in the assignment of issues to jurisdiction results. Rules for assigning matters to jurisdictions are always catching up with the ongoing evolution of jurisdictions (See box 8.1).

My colleagues Frank Baumgartner and Mike MacLeod and I have developed a quantitative method for tracing the evolution of committee jurisdictions (Baumgartner, Jones, and MacLeod 2000; see also Hardin 1998). We have developed a set of content categories (macroeconomics, social welfare, health, etc.) that may be used to trace policy change reliability across a long period of time. Like the essential ambiguity associated with policy jurisdictions, our system contains elements of arbitrariness, even if this arbitrariness is of the academic rather than political variety. But the system has the decided advantage of treating policymaking documents—statutes, budgets, hearings, and the like—similarly across time in assignment to policy content categories.

By applying the system to legislative hearings and noting the committee that held the hearing, we may observe changes in the nature of the jurisdictions of committees. We hypothesized that as time progressed, and Congress took on more and more new issues, committee jurisdictions would be increasingly muddled. This follows because each issue is not

Box 8.1: The Jurisdictional Assignment
of Education

The House of Representatives' rule X from the 105th Congress can be summarized as follows: "Education matters generally," go to the Committee on Education and the Workforce (X-f-6). However, activities having to do with agricultural colleges and experiment stations, agricultural research, agricultural education extension services, and home economics are referred to the Committee on Agriculture (X-a-4, 5, 6, 16). Biomedical research goes to Commerce (X-e-1); international education goes to International Relations (X-i-8); mining schools and experiment stations are under the jurisdiction of the Committee on Resources (X-l-14); the National Science Foundation, science scholarships, and scientific research in general go to the Committee on Science (X-n-10, 13, 14); education of veterans, of course, goes to Veterans' Affairs (X-r-3). Defense research projects, often done on college campuses, go to Armed Services, naturally. Finally, according to rule X, section 3, clause c, "The Committee on Education and the Workforce shall have the function of reviewing, studying, and coordinating, on a continuing basis, all laws, programs, and Government activities dealing with or involving domestic educational programs and institutions, and programs of student assistance, which are within the jurisdiction of other committees."

Education is one of the simplest jurisdictional cases for Congress. In other words, for the case that appears to be one of the simplest, there are at least eight committees with rule X authority over some parts of education matters generally. This does not include tax issues such as the tuition credit in the 1997 deficit reduction bill; tax matters, relating to education or anything else, go to Ways and Means (Baumgartner, Jones, and MacLeod 2000).

clearly defined in terms of the existing committee jurisdictions. A kind of policy entropy would infect the jurisdictional structure. The evolution of jurisdictions seemed pretty well governed by increasing entropy (although a decline into complete entropy would imply a completely useless committee system, an unlikely occurrence).

Figure 8.1 displays the strong jurisdictional entropy that has affected congressional jurisdictions since the Legislative Reform Act of 1948. The graph measures the clarity of jurisdictions (essentially by how many issues each committee shares with other committees) across time (each

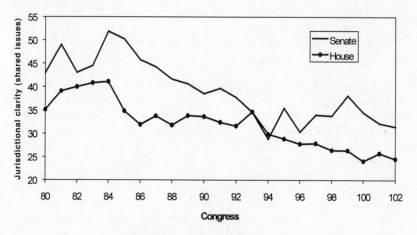

Figure 8.1   The Decline of Clarity in Congressional Committee
Jurisdictions
Source: Baumgartner, Jones, and MacLeod 2000

Congress lasts for two years). Decline in clarity implies an increase in entropy. Decline in the clarity of jurisdictions was especially severe from the late 1950s (around the term of the 86th Congress) through the early 1980s, when the national government was considering numerous new topics for policy action—science and technology, transportation, civil rights, the environment.

It might seem as if increasingly interlocked jurisdictions would lead to "gridlock," but in fact jurisdictional entropy is a mixed blessing from the perspective of political responsiveness to the emergence of new issues. On the one hand, jurisdictional difficulties are magnified in importance. On the other hand, a moderately entropic jurisdictional system allows for the raising of a policy issue within more than one jurisdiction, thereby making it less likely that political interests controlling one jurisdiction can keep an emerging issue off the policy agenda (Baumgartner and Jones 1993).

Congressional committee jurisdictions are but one example of a problem endemic to governments. Limits on the attention spans and knowledge bases of policymakers make a system of policymaking jurisdictions necessary. Controlling the excesses of power and encouraging the involvement of citizens argues for deconcentration of policymaking authority. But, because the world is complex, it is not possible to assign policy responsibility in a straightforward and unambiguous manner to policymaking jurisdictions. Political institutions reflect the limits of decision makers—their attention spans and knowledge bases, as well as their ambitions for themselves and the organizations they control. These factors can "feed back" into the institutions, causing them to evolve.

Institutions as Preference Creators

In a wide-ranging essay on the role of trust in democratic governance, Margaret Levi notes that institutions can change preferences as they evolve, and democratic institutions change preferences in predictable directions. "By delimiting behavioral choices, institutions—democratic or not—reveal what actions the collectivity believes are acceptable. They set new standards of behavior for both government and citizens" (1998, 94). Institutions are not just a set of rules governing behavior; they also have substantive impacts on the preferences of the governors and the governed (Levi 1997).

Preference creation is a far more difficult issue to address than incentive creation. In particular, preference creation cannot be explained at all within a framework of comprehensive rational choice. If preferences are not fixed, then the system becomes far less useful. It is also difficult to discuss the divergence between rational adaptation and bounded rationality.

Given the difficulty that preference creation causes for the systematic analysis of institutions, we ought not to use the concept unless it is absolutely necessary. It is not necessary to talk about preference creation if, for example, preferences include multiple attributes and the weights or saliences of the attributes change in response to changing circumstances (Jones 1994). Even after taking into account changes in the saliences of attributes, the preference creation problem will not disappear. We may explain preference creation using the standard facets of bounded rationality—in particular, habituation and cognitive and emotional identification with means. Moral argumentation is critical in establishing what Philip Tetlock calls "taboo trade-offs" (you can't own slaves, buy children, or pay a substitute to serve your prison time) (Levi 1998, 94).

The phenomenon of preference creation via the evolution of political and social institutions further illustrates the difficulties of the approach of evolutionary psychologists (discussed in chapter 2). Evolutionary psychologists posit substantive, domain-specific solution mechanisms to evolutionary problems, and downplay the general problem-solving, dynamic adaptive abilities of humans. But institutionally created preferences require the intervention of adaptive behavior as people's goals adjust to changing circumstances. What is more important in understanding human behavior in modern political and economic systems: the fact that men and women "differ dramatically in the frequency and content of sexual fantasy" (Buss 1995, 8), or that both sexes have developed a socially created aversion to owning other people?[2]

Preference creation is likely related to the general mechanism of organizational identification (or identification with means): the tendency of people to infuse strategies, not just goals, with emotional and cognitive meaning. There may also be a backdrop of the moral sense: we might conceive of preference creation as amplifying and canalizing substantive "limits" on rational adaptation (see chapter 5).

The issue is much thornier than the limited research on the topic would suggest. If preferences are not fixed, then they are part of the dynamic adjustment process. The evolution of institutions also affects the evolution of wants.

Appropriate Behavior

A great facilitator of human interactions in organizational life is the human tendency to follow rules. Developmental psychologists have observed how early in life children absorb rules and identify with them. Organizations work more smoothly than they might because of human rule-following tendencies. Norms of behavior develop that act to structure interactions between individuals, influencing beliefs and behavior. Studies by Jennifer Hochschild indicate that people's judgments about distributive justice are strongly influenced by norms: "[W]e can best understand people's distributive judgments by looking not at their general ideologies or class position, but at the distributive norms they apply to particular domains of life (Hochschild 1981, 82).

There are two sources of rule-following behavior. We follow rules because it is a rational thing to do; it saves us the costs of analysis and search. Rule following is connected to the preparation-deliberation trade-off discussed earlier in this book. Prepared strategies are stored as rules; rules in organizations are, in effect, handed to organizational members to encode and use as prepared strategies.

We also follow rules because we want to be cooperative. This reason for rule following is the probably inherited tendency of people to over-cooperate (in comparison to self-centered rational adaptation). James March notes that much human decision making is governed by the criterion of appropriateness.[3] Individuals "follow rules or procedures that they

---

2. Readers who think I chose selectively are invited to peruse Buss's list (1995).

3. March calls it a "logic" and contrasts it with the "logic of consequences." The logic of consequences includes all goal-oriented behavior, rational and intendedly rational. March was correct to highlight the different bases for decision making, but I would treat appropriateness as a limit on rational adaptation, albeit a substantive rather than a procedural one. See Goodin 1999 for a different view.

see as appropriate to the situation in which they find themselves. Neither preferences as they are normally conceived nor expectations of future consequences enter directly into the calculus" (March 1994, 57). Rule following and the criterion of appropriateness have important consequences for how people relate to one another in institutions and how those institutions operate. (March and Olsen 1989, 1995).

It may not be too much of a stretch to suggest that the criterion of consequences, according to which human action is intendedly goal directed, is grounded in human adaptability and procedural limits on it. The criterion of appropriateness is grounded in the major inherited limitation on human self-centered adaptability: sociability. There is of course much more to human nature, but perhaps these two facets are enough to understand the linkages between our genes and our current decision making in the formal institutions that canalize our behaviors.

Conclusions

Formal institutions create task environments for participants, ensuring that they coordinate behaviors in order to solve problems. Institutions themselves evolve. Evolution proceeds in response to changing external demands on the organization as well as through the creative actions of individual participants.

The fact that so much of human activity occurs within and among institutions means that the link between genes and any given decision is stretched thin. Institutions ensure that modern humans escape the limits imposed on them by their genetic inheritances. But, like all systems, institutions must mold the material upon which they are built—human nature. The best of institutions both free humans from their limitations, coordinate complex behaviors, and channel these behaviors.

Capitalist markets and liberal democracies reflect the self-centered nature of humankind, yet direct selfish behaviors toward productive ends. This process has been often recognized in social science writing. Less recognized is the reliance on these institutions on the inherited willingness of people to cooperate with one another. Neither complex markets nor democracies can possibly work without more cooperation and trust than self-centered individuals operating in the "shadow of the future" can provide.

CHAPTER 9

Overestimation, Neglect, and Rationality

In 1964, two young physicists at Bell Laboratories pointed the first powerful radio telescope at the sky. The instrument was available because of Bell Telephone's interest in the new technology of communications transmission via artificial satellite. The two radio astronomers, Arno Penzias and Robert Wilson, wanted to map the distribution of hydrogen between the stars in the Milky Way. But something annoying happened: the instrument detected a uniform radio noise, an aggravating background buzz, no matter what direction the astronomers pointed the instrument.

It seemed at first that the instrument was at fault. After repeated tests confirmed the reliability of the instrument, the Bell researchers admitted that the background radiation was real. And, indeed, it *was* real, and one of the truly great scientific discoveries of the century. The annoying background radiation, with a temperature of 2.7 degrees Kelvin, was in fact the residue of the creation of the universe predicted by physicist George Gamow's "Big Bang" theory. No longer was there any doubt that, in fact, there was an instant of creation of the universe; the "steady state" theory was unceremoniously dumped on the ashbin of scientific history as an interesting, but wrong, idea.

So what does background radiation have to do with the study of human behavior in organizational settings? The lessons are twofold. First, and most obvious, is that an appeal to facts can settle scientific controversy. The second lesson is metaphor: the past is carried through in human affairs, too, and sometimes the most distant past is the most important. The raw material of rational organizational life is human nature, which is not always so rational.

DECISION MAKING is premised on information, but people do not process information in a smooth and seamless manner. Disproportionate information processing interferes with rational adaptive choice. Disproportionate information processing and its consequent effect on decision making are based in human biology and evolutionary dynamics. Some of these limitations are procedural; like attention spans, they affect how we make decisions. Others are substantive; they affect the goals we bring into the process.

In no cases does biology determine outcomes. Biology is not destiny. But biology leaves its imprint in ways that affect how we respond to the current environment we face. It prepares us to learn some associations readily and resist others, particularly where we are emotionally involved in a previously learned association. Because of biology, all rewards are not equivalent, even if an objective observer would judge them to be equivalent. Because of biology, especially attention bottlenecks and emotional identifications, we often have difficulty in making trade-offs in choice situations.

This does not mean that people are incompetent decision makers. Reading much of the psychology literature, and in particular the literature criticizing the expected utility model, one gets the impression that people are really bad decision makers—even when these criticisms are carefully stated (as in Pios 1993). Some people are really bad decision makers, but most are not. Our behavior is canalized by biology, but not determined by it. We can get out of the canal, albeit this usually requires conscious effort or some mental restructuring of incentives (as in the case of mental accounting, discussed in chapter 2). More important, much of our cognitive architecture is adaptive, not maladaptive, in the modern world. The modular structure of the human brain does not foreclose a general problem-solving mechanism. Indeed, recent research indicates that general intelligence itself is modular, with a locus in the lateral prefrontal cortex (Duncan et al. 2000).

Exactly what does this mean for governance and political choice? Mathematician Benoit Mandelbrot goes to the very heart of the manner almost off-handedly: "Man finds it difficult to avoid oscillating between overestimation and neglect" (1997, 28). But Mandelbrot's observation, however casually stated, cannot have been arrived at casually. His entire mathematical edifice centers on the existence of unexpected punctuations and "wild randomness" as a central component of natural change (Mandelbrot 1997, 1999).

Were everything else put aside—uncertainty, the decision costs imposed by any transaction and magnified by the operation of governmental institutions, the political advantage given to vested interests—at base, there *still* would be an episodic and disjointed character to human action. And, as a direct consequence, the activities of modern, rationalized, complex organizations would still be disjointed, "oscillating between over-

estimation and neglect." Ironically, in relation to the demands and opportunities in the environment, there is both too much stability and too
much change.

In comparison to hypothetical rational actors, intendedly rational actors will adjust to changing circumstances in a disjointed and episodic
manner. Hypothetically rational actors may adjust disjointedly, but only
if the environment changes in a disjointed manner. An intendedly rational actor will adjust disjointedly even when the environment changes
continuously. Unlike the rational actor, the bounded actor must adjust
both to changes in the external environment and to his or her internal
environment.

Social scientists can no longer afford to ignore the biological raw
material on which the complex institutions of modern polities and economies are built. This emphatically does not mean ignoring adaptive goal-
oriented behavior, but it does mean coming to terms with the discontinui-
ties in human action that are driven by human cognitive architecture.

Decision Criteria

There are two different, potentially conflicting, criteria for judging a decision. One is the criterion of consequences. We judge a potential outcome in terms of its consequences for us. The second is the criterion of
appropriateness: is the choice under consideration appropriate for the circumstances? (See March 1994 and March and Olsen 1995, for extended
discussions of this distinction.)

The criterion of consequences is affected by our adaptive capacity and
the current task environment, and is constrained by the procedural limitations on adaptability discussed in this book. These limitations are both
cognitive and emotional, but let us recall that the term "limitations" refers
to constraints on fully rational adjustment. It emphatically does not mean
that one should put aside one's emotions in decision making (although
there can be excesses). Given the human cognitive limits of short-term
memory, attention, retrieval from long-term memory, and the fundamental role of learning, emotional states are an absolute necessity for intendedly rational thought. Through emotions, priorities are set and motivation
supplied. Emotions allocate our short-term memories; they govern our
attentiveness. Because attentiveness and consciousness are so intimately
related (see Crick 1994), it is likely that consciousness and emotion are
intimately bound together.

The criterion of appropriateness is affected by the substantive limits on
adaptation, as discussed in chapter 4. It is influenced by our (probably
inherited, but clearly socially reinforced) propensity toward sociability.
"Is this decision right, proper, or appropriate?" "How will I be viewed by

others?"[1] The criteria of appropriateness can add additional constraints to rational adaptation, because it adds a moral constraint to choice. (This moral constraint may or may not be admirable by modern, democratic standards. It may involve complete loyalty to one's group, but unrestrained aggression toward others. The only point here is that values can channel rational, goal-oriented behavior.)

Both criteria can be seen as based in evolutionary efficiency.[2] Clearly current adaptive capacity—the ability to understand the structure of a decision-making situation and to calculate costs and benefits of action—can be seen as efficient in evolutionary terms. Limitations on adaptation may also be efficient—because of the need to exclude irrelevant stimuli (via limits in attention and short-term memory) and the need to prioritize (requiring emotion, given that comprehensive attention is sacrificed). Of course each of these facets may involve unfortunate trade-offs for the organism. Attention fixation may exclude suddenly relevant stimuli (a predator).

It may be less appreciated that the criterion of appropriateness has an evolutionary basis. If, however, sociability offers selective advantages to individuals, that is, if social learning is efficient as a transmitter of information, then the role of natural selection becomes relevant in the development of rules of social interaction and a sense of morality. These become the criteria against which we judge our behavior, in addition to the self-centered consequences of the proposed plan of action.

A Behavioral Approach

The critics of rational choice almost unanimously recommend replacement of the rational choice assumptions with something more realistic. Behavioral economist Colin Camerer recommends replacement assumptions that "allow economic agents to be impulsive and myopic, to lack self-control, to keep track of earning and spending in separate 'mental accounting' categories, to care about the outcomes of others (both enviously and altruistically), to construct preferences from experience and observation, to sometimes misjudge probabilities, to take pleasure and pain from the difference between their economic state and some set of reference points, and so forth" (1998, 56).

This is indeed a proper approach, with two caveats. The first is that

---

1. The first of these questions is pure appropriateness. The second mixes appropriateness and consequential criteria, since self-interest is involved.

2. Evolution doesn't "select for" anything. It eliminates less adaptive features. Efficiency in evolution may occur, but it is not demonstrated. Moreover, any adaptation may or may not be in equilibrium—that is, it may be on its way out. Evolution takes time.

behavioralists not fall into the "and so forth" trap of trying to tie all sorts of outcomes to particular laboratory findings or field observations of behavior. Otherwise we commit the "laundry list" fallacy in a new guise. The second caveat is that we pay close attention to the principle of intended rationality: that people really are in the main adapting to the task environment they face.

That the task environment of decision making affects the nature of decision making is not in doubt. Work by psychologists Beach and Mitchell (1978), Christensen-Szalanski (1978), and Payne, Bettman, and Johnson (1993) has shown that people use a repertory of decision-making strategies, depending on the circumstances. And these circumstances involve, in part, the anticipated costs of using the strategy versus the anticipated benefits from the decision. The task environment must be understood in order to predict human behavior—even though at this point in the development of the social sciences, comparing frequency distributions of behavior is probably more productive than trying to predict particular actions.

The Task Environment

For most people most of the time, the task environment is specified by formal institutions: school, work, church, synagogue, mosque, government. Because these institutions are adapting themselves, the task environment people face is itself changing. The more change there is, the less structured the task environment facing the decision maker, and the more difficult the adaptive process. If we want to find small deviations between the adaptive model and human action, let us look for the most structured task environments. If we want to find disjointed, episodic adaptation, and even maladaptation, let us examine task environments that are rapidly changing.

The relationship between the task environment and human purposeful behavior is strongest under two conditions: the time available for adaptation is generous and the task environment—the goals, constraints, and general relationship between strategies and goals—are clear. By studying institutions where task environments are clear, we are in a much better position to assess the potentials and limits of human adaptive behavior in modern complex social systems.

Institutions help to clarify the task environment, hence they are great aids to human adaptability. But they also act to limit the time allocated to any given task via the mechanism of task performance rules. In the name of neutral efficiency, formal organizations routinize many of their tasks under the general assumption that the task performed is related to the goals of the organization. The human tendency to identify with the task performance rule, as a specific and behavioral manifestation, rather than the more general and abstract goals of the organization, causes a potential problem. Rules can become drags on the adaptability of the entire organization if they get out of phase with a changing task environment.

Similarly, humans routinize the connection between stimulus and response. When decision making is relegated to the level of Newell's cognitive band, most thought goes into recognizing and categorizing a stimulus. Once the stimulus is categorized—"understood"—the connection to behavior is determined. There is no thought, no search among alternatives, in response to a stimulus. This can be efficient in a static environment, but it can cause problems when the task environment is dynamic.

Attention is the mechanism that causes us to shift a task from the cognitive to the intendedly rational band of action. Attention can be brought under conscious control, but oftentimes it is not. In either case, attention governs accessibility to the conscious serial processing capacity of humans; in a similar fashion, agenda setting governs access to the serial processing (policymaking) capacity of formal organizations. The two phenomena are causally related.

In a complex world with many variables changing "in parallel," and limited channel capacity for conscious reflection, it is inevitable that a human decision maker will respond episodically to the flow of information from the environment. This will be the case even if that flow is smooth and incremental. Because of this, an objective task environment cannot be translated smoothly into a decision-making output.

Fundamental Equations of Human Behavior

Decision makers are goal directed and intend to pursue those goals rationally. Intended rationality incorporates four components. They are (1) the actor's goals, (2) the task environment, (3) the problem space constructed by the decision maker, and (4) the limits imposed by the cognitive/emotional architecture of human decision makers.

The behavior of a fully rational decision maker would be completely determined by the task environment. If we know the environment and the goals of the decision maker, then we may deduce the actions that the decision maker will take. For boundedly rational actors, however, we will need to know something about the cognitive and emotional architecture.

Addressing these aspects of human nature is conditioned on whether the task environment is relatively fixed or not. First, in relatively fixed task environments, such as asset markets and democratic elections, observed behavior (B) of actors may be divided into two mutually exclusive and exhaustive categories: (1) rational goal-attainment (G), and (2) limited rationality (L). This leads to the fundamental equation for fixed task environments:

$$B = G + L.$$

Second, in uncertain, ambiguous, or contradictory task environments, behavior is a function of goals, processing limits, and the connection between the decision maker's problem space and the task environment (objectively characterized). The fundamental equation may be characterized in multiplicative terms, the interaction between goals, processing limits, and the conception of the problem:

$$B = G \times L \times P.$$

In relatively fixed task environments, we should be able to divide behavior into adaptive, goal-oriented behavior and behavior that is a consequence of processing limits, and measure the deviation. This approach relies on a good theory of goal-directed behavior and of human limitations on adjustment. More complex task environments require more complex models of the interaction between goals, cognitive processing characteristics, and the conception of the problem.

Microfoundations for Macroanalysis

The analysis of organizations and institutions in social science must have a microfoundation in the actions and interactions of individual humans. The most systematic foundation, rational choice, is behaviorally wrong. It assumes that we respond only to the current situation and, in effect, that the "background radiation" of our biological inheritances is irrelevant.

This assumption greatly interferes with more rapid progress in the social and behavioral sciences. It leads to parallel languages, in which behavioral scientists underappreciate adaptive human behavior in complex institutions, and social scientists either ignore microfoundations or rest their analyses on an off-base behavioral assumption. Social scientists steeped in the rational choice approach assume they can explain all behavior with reference to incentives in the environment, linking behavior to supposed external stimuli in an ad hoc and arbitrary manner.

In the end, the balance between human behavior based in external, objective incentives and that connected to the internal cognitive architecture is an empirical question, and can only be settled through rigorous behavioral studies. This requires sensitivity to the mechanisms of human cognition, but it also requires an understanding of the institutional environment within which decisions are made.

REFERENCES

Alt, James, Margaret Levi, and Elinor Ostrom, eds. 1999. *Competition and Cooperation: Conversations with Nobelists about Economics and Political Science*. New York: Russell Sage.

Althaus, Scott. 1998. Information Effects in Collective Preferences. *American Political Science Review* 92 : 545–58.

Alvarez, R. Michael, and John Brehm. In press. *Hard Choices, Easy Answers*.

Amade, S. M., and Bruce Bueno de Mesquita. 1999. The Rochester School: The Origins of Positive Political Theory. In *Annual Review of Political Science*, vol. 2, ed. Nelson Polsby. Palo Alto: Annual Reviews.

Anderson, John R. 1983. *The Architecture of Cognition*. Cambridge: Harvard University Press.

Anton, Thomas. 1966. *The Politics of State Expenditures in Illinois*. Urbana: University of Illinois Press.

Aldrich, John. 1995. *Why Parties?* Chicago: University of Chicago Press.

Arnold, Douglas. 1990. *The Logic of Congressional Action*. New Haven: Yale University Press.

Asch, Solomon. 1952. *Social Psychology*. Englewood Cliffs, N.J.: Prentice-Hall.

Axelrod, Robert. 1970. *Conflict of Interest*. Chicago: Markham.

———. 1984. *The Evolution of Cooperation*. New York: Basic Books.

———. 1997. *The Complexity of Cooperation*. Princeton: Princeton University Press.

Bak, Per. 1996. *How Nature Works*. New York: Springer-Verlag.

Barnard, Chester. 1938. *The Functions of the Executive*. Cambridge: Harvard University Press.

Bartels, Larry M. 1996. Uninformed Votes: Information Effects in Presidential Elections. *American Journal of Political Science* 40 : 194–230.

Baumgartner, Frank R., and Bryan D. Jones. 1993. *Agendas and Instability in American Politics*. Chicago: University of Chicago Press.

Baumgartner, Frank R., Bryan D. Jones, and Michael MacLeod. 1998. Lessons from the Trenches: Quality, Reliability, and Usability in a New Data Source. *The Political Methodologist*.

———. 2000. Jurisdictional Evolution in the Legislative Process. *Journal of Politics* 62 : 321–49.

Beach, Lee Roy, and Terrence Mitchell. 1978. A Contingency Model for the Selection of Strategies. *Academy of Management Review* 3:439–49. Reprinted in *Image Theory,* ed. Lee Roy Beach (Mahwah, N.J.: Lawrence Erlbaum).

———. 1998. The Basics of Image Theory. In *Image Theory,* ed. Lee Roy Beach. Mahwah, N.J.: Lawrence Erlbaum.

Becker, Gary S. 1976. *The Economic Approach to Human Behavior.* Chicago: University of Chicago Press.

Bendor, Jonathan. 1985. *Parallel Systems: Redundancy in Government.* Berkeley: University of California Press.

Bennett, W. Lance. 1990. Toward a Theory of Press-State Relations in the United States. *Journal of Communication* 40:103–25.

Berelson, Bernard, Paul Lazarsfeld, and William McPhee. 1954. *Voting: A Study of Opinion Formation in a Presidential Campaign.* Chicago: University of Chicago Press.

Berry, William D. 1990. The Confusing Case of Budgetary Incrementalism: Too Many Meanings for a Single Concept. *Journal of Politics* 52:167–96.

Brehm, John, and Scott Gates. 1997. *Working, Shirking, and Sabotage.* Ann Arbor: University of Michigan Press.

Burnham, Walter Dean. 1970. *Critical Elections and the Mainsprings of American Democracy.* New York: Norton.

Burstein, Paul. 1998. *Discrimination, Jobs, and Politics.* Chicago: University of Chicago Press.

Buss, David. 1995. Evolutionary Psychology: A New Paradigm for Psychological Science. *Psychological Inquiry* 6:1–30.

Camerer, Colin F. 1998. Behavioral Economics and Nonrational Organizational Decision Making. In *Debating Rationality,* ed. Jennifer J. Halpern and Robert N. Stern. Ithaca: Cornell University Press.

Camerer, Colin F., and Richard F. Thaler. 1995. Ultimatums, Dictators, and Manners. *Journal of Economic Perspectives* 9:209–19.

Campbell, Angus, Philip Converse, Warren Miller, and Donald Stokes. 1960. *The American Voter.* New York: John Wiley.

———. 1966. *Elections and the Political Order.* New York: John Wiley.

Campbell, Donald T. 1975. On the Conflicts between Biological and Social Evolution and Moral Tradition. *American Psychologist* 30:1103–26.

Campbell, John Y., Andrew W. Lo, and A. Craig MacKinlay. 1997. *The Econometrics of Financial Markets.* Princeton: Princeton University Press.

Caporeal, Linda. 1997. The Evolution of Truly Social Cognition: The Core Configurations Model. *Personality and Social Psychology Review* 1:276–98.

Caporeal, Linda, Robyn M. Dawes, John M. Orbell, and Alpohns van de Kragt. 1989. Selfishness Examined: Cooperation in the Absence of Egoistic Incentives. *Behavioral and Brain Sciences* 12:683–739.

Carpenter, Daniel. 1996. Adaptive Signal Processing, Hierarchy, and Budgetary Control in Federal Regulation. *American Political Science Review* 90:283–302.

Chisholm, Donald. 1995. Problem Solving and Institutional Design. *Journal of Public Administration Research and Theory* 5:451–91.

Chong, Dennis. 1991. *Collective Action and the Civil Rights Movement.* Chicago: University of Chicago Press.

———. 1993. How People Think, Feel, and Reason about Civil Liberties. *American Journal of Political Science* 37:867–99.

Christensen-Szalanski, Jay. 1978. Problem-Solving Strategies: A Selection Mechanism, Some Implications, and Some Data. *Organizational Behavior and Human Performance* 22:307–23. Reprinted in *Image Theory,* ed. Lee Roy Beach (Mahwah, N.J.: Lawrence Erlbaum).

———. 1991. *Collective Action and the Civil Rights Movement.* Chicago: University of Chicago Press.

Clark, Andy. 1997. *Being There: Putting Brain, Body, and World Back Together Again.* Cambridge: MIT Press.

Coase, Ronald. 1990. *The Firm, the Market, and the Law.* Chicago: University of Chicago Press.

Cobb, Roger, and Charles Elder. [1972] 1983. *Participation in American Politics.* Baltimore: Johns Hopkins University Press.

Cobb, Roger, Jennie-Keith Ross, and Mark Howard Ross. 1976. Agenda Building as a Comparative Political Process. *American Political Science Review* 70: 126–38.

Cobb, Roger, and Marc Howard Ross, eds. 1997. *Cultural Strategies of Agenda Denial.* Lawrence: University Press of Kansas.

Cohen, Michael, James G. March, and Johann Olsen. 1972. A Garbage Can Model of Organizational Choice. *Administrative Science Quarterly* 17:1–25.

Converse, Philip. 1964. The Nature of Belief Systems in Mass Publics. In *Ideology and Discontent,* ed. David E. Apter. London: Collier-MacMillan.

Cootner, Paul. 1964. *The Random Character of Stock Market Prices.* Cambridge: MIT Press.

Cosmides, Leda, John Tooby, and Jerome Barkow. 1992. Introduction: Evolutionary Psychology and Conceptual Integration. In *The Mind, the Brain, and Complex Adaptive Systems,* ed. Harold J. Morowitz and Jerome L. Singer. Reading, Mass.: Addison-Wesley.

Coulter, Philip. 1988. *Political Voice: Citizen Demand for Urban Services.* University: University of Alabama Press.

Crecine, John P. 1969. *Government Problem-Solving: A Computer Simulation of Government Budgeting.* Chicago: Rand-McNally.

Crick, Francis. 1994. *The Astonishing Hypothesis.* New York: Charles Scribner's.

Cyert, Richard M., and James G. March. 1963. *A Behavioral Theory of the Firm.* Englewood Cliffs, N.J.: Prentice-Hall.

Dahl, Robert. 1967. The City in the Future of Democracy. *American Political Science Review* 61:953–70.

Damasio, Antonio R. 1994. *Descartes' Error.* New York: Putnam's.

———. 1999. *The Feeling of What Happens.* New York: Harcourt Brace.

Davis, Otto A., M. A. H. Dempster, and Aaron Wildavsky. 1966. A Theory of the Budget Process. *American Political Science Review* 60:529–47.

———. 1974. Towards a Predictive Theory of Government Expenditure:

U.S. Domestic Appropriations. *British Journal of Political Science* 4:419–52.

Dawes, Robyn M. 1988. *Rational Choice in an Uncertain World.* Fort Worth: Harcourt Brace College Publishers.

Dodd, Lawrence C. 1994. Political Learning and Political Change: Understanding Development across Time. In *The Dynamics of American Politics,* ed. Lawrence C. Dodd and Calvin Jilson. Boulder, Colo.: Westview Press.

Downs, Anthony. 1957. *An Economic Theory of Democracy.* New York: Harper-Row.

———. 1993. The Origins of *An Economic Theory of Democracy.* In *Information, Participation, and Choice,* ed. Bernard Groffman, 197–99. Ann Arbor: University of Michigan Press.

Drewel, Lindsay. 1999. Constituent Relations. Seattle: Department of Political Science, University of Washington.

Dugatin, Lee. 1999. *Cheating Monkeys and Citizen Bees.* New York: Free Press.

Duncan, John, Rüdiger Seitz, Jonathan Kolodny, Daniel Bor, Hans Herzog, Ayesha Ahmed, Fiona Newell, and Hazel Emslie. 2000. A New Basis for General Intelligence. *Science* 289:457–60.

Edwards, Ward. 1968. Conservatism in Human Information Processing. In *Formal Representation of Human Judgment,* ed. Benjamin Kleinmuntz, 17–52. New York: John Wiley.

Elster, Jon. 1979. *Ulysses and the Sirens.* Cambridge: Cambridge University Press.

Eulau, Heinz. 1963. *The Behavioral Persuasion in Politics.* New York: Random House.

Fairchild, Roy P., ed. 1966. *The Federalist Papers.* 2d ed. Garden City: Doubleday.

Fama, Eugene F. 1970. Efficient Capital Markets: A Review of Theory and Empirical Work. *Journal of Finance* 25.

Farnham, Barbara. 1994. *Avoiding Losses, Taking Risks.* Ann Arbor: University of Michigan Press.

Fenno, Richard. 1966. *The Power of the Purse.* Boston: Little, Brown.

Ferejohn, John, and James Kuklinski, eds. 1990. *Information and the Democratic Process.* Urbana: University of Illinois Press.

Fiorina, Morris. 1996. *Divided Government.* Boston: Allyn and Bacon.

Fiorina, Morris, and Kenneth Shepsle. 1989. Formal Theories of Leadership. In *Leadership and Politics,* ed. Bryan D. Jones. Lawrence: University Press of Kansas.

Fishburn, Peter. 1988. *Nonlinear Preference and Utility Theory.* Baltimore: Johns Hopkins University Press.

Fiske, Susan. 1981. Social Cognition and Effect. In *Cognition, Social Behavior, and the Environment,* ed. John H. Harvey. Hillsdale, N.J.: Lawrence Erlbaum.

———. 1992. Cognitive Theory and the Presidency. In *Researching the Presidency,* ed. George Edwards, John Kessel, and Bert Rockman. Pittsburgh: University of Pittsburgh Press.

Fiske, Susan, and Shelly Taylor. 1991. *Social Cognition.* New York: McGraw-Hill.

Flemming, Roy. 1998. Contested Terrains and Regime Politics: Thinking about

America's Trial Courts and Institutional Change. *Law and Social Inquiry* 23: 941–65.

Fodor, Jerry. 1980. *Modularity of Mind*. Cambridge: MIT Press.

Friedman, Jeffrey. 1996. Economic Approaches to Politics. In *The Rational Choice Controversy*, ed. Jeffrey Friedman, 1–24. New Haven: Yale.

Gant, Michael, and Norman Luttbeg. 1991. *Trends in American Electoral Behavior*. Itasca, Ill.: Peacock.

Garcia, John, Brenda K. McGowan, and Kenneth F. Green. 1972. Biological Constraints on Conditioning. In *Biological Bases of Learning*, ed. Martin Seligman and Joanne L. Hager. New York: Appleton-Centruy-Crofts.

Garrett, Laurie. 1995. *The Coming Plague*. New York: Penguin.

Gazzaniga, Michael S. 1998. *The Mind's Past*. Berkeley: University of California Press.

Gell-Mann, Murray. 1995. Complex Adaptive Systems. In *The Mind, the Brain, and Complex Adaptive Systems*, ed. Harold J. Morowitz anad Jerome L. Singer. Reading, Mass.: Addison-Wesley.

Gerber, Alan, and Donald Green. 1999. Misperceptions about Perceptual Bias. *Annual Review of Political Science* 2:189–210.

Gibson, J. J. 1979. *The Ecological Approach to Visual Perception*. Boston: Houghton-Mifflin.

Gist, John R. 1982. "Stability" and "Competition" in Budgetary Theory. *American Political Science Review* 76:859–72.

Gode, D. J., and S. Sunder. 1993. Allocative Efficiency in Markets with Zero Intelligence Traders. *Journal of Political Economy* 101:119–27.

Goodin, Robert E. 1999. Rationality Redux: Reflections on Herbert Simon's Vision of Politics. In *Competition and Cooperation: Conversations with Nobelists about Economics and Political Science*, ed. James Alt, Margaret Levi, and Elinor Ostrom. New York: Russell Sage.

Gottlieb, Gilbert. 1996. Developmental Psychobiological Theory. In *Developmental Science*, ed. Robert B. Cairns, Glen H. Elder, Jr., and E. Jane Costello. Cambridge: Cambridge University Press.

Gould, Stephen. 1980. Sociobiology and the Theory of Natural Selection. In *Sociobiology: Beyond Nature-Nurture?* ed. George Barlow and James Silverberg. Boulder, Colo.: Westview Press.

Granberg, Donald, and Thad A. Brown. 1989. On Affect and Cognition in Politics. *Social Psychology Quarterly* 52:171–82.

Green, Donald, and Ian Shapiro. 1994. *Pathologies of Rational Choice Theory*. New Haven: Yale University Press.

Green, Mart T., and Fred Thompson. In Press. Organizational Process Models of Budgeting. In *Research in Public Administration*, ed. John Bartle. San Francisco: JAI Press.

Guilford, J. P. 1954. *Psychometric Methods*. New York: McGraw-Hill.

Güth, Werner, and Reinhard Teitz. 1990. Ultimatum Bargaining Behavior: A Survey and Comparison of Experimental Results. *Journal of Economic Psychology* 11:417–49.

Hager, Gregory L., and Jeffrey Talbert. 2000. Look for the Party Label. *Legislative Studies Quarterly* 25:75–99.

Hall, Richard. 1996. *Participation in Congress*. New Haven: Yale University Press.

Halpern, Jennifer, and Robert Stern. 1998. Beneath the Social Science Debate: Economic and Social Notions of Rationality. In *Debating Rationality*. Ithaca: Cornell University Press.

Hammond, Thomas. 1990. In Defense of Luther Gulick's "Notes on a Theory of Organization." *Public Administration Review* 68:143–73.

Hammond, Thomas, and Gary J. Miller. 1987. The Core of the Constitution. *American Political Science Review* 81:1155–74.

Hardin, Garrett. 1968. The Tragedy of the Commons. *Science* 162:1243–88.

Hardin, John. 1998. Advocacy versus Certainty: The Dynamics of Committee Jurisdiction Concentration. *Journal of Politics* 60:374–97.

Heimann, Larry. 1993. Understanding the *Challenger* Disaster: Organizational Structure and the Design of Reliable Systems. *American Political Science Review* 87:421–35.

———. 1997. *Acceptable Risks*. Ann Arbor: University of Michigan Press.

Hinde, Robert A. 1991. *Cooperation and Prosocial Behavior*. Cambridge: Cambridge University Press.

Hinich, Melvin, and Michael Munger. 1994. *Ideology and the Theory of Political Choice*. Ann Arbor: University of Michigan Press.

Hirshleifer, David. 1995. The Blind Leading the Blind: Social Influence, Fads, and Informational Cascades. In *The New Economics of Human Behavior*, ed. Mariano Tommasi and Kathryn Ierulli. Cambridge: Cambridge University Press.

Hirsz, Verlin B., and R. Scott Tisdale. 1997. The Emerging Conceptualization of Groups as Information Processors. *Psychological Bulletin* 121:43–64.

Hochschild, Jennifer. 1981. *What's Fair?* Cambridge: Harvard University Press.

Holland, John. 1995. Can There Be a Unified Theory of Complex Adaptive Systems? In *The Mind, the Brain, and Complex Adaptive Systems,* ed. Harold J. Morowitz and Jerome L. Singer. Reading, Mass.: Addison-Wesley.

Holland, John, and John E. Miller. 1991. Artificial Adaptive Agents in Economic Theory. *American Economic Review* 81:365–70.

Hutchins, Edwin. 1995. *Cognition in the Wild*. Cambridge: MIT Press.

Iyengar, Shanto. 1990. Shortcuts to Political Knowledge: Selective Attention and the Accessibility Bias. In *Information and the Democratic Process,* ed. John Ferejohn and James Kuklinski, 160–85. Urbana: University of Illinois Press.

———. 1991. *Is Anyone Responsible?* Chicago: University of Chicago Press.

Iyengar, Shanto, and Donald Kinder. 1987. *News that Matters*. Chicago: University of Chicago Press.

Jervis, Robert. 1970. *The Logic of Images in International Relations*. Princeton: Princeton University Press.

———. 1976. *Perception and Misperception in International Politics*. Princeton: Princeton University Press.

Jones, Bryan D. 1980. *Service Delivery in the City: Citizen Demand and Bureaucratic Rules*. New York: Longman.

———. 1985. *Governing Buildings and Building Government: A New Perspective on the Old Party.* University: University of Alabama Press.

———. 1994. *Reconceiving Decision-Making in Democratic Politics.* Chicago: University of Chicago Press.

———. 1996. Attributes, Alternatives, and the Flow of Ideas: Information Processing in Politics. Paper presented at the American Political Science Association Meetings, San Francisco, Calif.

———. 1999a. Bounded Rationality, Political Institutions, and the Analysis of Outcomes. In *Competition and Cooperation: Conversations with Nobelists about Economics and Political Science,* ed. James Alt, Margaret Levi, and Elinor Ostrom. New York: Russell Sage.

———. 1999b. Bounded Rationality. In *Annual Review of Political Science,* vol. 2, ed. Nelson Polsby. Palo Alto: Annual Reviews.

Jones, Bryan D., and Lynn Bachelor. 1994. *The Sustaining Hand.* 2d ed. Lawrence: University Press of Kansas.

Jones, Bryan D., Frank R. Baumgartner, and Jeffrey Talbert. 1993. The Destruction of Issue Monopolies in Congress. *American Political Science Review* 87: 657–71.

Jones, Bryan D., Frank R. Baumgartner, and James L. True. 1996. The Shape of Change: Punctuations and Stability in U.S. Budgeting, 1947–94. Paper presented at the Annual Meeting of the Midwest Political Science Association Chicago, Illinois.

———. 1999. Policy Punctuations: U.S. Budget Authority, 1947–95. *Journal of Politics* 60: 1–30.

Jones, Bryan D., Saadia R. Greenberg, Clifford Kaufman, and Joseph Drew. 1977. Bureaucratic Response to Citizen-Initiated Contacts: Environmental Enforcement in Detroit. *American Political Science Review* 71: 148–65.

Jones, Bryan D., and Tracy Sulkin. 2000. Representation, Information, and Public Policy. Seattle: Center for American Politics and Public Policy.

Jupille, Joseph H. 2000. Procedural Politics: Issues, Interests, and Institutional Change in the European Union. Ph.D. diss., University of Washington, Seattle.

Kagel, John, Raymond Battalio, and Leonard Green. 1995. *Economic Choice Theory.* New York: Cambridge University Press.

Kagel, John, and Dan Levin. 1986. The Winner's Curse and Public Information in Common Value Auctions. *American Economic Review* 76: 894–920.

Kahneman, Daniel, and Amos Tversky. 1979. Prospect Theory: An Analysis of Decision-Making under Risk. *Econometrica* 47: 263–91.

———. 1983. Choices, Values, and Frames. *American Psychologist* 39: 341–50.

Key, V. O., Jr. 1955. A Theory of Critical Elections. *Journal of Politics* 17: 3–18.

Key, V. O., Jr., with Milton Cummings. 1966. *The Responsible Electorate.* Cambridge: Belknap Press of Harvard University Press.

Kiewiet, D. Roderick. 1983. *Macroeconomics and Micropolitics.* Chicago: University of Chicago Press.

Kinder, Donald, and D. Roderick Kiewiet. 1979. Economic Discontent and Political Behavior: The Role of Personal Grievances and Collective Economic

Judgments in Congressional Voting. *American Journal of Political Science* 23: 495–527.

Kindleberger, Charles P. 1996. *Manias, Panics, and Crashes.* New York: John Wiley.

King, David. 1997. *Turf Wars.* Chicago: University of Chicago Press.

Kingdon, John. [1984] 1996. *Agendas, Alternatives, and Public Policies.* 2d ed. Boston: Little, Brown.

Krehbiel, Keith. 1991. *Information and Legislative Organization.* Ann Arbor: University of Michigan Press.

LaHerrere, Jean, and Didier Sornette. 1998. Stretched Exponentials in Nature and Economy: "Fat Tails" with Characteristic Scales. *European Physical Journal* B2:525–39.

Laitin, David. 1999. Identity Choice under Conditions of Uncertainty. In *Competition and Cooperation: Conversations with Nobelists about Economics and Political Science,* ed. James Alt, Margaret Levi, and Elinor Ostrom. New York: Russell Sage.

Lancaster, Kelvin. 1971. *Consumer Demand: A New Approach.* New York: Columbia University Press.

———. 1979. *Variety, Equity, and Efficiency: Product Variety in an Industrial Society.* New York: Columbia University Press.

Landau, Martin. 1969. Redundancy, Rationality, and the Problem of Duplication and Overlap. *Public Administration Review* 29:346–58.

Larkey, Patrick. 1977. *Evaluating Public Programs.* Princeton: Princeton University Press.

Lazarsfeld, Paul, Bernard Berelson, and Helen Gaudet. 1944. *The People's Choice.* New York: Duell, Sloan, and Pearce.

Levi, Margaret. 1997. *Consent, Dissent, and Patriotism.* Cambridge: Cambridge University Press.

———. 1998. A State of Trust. In *Trust and Governance,* ed. Valerie Braithwaite and Margaret Levi. New York: Russell Sage.

Levitt, Barbara, and James G. March. 1988. Organizational Learning. *Annual Review of Sociology* 14:319–40.

Levy, Jack S. 1997. Prospect Theory, Rational Choice, and International Relations. *International Studies Quarterly* 41:87–112.

Lewontin, R. C. 1998. The Evolution of Cognition: Questions We Will Never Answer. In *Methods, Models, and Conceptual Issues: An Invitation to Cognitive Science,* vol. 4, ed. Don Scarborough and Saul Sternberg. Cambridge: MIT Press.

Lindblom, Charles E. 1959. The Science of Muddling Through. *Public Administration Review* 19:79–88.

Lodge, Milton. 1995. Toward a Procedural Model of Candidate Evaluation. In *Political Judgment,* ed. Milton Lodge and Kathleen McGraw. Ann Arbor: University of Michigan Press.

Lodge, Milton, Kathleen M. McGraw, and Patrick Stroh. 1989. An Impression-Driven Model of Candidate Evaluation. *American Political Science Review* 83: 399–419.

Lodge, Milton, and Patrick Stroh. 1993. Inside the Mental Voting Booth: An Impression-Driven Process Model of Candidate Evaluation. In *Explorations in Political Psychology*, ed. Shanto Iyengar and William J. McGuire. Durham: Duke University Press.

Lounamaa, Perth H., and James G. March. 1985. Adaptive Coordination of a Learning Team. *Management Science* 33:107–23.

Lowenstein, George, and Jon Elster. 1992. *Choices over Time*. New York: Russell Sage.

Luce, R. Duncan. 1992. A Path Taken: Aspects of Modern Measurement Theory. In *From Learning Theory to Connectionist Theory*, ed. Alice Healy and Stephen Kosslyn. Hillsdale, N.J.: Lawrence Erlbaum.

———. 1995. Four Tensions Concerning Mathematical Modeling in Psychology. *Annual Review of Psychology* 46:1–26.

Lupia, Arthur. 1994. Shortcuts versus Encyclopedias: Voting Behavior in California Insurance Reform Elections. *American Political Science Review* 88:63–76.

Lupia, Arthur, and Matthew McCubbins. 1998. *The Democratic Dilemma*. Cambridge: Cambridge University Press.

Lux, Thomas. 1995. Herd Behaviour, Bubbles, and Crashes. *Economic Journal* 105:881–96.

———. 1998. The Socio-Economic Dynamics of Speculative Markets. *Journal of Economic Behavior and Organization* 33:145–65.

McCarthy, John. 1956. The Inversion of Functions Defined by Turing Machines. In *Automata Studies*, ed. Claude Shannon and John McCarthy. Princeton: Princeton University Press.

McCombs, Maxwell E., and Donald Shaw. 1972. The Agenda Setting Function of the Mass Media. *Public Opinion Quarterly* 36:176–87.

MacKuen, Michael B., W. Russell Neuman, and George E. Marcus. 1997. Affective Intelligence and Rational Choice. Paper presented at the Midwest Political Science Association, Chicago.

MacRae, Duncan. 1958. *Dimensions of Congressional Voting*. Berkeley and Los Angeles: University of California Press.

Malkiel, Burton G. 1996. *A Random Walk Down Wall Street*. New York: Norton.

Mandelbrot, Benoit. 1997. *Fractals and Scaling in Finance*. New York: Springer.

———. 1999. *Multifractals and 1/f Noise*. New York: Springer.

March, James G. 1978. Bounded Rationality, Ambiguity, and the Engineering of Choice. *Bell Journal of Economics* 9:578–608.

———. 1994. *A Primer on Decision-Making*. New York: Free Press.

March, James G., and Johann Olsen. 1976. *Ambiguity and Choice in Organizations*. Bergen: Universitätsforlaget.

———. 1989. *Rediscovering Institutions*. New York: Free Press.

———. 1995. *Democratic Governance*. New York: Free Press.

March, James G., and Herbert A. Simon. 1958. *Organizations*. New York: John Wiley.

Marcus, George E., and Michael McKuen 1993. Anxiety, Enthusiasm, and the Vote. *American Political Science Review* 87:688–701.

Marcus, George E., and Wendy Rahn. 1990. Emotions and Democratic Politics. *Research in Micropolitics* 3:29–58.

Margolis, Howard. 1987. *Patterns, Thinking, and Cognition.* Chicago: University of Chicago Press.

Masters, Roger D. 1989. *The Nature of Politics.* New Haven: Yale University Press.

———. 1998. *Fortune Is a River.* New York: Free Press.

Matthews, Donald. 1960. *U.S. Senators and Their World.* Chapel Hill: University of North Carolina Press.

May, Peter. 1992. Policy Learning and Failure. *Journal of Public Policy* 12:331–54.

———. 1999. Fostering Policy Learning: A Challenge for Public Administration. *International Review of Public Administration* 4:21–31.

Mayer, William G. 1995. Changes in Elections and the Party System: 1992 in Perspective. In *The New American Politics,* ed. Bryan D. Jones. Boulder, Colo.: Westview Press.

Mayhew, David. 1974. *The Electoral Connection.* New Haven: Yale University Press.

Mayr, Ernst. 1997. *This Is Biology.* Cambridge: Belknap Press of Harvard University Press.

Meltsner, Arnold. 1971. *The Politics of City Revenue.* Berkeley: University of California Press.

Meltzer, Allen H., and Scott F. Richard. 1978. Why Government Grows (and Grows) in a Democracy. *Public Interest* 52:116.

Mill, J. S. [1863] 1956. *On Liberty.* Edited by Currin V. Shields. Indianapolis: Bobbs-Merrill.

Miller, Gary J., and Joe A. Oppenheimer. 1982. Universalism in Experimental Communities. *American Political Science Review* 76:561–74.

Miller, George. 1956. The Magic Number Seven, Plus or Minus Two: Some Limits on our Capacity for Processing Information. *Psychological Review* 63:81–97.

Miller, Warren E., and J. Merrill Shanks. 1996. *The New American Voter.* Cambridge: Harvard University Press.

Mintz, Alex. 1993. The Decision to Attack Iraq: A Noncompensatory Theory of Decision Making. *Journal of Conflict Resolution* 37 (December): 595–618.

Mladenka, Kenneth. 1978. Rules, Service Equity, and Distributional Decisions. *Social Science Quarterly* 59:192–202.

Mondak, Jeffrey J. Cognitive Heuristics, Heuristic Processing, and Efficiency in Political Decision-Making. *Research in Micropolitics* 4:117–42.

Nardulli, Peter. 1995. The Concept of a Critical Realignment, Electoral Behaviors, and Political Change. *American Political Science Review* 89:10–22.

Natchez, Peter B., and Irvin C. Bupp. 1973. Policy and Priority in the Budgetary Process. *American Political Science Review* 67:951–63.

Newell, Allen. 1968. Judgment and Its Representation. In *Formal Representation and Human Judgment,* ed. Benjamin Kleinmuntz. New York: John Wiley.

———. 1990. *Unified Theories of Cognition.* Cambridge: Harvard University Press.

Newell, Allen, and Herbert A. Simon. 1972. *Human Problem Solving.* Englewood Cliffs, N.J.: Prentice-Hall.

Niskanan, William. 1971. *Bureaucracy and Representative Government.* Chicago: Aldine-Atherton.

Nordhaus, William. 1975. The Political Business Cycle. *Review of Economic Studies* 42:169–90.

North, Douglas. 1981. *Structure and Change in Economic History.* New York: Norton.

———. 1990. *Institutions, Institutional Change, and Economic Performance.* Cambridge: Cambridge University Press.

Olson, Mancur. 1965. *The Logic of Collective Action.* Cambridge: Harvard University Press.

Ordeshook, Peter. 1993. The Development of Contemporary Political Theory. In *Political Economy: Institutions, Competition, and Representation,* ed. William A. Barnett, Melvin J. Hinich, and Norman J. Schofield. Cambridge: Cambridge University Press.

Ostrom, Elinor. 1990. *Governing the Commons.* Cambridge University Press.

———. 1998. A Behavioral Approach to the Rational Choice Theory of Collective Action. *American Political Science Review* 92:1–22.

———. 1999. Coping with Tragedies of the Commons. *Annual Review of Political Science* 2:493–535.

Ostrom, Elinor, Roy Gardner, and James Walker. 1994. *Rules, Games, and Common Pool Resources.* Ann Arbor: University of Michigan Press.

Ostrom, Vincent. 1997. *The Meaning of Democracy and the Vulnerability of Democracies.* Ann Arbor: University of Michigan Press.

Padgett, John F. 1980. Bounded Rationality in Budgetary Research. *American Political Science Review* 74:354–72.

———. 1981. Hierarchy and Ecological Control in Federal Budgetary Decision Making. *American Journal of Sociology* 87:75–128.

Page, Benjamin, and Robert Y. Shapiro. 1992. *The Rational Public.* Chicago: University of Chicago Press.

Pareto, Vilfredo. 1935. *Mind and Society* [Trattato di Sociologia generale]. Ed. Arthur Livingston. New York: Harcourt, Brace.

Payne, John W., James R. Bettman, and Eric J. Johnson. 1993. *The Adaptive Decision-Maker.* New York: Cambridge University Press.

Percy, Stephen. 1985. *Demand Processing and Performance in Public Agencies.* University: University of Alabama Press.

Piattelli-Palmarini, Massimo. 1994. *Inevitable Illusions.* New York: John Wiley.

Pierce, John R. 1980. *An Introduction to Information Theory.* 2d rev. ed. New York: Dover.

Pinker, Steven. 1997. *How the Mind Works.* New York: Norton.

Pios, Scott. 1993. *The Psychology of Judgment and Decision Making.* New York: McGraw-Hill.

Plott, Charles R. 1976. Axiomatic Social Choice Theory. *American Journal of Political Science* 20:511–96.

———. 1991. Will Economics Become an Experimental Science? *Southern Economic Journal* 57:901–20.

Plott, Charles R., and Shyam Sunder. 1982. Efficiency of Experimental Security Markets with Insider Trading. *Journal of Political Economy* 90:663–98.

Poole, Keith, and Howard Rosenthal. 1997. *Congress: A Political-Economic History of Roll Call Voting.* New York: Oxford University Press.

Popkin, Samuel. 1991. *The Reasoning Voter.* Chicago: University of Chicago Press.

Potoski, Matthew, and Jeffrey Talbert. 1998. The Dimensional Structure of Policy Outputs: Distributive Policy and Roll Call Voting. Paper presented at the Southern Political Science Association Meetings, Atlanta.

Rahn, Wendy. 1995. Candidate Evaluation in Complex Information Environments. In *Political Judgment,* ed. Milton Lodge and Kathleen McGraw. Ann Arbor: University of Michigan Press.

Riker, William. 1962. *The Theory of Political Coalitions.* New Haven: Yale University Press.

———. 1982. *Liberalism versus Populism.* Prospect Heights, Ill.: Waveland Press.

Rochefort, David, and Roger Cobb, eds. 1994. *The Politics of Problem Definition.* Lawrence: University Press of Kansas.

Rubinstein, Ariel. 1998. *Modeling Bounded Rationality.* Cambridge: MIT Press.

Quattrone, George A., and Amos Tversky. 1988. Contrasting Rational and Psychological Analyses of Political Choice. *American Political Science Review* 3:719–36.

Sabatier, Paul, and Hank Jenkins-Smith. 1993. *Policy Change and Learning.* Boulder, Colo.: Westview Press.

Samuelson, Paul. 1965. Proof that Properly Anticipated Prices Fluctuate Randomly. *Industrial Management Review* 6:41–49.

Sanger, David E. 1999. Fed Chief Warns about Stocks and Tax Cuts. *New York Times,* 23 July.

Sargent, Thomas. 1993. *Bounded Rationality in Macroeconomics.* Oxford: Oxford University Press.

Schattschneider, E. E. 1960. *The Semi-Sovereign People.* New York: Holt, Reinhardt, and Winston.

Schneider, Mark, Paul Teske, Melissa Marschall, Michael Mintrom, and Christine Roch. 1997. Institutional Arrangements and the Creation of Social Capital. *American Political Science Review* 91:82–91.

Seligman, Martin, and Joanne L. Hager. 1972. Introduction to *Biological Boundaries of Learning,* ed. Martin Seligman and Joanne L. Hager. New York: Appleton-Century-Crofts.

Shannon, Claude, and Warren Weaver. 1949. *The Mathematical Theory of Communication.* Urbana: University of Illinois Press.

Shaw, Donald, and Maxwell McCombs. 1977. *The Emergence of American Political Issues.* St.Paul, Minn.: West Publishing.

Shefrin, Hersh. 2000. *Beyond Greed and Fear.* Boston: Harvard Business School Press.

Shepard, Roger N. 1964. Attention and the Metric Structure of the Stimulus. *Journal of Mathematical Psychology* 1:54–87.

———. 1990. *Mind Sights*. San Francisco: Freeman.

———. 1992. The Perceptual Organization of Colors. In *The Mind, the Brain, and Complex Adaptive Systems*, ed. Harold J. Morowitz and Jerome L. Singer. Reading, Mass.: Addison-Wesley.

Shiffren, Richard M., and Walter Schneider. 1977. Controlled and Automatic Human Information Processing II. *Psychological Review* 84:127–90.

Shiller, Robert J. 2000. *Irrational Exuberance*. Princeton: Princeton University Press.

Shleifer, Andrei. 2000. *Inefficient Markets: An Introduction to Behavioral Finance*. New York: Oxford University Press.

Simon, Adam. 1999. Dynamics in Processing Everyday Political Messages. Occasional Paper. Seattle: Center for American Politics and Public Policy, University of Washington.

Simon, Herbert A. 1947. *Administrative Behavior*. New York: Macmillan.

———. 1957. *Models of Man*. New York: John Wiley.

———. 1977. The Logic of Heuristic Decision-Making. In *Models of Discovery*, ed. R. S. Cohen and M. W. Wartofsky. Boston: D. Reidel.

———. 1979. Rational Decision-Making in Business Organizations. *American Economic Review* 69:495–501.

———. 1983. *Reason in Human Affairs*. Stanford: Stanford University Press.

———. 1985. Human Nature in Politics: The Dialogue of Psychology with Political Science. *American Political Science Review* 79:293–304.

———. 1989. *Models of Thought*. Vol. 2. New Haven: Yale University Press.

———. 1990. A Mechanism for Social Selection and Successful Altruism. *Science* 250:1665–68.

———. 1993. Altruism and Economics. *American Economic Review* 83:151–61.

———. 1995a. Near Decomposability and Complexity: How a Mind Becomes a Brain. In *The Mind, the Brain, and Complex Adaptive Systems*, ed. Harold J. Morowitz and Jerome L. Singer. Reading, Mass.: Addison-Wesley.

———. 1995b. Rationality in Political Behavior. *Political Psychology* 16:45–61.

———. 1996a. *Models of My Life*. Cambridge: MIT Press.

———. 1996b. *The Sciences of the Artificial*. 3d ed. Cambridge: MIT Press.

———. 1997a. Bounded Rationality. In *Models of Bounded Rationality*, vol. 3, ed. Herbert A. Simon. Cambridge: MIT Press.

———. 1997b. Motivation and the Theory of the Firm. In *Models of Bounded Rationality*, vol. 3, ed. Herbert A. Simon. Cambridge: MIT Press.

———. 1997c. Organizations and Markets. In *Models of Bounded Rationality*, vol. 3, ed. Herbert A. Simon. Cambridge: MIT Press.

———. 1998. Theory Generation as a Task in Science. Presented at the Conference on Taking Economics Seriously, Carnegie-Mellon University, Pittsburgh, 11 April.

———. 1999. The Potlatch between Political Science and Economics. In *Competition and Cooperation: Conversations with Nobelists about Economics and Political Science*, ed. James Alt, Margaret Levi, and Elinor Ostrom. New York: Russell Sage.

Skinner, B. F. [1948] 1962. *Walden Two*. New York: Macmillan.

————. 1974. *About Behaviorism.* New York: Alfred A. Knopf.

Smith, Vernon L., Gerry L. Suchanek, and Arlington W. Williams. 1988. Bubbles, Crashes, and Endogenous Expectations in Experimental Spot Asset Markets. *Econometrica* 56:1119–51.

Sniderman, Paul M., Richard A. Brody, and Philip E. Tetlock. 1991. *Reasoning and Choice: Explorations in Political Psychology.* Cambridge: Cambridge University Press.

Sober, Elliott, and David Sloan Wilson. 1998. *Unto Others: The Evolution and Psychology of Unselfish Behavior.* Cambridge: Harvard University Press.

Somit, Albert, and Steven A. Peterson. 1999. A (Darwinian) Tale of Two Theories. *PS* 32 (1): 39–44.

Slovic, Paul. 1990. Choice. In *Thinking: An Invitation to Cognitive Science,* vol. 3, ed. Daniel N. Osherson and Edward E. Smith. Cambridge: MIT Press.

Steinbruner, John D. 1974. *The Cybernetic Theory of Decision: New Dimensions of Political Analysis.* Princeton: Princeton University Press.

Stevens, S. S. 1975. *Pyschophysics.* New York: John Wiley.

Stimson, James, Michael MacKuen, and Robert Erickson. 1995. Dynamic Representation. *American Political Science Review* 89:543–64.

Stone, Clarence. 1993. Urban Regimes and the Capacity to Govern: A Political Economy Approach. *Journal of Urban Affairs* 15:1–28.

Su, Tsai-Tsu, Mark S. Kamlet, and David Mowery. 1993. Modeling U.S. Budgetary and Fiscal Outcomes: A Disaggregated, Systemwide Perspective. *American Journal of Political Science* 37:213–45.

Symons, Donald. 1992. On the Use and Misuse of Darwinism in the Study of Human Behavior. In *The Adapted Mind,* ed. Jerome H. Barkow, Leda Cosmides, and John Tooby. New York: Oxford University Press.

Talbert, Jeffrey, and Matthew Potoski. 2000. Setting the Legislative Agenda: The Dimensional Structure of Bill Sponsoring and Floor Voting. Paper presented at the Midwest Political Science Association, Chicago.

Taylor, Michael. 1976. *Anarchy and Cooperation.* London: John Wiley.

————. 1987. *The Possibility of Cooperation.* Cambridge: Cambridge University Press.

Thaler, Richard H. 1988. Anomalies: The Ultimatum Game. *Journal of Economic Perspectives* 2:195–206.

————. 1991. *Quasi Rational Economics.* New York: Russell Sage.

————. 1992. *The Winner's Curse: Paradoxes and Anomalies of Economic Life.* Princeton: Princeton University Press.

Thatch, W. T., H. P. Goodkin and J. G. Keating. 1992. The Cerebellum and the Adaptive Coordination of Movement. *Annual Review of Neuroscience* 15: 403–42.

Thompson, Fred. 1979. American Legislative Decision Making and the Size Principle. *American Political Science Review* 73:1100–108.

Thompson, William. 1996. Foreign Policy, the End of the Cold War, and the 1992 Election. In *The New American Politics,* ed. Bryan D. Jones. Boulder, Colo.: Westview Press.

Thorngate, Warren. 1988. On Paying Attention. In *Recent Trends in Theoretical*

Psychology, ed. William J. Baker, L. P. Moos, and H. J. Stam. New York: Springer-Verlag.

Thurmaier, Kurt. 1995. Decisive Decision Making in the Executive Budget Process: Analyzing the Political and Economic Propensities of Central Budget Bureau Analysts. *Public Administration Review* 55:448–60.

Thurstone, L. L. 1947. *Multiple Factor Analysis.* Chicago: University of Chicago Press.

Tooby, John, and Leda Cosmides. 1992. Cognitive Adaptations for Social Exchange. In *The Adapted Mind,* ed. Jerome H. Barkow, Leda Cosmides, and John Tooby. New York: Oxford University Press.

True, James L. In Press. Avalanches and Incrementalism. *American Review of Public Administration.*

True, James L., Bryan D. Jones, and Frank R. Baumgartner. 1999. Punctuated Equilibrium Theory. In *Theories of the Policy Process,* ed. Paul Sabbatier. Boulder, Colo.: Westview Press.

Truman, David. 1951. *The Governmental Process.* New York: Alfred A. Knopf.

Tversky, Amos. 1972. Elimination by Aspects: A Theory of Choice. *Psychological Review* 79:281–99.

Tversky, Amos, Shmuel Sattath, and Paul Slovic. 1988. Contingent Weighting in Judgment and Choice. *Psychological Review* 95:371–84.

VanBerg, Viktor. 1993. Rational Choice, Rule Following, and Institutions: An Evolutionary Perspective. In *Rationality, Institutions, and Economic Methodology,* ed. Uskali Maki, Bo Gustafsson, and Christian Knudsen. London: Routledge.

———. 1999. Rational Choice and Rule- or Program-Based Behavior: Alternate Paradigms. Department of Economics, Albert-Ludwigs Universität Freiburg.

Wanat, John. 1974. Bases of Budgetary Incrementalism. *American Political Science Review* 68:1221–28.

Whitman, Donald. 1995. *The Myth of Democratic Failure.* Chicago: University of Chicago Press.

Wildavsky, Aaron. 1964. *The Politics of the Budgetary Process.* Boston: Little, Brown.

Wilson, E. O. 1998. *Consilience.* New York: Alfred A. Knopf.

Wilson, James Q. 1980. *The Politics of Regulation.* New York: Basic Books.

———. 1993. *The Moral Sense.* New York: Free Press.

Wlezien, Christopher. 1995. The Public as Thermostat: Dynamics of Preferences for Spending. *American Journal of Political Science* 39:981–1000.

Young, Paul. 1987. *The Nature of Information.* New York: Praeger.

Zaller, John. 1992. *The Nature and Origins of Mass Opinion.* Cambridge: Cambridge University Press.